English Result

Pre-intermediate Student's Book

Mark Hancock & Annie McDonald

OXFORD
UNIVERSITY PRESS

Contents 3

Contents 5

WHAT'S IN A NAME?

1 In **Iceland**, people don't have a family surname. They use their father's first name. For example Björk Guðmundsdóttir is the daughter of Guðmund.

2 In **Russia**, people have both their father's name and a surname. For example, the second name in Maria Yuryevna Sharapova comes from her father's name, Yuri.

3 **British and American** people usually have a first name, a middle name and the surname of their father. They often write their first name and middle name as initials. For example, the writer Joanne Kathleen Rowling is called J. K. Rowling on her books.

4 In **Spanish-speaking** countries, children use the surnames of both their parents. For example, Gabriel García Márquez's father's surname was García. His mother's surname was Márquez.

5 People from **China** write their surname before their first name. For example Jackie Chan's name is Chan Kong-Sang. 'Jackie' is just a nickname.

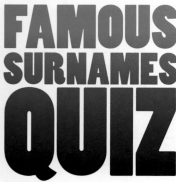

FAMOUS SURNAMES QUIZ

You know the **names**, but do you know the **people**?

How to talk about names

G possessive 's   V family; parts of names

A   Read and use what you know

1 Look at **What's in a name?** opposite. Match the people in photos a–e with these names.

- [b] Gabriel García Márquez, writer
- [a] J. K. Rowling, writer
- [e] Björk, singer
- [d] Jackie Chan, film actor
- [c] Maria Sharapova, tennis player

2 What do you know about the people in exercise 1? Tell a partner.

Example   Gabriel García Márquez is from Colombia.

3 Read **What's in a name?** opposite. Match photos a–e with texts 1–5.

4 Match these names with sentences 1–6. Work with a partner.

Jackie   Rowling   Joanna   Yuryevna
Kathleen   Márquez   Maria   Guðmundsdóttir

1 This is a surname. *Rowling, Márquez*
2 These are first names.
3 This is a middle name.
4 These names come from a father's first name.
5 This is a mother's surname.
6 This is a nickname.

5 Ask and answer with a partner.

1 Have you got a middle name?
2 How many surnames have you got?
3 Have you got a nickname?
4 Is any part of your name the same as your father or mother's name?
5 Do you like your name?
6 Is your name common in your country?
7 Does your name mean anything?

B   Grammar possessive 's

6 Complete the box.

male	female
father	mother
son	daughter
husband	wife
brother	sister
uncle	aunt
grandfather	grandmother
	cousin

7 Tell your partner about your family. Use *I've got*.

Example I've got three brothers.

8 Complete the grammar box.

singular nouns	plural nouns
My father's name is Jerry. My grandmother's name is Alice.	My brothers' names are Ben and Tom. Our daughters' names are Kylie and Nina.

To make a singular noun possessive, add *'s*.
To make a plural noun possessive, add *s'*.

9 What about your family's names? Ask and answer with a partner.

Example   **A** What are your sisters' names?
            B Maria and Sonia.

10 Complete the text with s, 's, or s'.

I've got two brothers¹. Their names² are Ruy and Edson. Ruy's³ middle name is José. Edson's⁴ middle name⁵ are Pedro and Paulo. My sister's⁶ name is Nélida but we call her Nelly. My parents'⁷ names⁸ are João and Maria.

More practice? **Grammar Bank** >> p.136.

C   Listen for key words

11 1A.1▶ Listen to the spellings. Find the names in the **Famous surnames quiz** opposite.

Audio H-O-N-D-A   **You** Honda!

12 1A.2▶ Listen to five quiz questions. Say the surname.

13 1A.3▶ Listen and complete.

A What's your ¹ *name* ?
B Chico.
A Is that your ² first name?
B Yes. It's ³ short for Francisco.
A Oh. And what's your ⁴ surname?
B My surnames are Oliveira Cardoso.
A Oliveira Cardoso?
B Yes. Oliveira's my mother's surname and Cardoso's my ⁵ father's surname.
A Oh I see. So it's Francisco Oliveira Cardoso?
B That's right. but just ⁶ call me Chico!

14 Check your answers in the audio script on >> p.150.

15 Say the conversation with a partner. Then say it again with information about you.

ABC Put it all together

16 Ask other people in the class about their names. Use the questions in exercises 5 and 13 to help you.

I can talk about names.

Tick ✓ the line.   with a lot of help   with some help   on my own   very easily

You're the detective!

ticket

letter

envelope

note

driving licence

I.D. card

business card

credit card

badge

passport

How to give and understand personal details

G present simple -s or -es ending v documents and personal details P when is -s an extra syllable?

A Vocabulary documents and personal details

1 What documents have you got with you now? Show or tell a partner.

2 Look at **You're the detective!** opposite. Complete this form about the person.

1	Surname	Watt
2	First name	CAROLINE
3	Age	30
4	Nationality	BRITISH
5	Date and place of birth	12.10.1981 LINCOLN
6	Address	29 WELDON ST., LOUTH
7	Telephone	509 483 8927
8	Marital status	MARRIED
9	Job	NURSE
10	Place of work	COUNTY HOSPITAL, LOUTH
11	Interests	TENNIS, CATS, THAI FOOD, COOKING

3 How do you know the information in 1–11? Say which documents helped you.

Example We know her birthday from her passport. We know her age from ...

B Listen for key information

4 **1B.1▶** Listen to Caroline. Which pieces of information from exercise 2 do you hear? Tick ✓ them.

5 Listen again. Complete the information for Caroline. Compare with a partner.

	Caroline	me
get up at		6 a.m
then	have shower	drink a coffee
and		smoke a cigarette
start work* at		9 am
finish work* at		18 pm
evening	play tennis	read books
		watch TV
go to bed at		12 pm.

* or school / university

6 Complete the 'Me' column and tell a partner about yourself.

Example I get up at 7 o'clock and then I brush my teeth.

C Grammar present simple -s or -es ending

7 Add these verbs to the grammar box.
finish start watch read

-s		-es	
I/you/we/they	he/she/it	I/you/we/they	he/she/it
get	gets	go	goes
finish	finishes	watch	watches
start	starts	finish	finishes

irregular	
I/you/we/they	he/she/it
have / are	has / is

8 Do you add -s or -es to these verbs? Decide with a partner.
arrive dance draw drink eat kiss make
paint play push sing teach think wash
More practice? **Grammar Bank** >> p.136.

D Pronunciation when is -s an extra syllable?

9 **1B.2▶** Do these pairs of sentences have the same or different numbers of syllables? Listen and count.
1 I sit and read. ☐4 She sits and reads. ☐4 *same*
2 You sing and dance. ☐4 She sings and dances. ☐5 *different*
3 We watch football. ☐4 He watches football. ☐5
4 They open and close. ☐4 It opens and closes. ☐5
5 I go swimming. ☐4 She goes swimming. ☐4
6 You start and finish. ☐4 It starts and finishes. ☐5

10 Listen again and repeat.

11 Write the verbs ending in -s from exercise 9 in this table.

The -s ending is not an extra syllable	The -s ending is an extra syllable
sits	dances

12 Look at your notes in exercise 5. Tell your partner how Caroline is different from you.

Example Caroline gets up at half past six. I get up at eight o'clock.

ABCD Put it all together

13 Ask three other students in the class about their normal day. Make notes like the table in exercise 5.

14 Work in small groups. Tell the others about the people you talked to in exercise 13. Listen and guess who the people are.

Example She gets up at eight o'clock. Then she ...

I can give and understand personal details.

Office Life

Episode one

1

Justin Hi. Are you new?
Anna Yes.
Justin When did you start?
Anna On Monday.

2

Justin Where do you work?
Anna Just along the corridor. What do you do?

3

Justin I'm a computer technician. I check the system for viruses.
Anna How often do you check it?
Justin Not very often. They don't pay me enough!

4

Anna So what are you doing now?
Justin I'm playing a computer game. Why not? The boss isn't looking!

5

Anna What's the boss like?
Justin I don't know her. She's new. But people say she's horrible.
Anna Really? What's her name?

6

Justin Anna Conde. But we call her Anaconda.
Anna Why do you call her that?
Justin Why do you think?!

7

Anna Where does she come from?
Justin I don't know. The zoo, probably!

8

Anna Hmm. And what's your name?
Justin Justin. And you?

9

Anna I'm Anna Conde – the new boss. And by the way, I think you've got a virus.
Holly Ouch!

Question words

Who?	Where?	When?	What?	Why?	Which?	How?

How to ask questions about people

A Read a comedy sketch

1 Work with a partner. Look at the photos opposite. Guess the answers to these questions.
   1 How old are the people?
   2 Are they friends?

2 Read **Office Life** opposite. Choose the best title for this episode. Compare with a partner.
   a The New Boss
   b Justin's Computer
   c Another Bad Day

3 Answer the questions with a partner.
   1 When does Justin understand that he's speaking to the new boss?
   2 Anna is angry. Why?

4 **Office Life** is a comedy sketch. Where do you think the audience will laugh? Write L.

5 **1C.1▶** Listen and check.

6 Cover the page opposite. Complete these questions from the story. Use *did*, *does*, *do*, *is*, and *are*. Then answer the questions with a partner.
   1 When ___*did*___ you start?
   2 Where _do_ you work?
   3 What _do_ you do?
   4 How often _do_ you check it?
   5 What _are_ you doing now?
   6 What _is_ the boss like?
   7 What _is_ her name?
   8 Why _do_ you call her that?
   9 Where _is_ she come from?
   10 What _is_ your name?

7 Read and check.

B Pronunciation rhythm in *Wh-* questions

8 Look at **Question words** opposite. Match them with these answers.

Why?	Because!
When?	Now!
Who?	You!
Where?	Here!
How?	Carefully!
Which?	That one!
What?	Nothing!

9 **1C.2▶** Listen and check. Which questions begin with /w/ and which begin with /h/?

10 Cover exercise 8 and test a partner.
   Example   A Where?   B Here!

11 **1C.3▶** Listen and repeat these questions. Keep the ●●●● rhythm.

●	●	●	●
Who	was	he	**with?**
Where	were	your	**keys?**
When	does	she	**start?**
What	do	they	**do?**
Why	are	you	**here?**
Which	is	her	**desk?**
How	did	it	**end?**

12 Act the **Office Life** conversation with a partner.

C Grammar *be* and *do* in questions

13 Write the red words from exercise 11 in the grammar box.

	questions with verb *be*		questions with other verbs	
	he/she/it	you/we/they	he/she/it	you/we/they
present	Where _is_ her car?	What _are_ their names?	What _does_ he do?	Where _do_ you work?
past	Where _was_ he born?	Who _were_ you with?	When _did_ they arrive?	

14 Match 1–8 with a–h.
   1 What's _h_   a she sit?
   2 Where do   b the boss?
   3 Which is   c the toilets?
   4 When did _f_   d you before?
   5 Where were _d_   e you sit?
   6 Who's _b_   f you start this job?
   7 Where does _a_   g your computer?
   8 Where are _c_   h your name?

15 Work with a partner. Do a role play. One of you is a new worker in the office and the other is Holly. Use questions from exercise 14 or think of others.
   More practice? **Grammar Bank** >> p.136.

ABC Put it all together

16 Write questions to ask your partner about their work, studies, family, home, and hobbies. Use the question words from exercise 8.
   Examples   Where do you work? What do you study?

17 Change partners and ask your new partner about their partner from exercise 16.

In the dictionary

noun

watch² /wɒtʃ/ *noun* **1** [C] a type of small clock that you usually wear around your wrist: *a digital watch* ◇ *My watch is a bit fast/slow* (trochę się śpieszy/spóźnia).

verb —

watch /wɒtʃ/ *verbo, nombre*
1 *vt, vi* observar, mirar ➔ *Ver nota en* MIRAR **2** *vt* (*TV, Dep*) ver **3** *vt, vi* (*espiar*) vigilar, observar
▸ *n* **1** reloj (*de pulsera*) ➔ *Ver dibujo en* RELOJ **2** vigilancia: *to keep (a close) watch over sth* vigilar (atentamente) algo **3** (turno de) guardia LOC *Ver* CLOSE² **watchful** *adj* vigilante, alerta — **adjective**

different meanings

watch² 0━ /wɒtʃ/ *noun*
1 (*plural* **watches**) a thing that you wear on your wrist so you know what time it is: *She kept looking at her watch nervously.* ➔ Look at the note at **clock**.

pronunciation

plural

leaf /li:f/ *s* (*pl* **leaves** /li:vz/) foglia LOC **take a leaf out of sb's book** prendere esempio da qn *Vedi anche* TURN **leafy** *agg* (-ier, -iest) ricco di foglie: *leafy vegetables* verdure a foglia

Extracts from *Oxford Pocket Słownik Kieszonkowy*, *Diccionario Oxford Pocket para estudiantes de inglés*, *Oxford Wordpower Dictionary* and *Dizionario Oxford Study per studenti d'inglese*.

Definitions!
Which one is *wrong*?

1 What does *book* mean?
A It means to get tickets, a room in a hotel or a table at a restaurant.
B A book is something that you read.
C It means the same as *fast*.

2 What does *park* mean?
A It's an adjective. It's the opposite of *long*.
B It's a place in a town with trees and grass.
C It's a verb. It means leave the car somewhere.

3 What does *left* mean?
A It's means the same as *difficult*.
B It's the opposite of *right*.
C It's the past of *leave*.

4 What does *match* mean?
A It means the same as *game*. For example, a *football match*.
B It's a kind of drink. It's similar to tea.
C It's a small piece of wood to light a cigarette or a fire.

5 What does *fit* mean?
A It's a verb. We say clothes or shoes fit if they are not too big and not too small.
B It's an adjective. It means the same as *healthy*.
C It's a noun. It's a kind of chair in a church.

6 What does *ring* mean?
A It's a noun. You wear a ring on your finger.
B It means the opposite of *large*.
C It means to call someone on the phone.

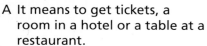

How to **talk about vocabulary**

G grammar in the dictionary   **V** definition words   **P** pronunciation in the dictionary

(handwritten top margin)
Salmon is a kind of fish.
Left is the opposite of right.
Son sounds the same as sun.
Easy is the opposite of difficult.
Apple is a kind of fruit.

A Think about words and meanings

1 Look at **In the dictionary** opposite. Find an example of each.
- 1 a noun = *leaf*
- 2 a verb =
- 3 an adjective =
- 4 a plural =

2 Complete the sentences with a partner. Use the pictures to help you.

1 I'm going to *watch* a football *match* on TV.

2 I'm going to *ring* 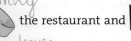 the restaurant and *book* a table.

3 Oscar always *leaves* 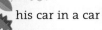 his car in a car *park.*

3 Complete the sentences. Use each word twice.
book cook leaves park watch

1 My mum works in a restaurant. She's a _cook_ .
2 You can't _park_ your car there.
3 The train _leaves_ at twelve.
4 I often read a _book_ before going to sleep.
5 Shall we _watch_ a DVD?
6 Did you _book_ a room in the hotel?
7 The garden is covered in _leaves_ .
8 We went for a walk in the _park_ .
9 My _watch_ says the time is 3.15.
10 You can _cook_ this in the microwave.

B Pronunciation in the dictionary

4 Match these words and their pronunciation. Then check in a dictionary.
buy son meet ~~write~~ knew sun
wait meat ~~right~~ new weight bye

- 1 /raɪt/ *write, right*   3 /weɪt/ *weight, wait*   5 /njuː/ *knew, new*
- 2 /sʌn/ *son, sun*   4 /baɪ/ *buy, bye*   6 /miːt/ *meet, meat*

5 Find the pronunciation of these words in the dictionary. Try to say the words.
debt receipt quay rough
det risit ki raf

6 **1D.1▶** Listen and check.

C Read definitions and respond

7 Look at **Definitions!** opposite. Work with a partner. Read the quiz and decide which definition (a, b or c) is wrong.

8 **1D.2▶** Listen and check your answers.

9 Make definitions from the table.

Write	means the same as	leave
Salmon	sounds the same as	sun
Left	is the opposite of	fruit
Son	is a kind of	difficult
Little	is the past of	small
Easy		right
Apple		fish

Example *Write* sounds the same as *right*.

(handwritten) Little means the same as small.
Left is the past of leave.

D Grammar in the dictionary

10 Write these words in the table.
bought verb ~~adjective~~ slowly noun children

	short for ...	example
adj	*adjective*	slow, quick
adv	adverb	slowly, quickly, well.
n	noun	child, table, apple
pl	plural	children, friends, sisters, feet
v	verb	buy, play, work,
pt	past tense	bought, played,

11 Complete the story with these words. Use a dictionary to help you.
asked boss checks job lazy new office questions rude stopped viruses well ~~works~~

Justin is a computer technician. He ¹ _works_ (v) in an ² _office_ (n) and he ³ _checks_ (v) the system for ⁴ _viruses_ (pl). He's ⁵ _lazy_ (adj) and doesn't do his ⁶ _job_ (n) very ⁷ _well_ (adj). Yesterday, Anna ⁸ _stopped_ (pt) at his desk and ⁹ _asked_ (pt) him some ¹⁰ _questions_ (pl). Justin said some very ¹¹ _rude_ (adj) things about the ¹² _new_ (adj) boss. He didn't know it, but Anna *is* the new ¹³ _boss_ (n)! The moral of the story is 'Always find out who you are talking to!'

ABCD Put it all together

12 Work in a four, organized as Pair A and Pair B. Pair A look at **Definitions!** on ≫ p.126. Pair B look at **Definitions!** on ≫ p.132. Add a wrong definition in questions 2 and 3 and complete the missing example in question 3.

13 Take turns to be A and B.
A Read out a question and the three possible answers, a, b and c.
B Guess which definition is wrong.

I can talk about vocabulary.

Tick ✓ the lines.   with a lot of help   with some help   on my own   very easily

Writing A learning biography

A Read for general meaning

1 Read the text. Don't worry about the spelling mistakes! What language is Cleo studying?

I'm studying ~~French~~ at the moment. It's the most important ~~langage~~ in West Africa, and I want to travel to Senegal and Mali next year.

I go to evening classes three times a week. We have a coursebook, and I ~~always~~ study it if I've got a free moment, on the bus for ~~example~~. I also have a ~~vocabary~~ notebook, and I ~~writ~~ new words in there, with an example sentence. I've got some CDs for listening practice, and I ~~listen~~ to them when I'm in the house cooking or cleaning. I ~~somtimes~~ listen to Radio Paris too, and I can ~~undestand~~ a little.

Cleo Roberts

2 Read the sentences. Are they *true* or *false*?
In the text, Cleo tells us ...
1 she wants to travel to Senegal next year. *True*
2 she goes to classes three mornings a week. F
3 she reads her coursebook on the bus. T
4 she reads her vocabulary notebook when she's cooking. F
5 she listens to French radio. T

3 Ask your partner these questions.
1 Why are you learning English?
2 When do you study your coursebook?
3 What do you write in your notebook?
4 How do you practise listening?

B Think about learning English

4 Work with a partner. What verbs can you use to talk about learning a language?
1 *write, read, send* email
2 listen, write, sing, songs
3 watch, listen, read DVDs
4 read, write books
5 play, write software computer games
6 write, read, review my notes revise, study
7 talk to, listen to, other students practice with
8 listen to the radio

5 Why and How? Answer the questions.
1 Why is Cleo studying this language?
2 How does she study it?

6 Here are some points about learning English. Do they answer the question *Why do you study?* or *How do you study?*
1 I write new words in a notebook. *How*
2 I want to visit Canada. Why
3 I listen to CDs in English on the bus. How
4 I watch DVDs in English. How
5 I need English in my work. Why
6 I need to read books in English at university. Why
7 I meet English speakers in a pub in my town. How
8 I learn the words of songs in English. How

7 **1E.1▶** Luisa is studying English. Listen and write *why* and *how* notes in the table.

Studying English		Luisa	me
Why?		want to go visit Canada	
How?	lessons	2 English	one per week
	study	homework	homework
	practice	spelling	

8 Write notes for you in the table.

C Check spelling

9 Correct the mistakes in Cleo's writing. Add one letter to each <u>underlined</u> word.

ABC Put it all together

10 Write a learning biography for you. Use your notes from exercise 8 to help you.

11 Check your spelling.

12 Give your paragraph to your partner. Do you do the same things?

I can write a learning biography.
Tick ✓ the line.   with a lot of help   with some help   on my own   very easily

Unit 1 Review

A Grammar

1 Possessive 's Add *s*, *'s*, *s'* or nothing in the spaces in this text. There are nine missing letters.

My name s ¹ is Flavio. I've got two sister s ² and a brother. My sister s ³ name s ⁴ are Maria and Celia. My brother s ⁵ name's ⁶ is Lucio. In my country, we take both our parent' s ⁷ surname s ⁸. Our mother s ⁹ surname s ¹⁰ comes first and our father' s ¹¹ surname s ¹² comes second. My surname s' ¹³ are Arantes and Ferreiro.

2 Present simple -*s* or -*es* endings Complete the text with the correct form of these verbs.

~~take~~ ~~watch~~ ~~get up~~ ~~go~~ ~~finish~~
~~sing~~ ~~have~~ ~~start~~ ~~read~~ ~~play~~

Keira ¹*gets up* early and ² took running. She ³ has breakfast and ⁴ goes the train to work. She ⁵ starts work at 9.00 and ⁶ finished at 5.30. In the evening, she ⁷ watched TV or ⁸ read a book. At the weekend, she ⁹ song and ¹⁰ played the piano in a band.

3 *be* and *do* in questions Complete the questions with these forms of *be* and *do*.

is   are   ~~was~~   were   do   does   did

1 What *was* on TV last night?
2 What did you do last weekend?
3 Where is my glasses?
4 Where are you born?
5 Where do you live now?
6 Where were your family come from?
7 Who does your favourite actor?

4 Pronouns and possessive adjectives Underline the correct word.

1 I've got a sister and a brother. They/**Their** names are Carol and Colin.
2 **I**/My parents' names are Pedro and Paula.
3 What's you/**your** name?
4 Chan Kong-Sang is from China. He/**His** nickname's Jackie.
5 We/**Our** names are Marta and Pablo. **We**/Our're from Spain.

5 Grammar in the dictionary Look at the underlined words in the text. Write the number next to the type of word.

adjective ☐   adverb ☐   noun ☐
plural noun ☐   verb ☐ 1   past tense ☐

Run is a verb. When people move¹ their feet² faster than walking they are running. People move quickly³ when they run. A cat⁴ can run faster⁵ than a mouse. Yesterday, a mouse ran⁶ into my garden.

B Vocabulary

6 Personal details Complete the form with your personal details.

1	Surname	OBERMILLER
2	First name	KINGA
3	Age	39
4	Nationality	POLISH
5	Date and place of birth	17.10.1972 WLOCLAWEK
6	Address	47 PARK ROAD
7	Telephone	07926043633
8	Marital status	HAPPY SINGLE
9	Job	ASSISTANT LAUNDRY
10	Place of work	BLC
11	Interests	PSYCHOLOGY, ESOTERIC, BOOKS, MOVIES,

7 Documents Find the words.

1 enot note   2 kittec ticket   3 volpenee envelope

5 ilastini
4 cencile licence

6 drac card   7 gebda badge   8 sportsap passport

8 Question pronouns Complete each question with a different question word.

A ¹ *Where* do you live?
B In Prague.
A ² Who do you live with?
B Nobody. I live alone.
A ³ What time do you get up?
B Eight o'clock.
A ⁴ When do you start work?
B Half past nine.
A ⁵ How do you get to work?
B By bus.
A ⁶ Which day of the week is your favourite?
B Sunday.
A ⁷ Why ?
B Because I can relax.

Day trips from Bangor

North Wales

1 Visit Anglesey's beautiful beaches, and enjoy watersports such as surfing, canoeing, diving, and windsurfing.

2 Go walking among the lakes, forests, and mountains of the Snowdonia National Park. The park covers 823 square miles and has some of the most beautiful countryside in Britain.

3 Visit the famous Swallow Falls on the Llugwy River, near the charming town of Betws-y-Coed.

4 See a village in Anglesey with one of the longest names in the world: Llanfairpwllgwyngyllgogerychwyrndrobwyllllantysiliogogogoch. The sign in the railway station is as long as the platform!

5 See the ruins of the church on Llanddwyn Island. The island was the home of Saint Dwynwen, the Welsh Saint Valentine.

6 Take the mountain railway to the top of Snowdon, the highest mountain in England and Wales. On a clear day, you can see England in one direction and Ireland in the other.

7 Walk down the 400 steps to the South Stack lighthouse on Holy Island. This lighthouse is one of the most spectacular in the country.

8 See the famous old castle at Conwy. King Edward built the castle in only four years.

Snowdon Mountain Railway

Return Fares

Llanberis to summit

Adults	£21.00
Children under 15	£14.00
Students	£17.00

Single Fares

Llanberis to summit

Adult	£14.00
Children under 15	£11.00
Students	£11.00

Journey times

One way	1 hour
Round trip	2½ hours
First train	9.00 a.m.

Distance

4½ miles (7½ kilometres)

Telephone 0870 4580033 ext 100   **Email** info@snowdonmountainrailway.co.uk

10 miles
10 kilometres

SNOWDON
3,560 ft
1085m

How to ask for tourist information

v tourist attractions **P** rhythm in *How* questions

A Read a tourist brochure

1 Read **Day trips from Bangor** opposite. Match the day trips with the photos.

2 Which trips opposite would you like to go on? Why? Compare with a partner.

3 Read **Snowdon Mountain Railway** and look at the map opposite. Answer the questions.
   1 How high is Snowdon?
   2 How far is the summit from Llanberis?
   3 How long is the round trip?
   4 How much is the single fare for a child?

B Vocabulary tourist attractions

4 Look at **Tourist attractions** opposite and find the things in the pictures. Which are not in any of the pictures?
   Example   mountain – pictures a and f

5 Which tourist attractions are man-made? Which are natural?

6 **2A.1▶** Listen and check. Then listen again and repeat.

7 Tell a partner about the tourist attractions in your area.

C Pronunciation rhythm in *How* questions

8 **2A.2** Listen and repeat the questions. Stress the word *How* <u>and</u> the adjective after it.

●	●	•	•
How	**high**	is	it?
How	**old**	is	it?
How	**far**	is	it?
How	**much**	are	they?
How	**long**	is	it?

9 Ask your partner questions from the box.

How	much	is	the fare from here to ... ?
	old	are	the highest mountain in ... ?
	far		it from your home to ... ?
	long		your journey home?
	high		*your ideas* ...

Example   **A** How long is your journey home?
            B Half an hour.

D Listen for specific information

10 **2A.3▶** Sara is a tourist visiting North Wales. Listen. Where is she?

11 Listen again and answer the questions.
   1 Why doesn't Sara want to walk up the mountain?
   2 How high is the mountain?
   3 How far is the station?
   4 How can you get to the station?
   5 How long's the round trip on the train?
   6 What's at the top of the mountain?
   7 Why doesn't Sara want to go on this trip?

12 Check your answers in the audio script on p.150. <u>Underline</u> useful questions in the conversation.

13 Role play.
   Student A
   Ask B for information about the Eiffel Tower. Go to **»** p.126.

   Student B
   Ask A for information about the London Eye. Go to **»** p.132.

ABCD Put it all together

14 Think of three tourist attractions you know. Write their names on a piece of paper.

15 Work with a partner. Think of questions to ask about tourist attractions.
   Examples   What's it called?
                Where is it?
                How old is it?

16 Change partners. Take turns to be **A** and **B**.
   Student A   You're a tourist. Ask for information about the three places on your partner's paper.
   Student B   You work in the tourist office. Answer **A**'s questions.

I can ask for tourist information.

Tick ✓ the line.   with a lot of help   with some help   on my own   very easily

The Travel Agent

How to describe places

G adjective order **V** fact and opinion adjectives **P** stress-timed rhythm

A Read and listen for detail

1 Do you know any tourist attractions in these countries? Compare ideas in small groups.

Scandinavia Spain Egypt the USA Mexico *your ideas*

2 Read **The Travel Agent** opposite. <u>Underline</u> the tourist attractions. Which countries in exercise 1 do they come from?

3 **2B.1▶** Listen and complete the missing adjectives in **The Travel Agent** text opposite.

4 Read the sentences. Write *true* or *false*.
1 The customers want to book a safari. *True*
2 Jen wants to sell a holiday in Scandinavia. T
3 The customers want to see insects. F
4 Jen describes Scandinavia to the customers. F
5 The customers aren't interested in a holiday in Scandinavia. T

B Grammar adjective order

5 Complete the rule with *before* or *after*.

That's a lovely little insect!

That's a horrible little insect!

Put the fact after the opinion.
Put the opinion before the fact.

6 Work with a partner. Find more fact and opinion adjectives in the picture story.

fact		opinion	
long	b_____	nice	p_____
b_____	o_____	h_____	f_____
w_____	l_____	b_____	

7 Tick ✓ the correct phrases. Correct the wrong phrases.
1 beautiful old railway
2 pretty white villages
3 white beautiful beaches *beautiful white beaches*
4 horrible little insects
5 water blue lovely *lovely blue water*
6 long nice safari *nice long safari*
7 pretty little island

8 **2B.2▶** Listen, check and repeat.

9 Work with a partner. Describe your pictures and find the differences. Decide which place would be better for a holiday.
Student A Look at the picture on **≫** p.126.
Student B Look at the picture on **≫** p.132.

More practice? **Grammar Bank** **≫** p.137.

C Pronunciation stress-timed rhythm

10 **2B.3▶** Listen and repeat the three rhythms.

rhythm 1 ● nice ● blue ● lakes

rhythm 2 ●● lovely ●● quiet ●● beaches

rhythm 3 ●●● interesting ●●● African ●●● animals

11 **2B.4▶** Listen and repeat. Are these rhythms 1, 2, or 3?
a **beau**tiful **col**ourful **vill**ages
b **fine old trees**
c **pret**ty **lit**tle **is**lands

D Listen to someone describing a place

12 **2B.5▶** Listen to Sara talking about her home. <u>Underline</u> where you think she lives.
The north of England
The south of Italy
The north of Spain
North-east Brazil

13 Listen again and tick ✓ the things Sara talks about.
☑ beaches ☐ lakes ☐ castles ☐ forests
☐ towns ☐ islands ☐ mountains

14 Work with a partner. Can you remember what adjectives she uses to describe the nouns in exercise 13? Read the audio script on **≫** p.151 and check.
Example beaches – nice, quiet

ABCD Put it all together

15 Make notes about a place to go on holiday. Use these ideas:
weather beaches food people things to do

16 Work in small groups. Describe your place and agree on the best one.

I can describe a place.
Tick ✓ the line. with a lot of help with some help on my own very easily

Weather

Noun	Adj
rain	rainy
snow	snowy
cloud	cloudy
fog	foggy
storm	stormy
sun	sunny
wind	windy
heat	hot
cold	cold

Temperature

high — hot
— warm
— cool
low — cold

Rainfall

heavy — wet
light —
— dry

a b c d

London Weather

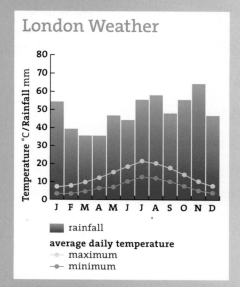

Temperature °C / Rainfall mm

J F M A M J J A S O N D

■ rainfall

average daily temperature
— maximum
— minimum

Afro hair

Going to Extremes

Nick Middleton, a geography lecturer at Oxford University, likes bad weather. In National Geographic's four-part TV series *Going to Extremes*, Nick travels to the places with the most extreme weather in the world – the hottest, coldest, wettest, and driest places.

In one episode of the series, Nick visits the Danakil in North East Ethiopia. The Danakil is a desert of salt. It's 100 metres lower than sea level and it's hot! The temperature is often higher than 50 degrees. The highest recorded temperature in the world is 57° in Libya. But the Danakil has <u>the highest</u> average temperature. In summer, it's never lower than 40°.

The local people, the Afar, are very tough. The men carry guns and long knives. But Nick finds their softer side: hair. These men spend two hours a day working on their big *Afro* hair. In this heat, they say, their hair is better than a hat.

In another episode of the series, Nick travels to the world's coldest inhabited place. In Oymyakon, Siberia, the average winter temperature is lower than minus 25°. Only Antarctica is colder, but nobody lives there. Nick also visits the wettest place in the world, Mawsynram in India, and the driest place, Arica in Chile.

How to compare the weather in different places

G comparative and superlative adjectives   **V** weather   **P** -er and -est endings

A Vocabulary weather

1 Look at **Weather** opposite. Use the words to describe the pictures.
Example Picture a = It's windy and sunny.

2 **2C.1▶** Listen. Are the sentences true where you are now?
Example 1 = It's raining. True! (or False!)

B Read for detail

3 Which are the hottest, coldest, wettest, and driest places you've visited? Tell a partner.

4 Read **Going to Extremes** opposite. Which four places does Nick Middleton visit?

5 Read again and answer the questions.
1 What's the highest recorded temperature in the world? *57° Libya*
2 Which has a higher average temperature, the Danakil or Libya? *Danakil*
3 What's the lowest summer temperature in the Danakil? *40°*
4 What's the average winter temperature in Oymyakon? *25°*
5 Which is colder, Siberia or Antarctica? *Antarctica is colder then Siberia*

C Grammar comparative and superlative adjectives

6 Read sentences a, b, and c and answer the questions.
a Antarctica is cold.
b Antarctica is colder than Siberia. (comparative)
c Antarctica is the coldest place in the world. (superlative)

Which sentence talks about:
1 one place compared with all other places? *C*
2 only one place? *A*
3 one place compared with another place? *B*

7 Complete the grammar box.

		comparative	superlative
one syllable	cold	colder	the coldest
	high	*higher*	*the highest*
one syllable ending vowel + consonant	wet	wetter	the wettest
	hot	*hotter*	*the hottest*
two or more syllables	extreme	more extreme	the most extreme
	uncomfortable	*more*	*the most*
But two syllables ending -y	windy	windier	the windiest
	heavy	*heavier*	*the heaviest*
irregular	good	better	*the biggest*
	bad	*worse*	the worst

8 Read **Going to Extremes** again. Underline the comparative and superlative adjectives.

9 Look at **London Weather** opposite. Complete these sentences with comparatives or superlatives.
1 (cold) January is the *coldest* month.
2 (wet) November is *wetter then* September.
3 (warm) July is *the warmest* month.
4 (dry) March is *drier then* February.
5 (high) In summer, the temperature is *higher then* 20°.
6 (low) In winter, the temperature is *lower then* 5°.

More practice? **Grammar Bank** >> p.137.

D Pronunciation -er and -est endings

10 **2C.2▶** Listen and say A, B, or C.

A	B	C
cold weather	colder weather	coldest weather
windy city	windier city	windiest city
heavy snow	heavier snow	heaviest snow
hot summer	hotter summer	hottest summer

11 Test a partner.
Example **A** Cold weather.   **B** A!

E Listen for specific information

12 What do you know about the climate in England and Australia? Tell a partner.

13 **2C.3▶** Listen. What do you learn about Alan Brent?

14 Listen again and complete the sentences about the weather in London and Sydney.
1 The rain is heavier in *Sydney*.
2 _____ is cloudier.
3 _____ is sunnier and hotter.
4 In Sydney, the most uncomfortable months are _____ and _____.
5 When Alan arrived in London, the temperature was _____.

ABCDE Put it all together

15 Look at **London Weather** again. Write notes to compare it with the weather in another place you know.
Example winter = Moscow colder than London

16 Tell your partner about your place compared to London. Use your notes to help you. Which place has better weather?

I can compare the weather in different places.

Tick ✓ the line.   with a lot of help   with some help   on my own   very easily

Souvenirs

bag cap cup fan key ring knife
mug plate postcard poster rug T-shirt

Handwritten labels around images: rug, mug, key ring, fan, mug, cup, knife, cap, plate, poster, T-shirt, bag, postcard

Souvenir Challenge
Can you guess where these souvenirs are from?

Map labels:

NORTH AMERICA
9 — The USA
7 — Mexico
CENTRAL AMERICA
Panama — 10
SOUTH AMERICA
Peru — 11

UK — 4 3 — Germany
EUROPE — 5 — Austria
Tunisia — 12
NORTH AFRICA
THE MIDDLE EAST
6 — Jordan
2 — Egypt

Russia — 8
ASIA
China — 1

Postcard

Hi James

Having a great time here in Cairo.

Today we visited the Khan el-Khalili Bazaar. It's one of the biggest bazaars in the world and we got lost! There are thousands of shops. I bought a leather jacket and a rug. We spent an hour in a carpet shop and the man gave us tea. Then he wasn't very happy because we left without buying anything!

Tomorrow, we're going to visit the Cairo opera on the island of Gezira.

See you next week

Love from Petra (and Bernie!)

How to talk about personal things

G past simple   v souvenirs, countries, and regions

A Vocabulary souvenirs, countries, and regions

1 Work with a partner. Think of the names of countries in each of these places.

Asia   North America
Central America   South America
Europe   The Middle East
North Africa

Example   Asia – China, India, Japan …

2 Look at **Souvenirs** opposite. Match them with the photos.
Example   Picture 1 – fan

3 **2D.1▶** Listen and check.

4 **2D.2▶** Listen to two people doing the **Souvenir Challenge** opposite. Which souvenir do they talk about?

5 Do the **Souvenir Challenge** quiz with a partner. Use the world map to help you.

6 Ask and answer in small groups.
Have you got any favourite souvenirs?
Are there any typical souvenirs in your home region?

B Read a postcard

7 Read **Postcard** opposite. Which souvenir in the photos did Petra buy?

8 Work with a partner. Do you think these sentences are *true* or *false*? If you think they are *false*, say why.
1 Petra lives in Cairo. F
2 Petra wrote the postcard before breakfast. F
3 Petra spent some money in the bazaar. T
4 Petra went there alone. F
5 The man in the carpet shop wanted Petra to pay for the tea. F

C Grammar past simple

9 Complete the sentences in the grammar box. Which verbs are irregular?

+	–	?
She went there alone.	She didn't go there alone.	Did she go there alone?
I bought a jacket.	I didn't buy a jacket.	Did you buy a jacket?
We visited the bazaar.	We didn't visit the bazaar.	Did you visit the bazaar?

10 Write the past form of these irregular verbs.

bring	*brought*	go	went
buy	bought	have	had
do	did	leave	left
find	found	send	sent
get		spend	
give	gave	take	took

11 Complete the conversation with the correct past simple form of one of these verbs.

buy do enjoy ~~get~~ give (x2) work

A Where *did* you *get* that T-shirt?
B My sister gave it to me.
A Where did she buy it?
B Panama. She worked there for three years.
A What did she do?
B She gave English classes.
A Did she enjoy it?
B Yes, she did.

More practice? **Grammar Bank** >> p.137.

D Listen for key words

12 **2D.3▶** Listen and read about Petra and James talking about one of the souvenirs in the photos opposite. Which one do they talk about? How do you know? Underline the key words in the conversation.

James   That's nice. I love the blue colour.
Petra   Mmm, yes.
J   Where did you get it?
P   My boyfriend gave it to me. Because of the two fish. I'm a Pisces.
J   Oh. Where did he get it?
P   He bought it on a beach in Mexico.
J   Mexico? Did you go with him?
P   No, I didn't go. I just got the plate!
J   Oh well. Better than nothing.

13 **2D.4▶** Listen to Petra and James talking about other souvenirs opposite. Which three do they talk about? Make notes of the key words.

ABCD Put it all together

14 Ask other students in the class about their personal things. Who bought their things in the most interesting places?
Example   A I like your glasses. Where did you get them?
            B I bought them at the duty free shop in Vienna airport.
            A Oh …

I can talk about personal things.

Tick ✓ the line.   with a lot of help   with some help   on my own   very easily

Writing A description of a region

A Read a description of a region

1 Read these emails. What things in the photo does Elvira mention?

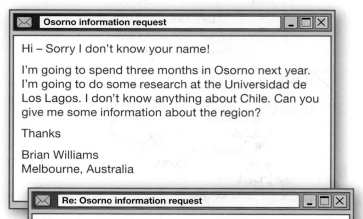

Osorno information request

Hi – Sorry I don't know your name!

I'm going to spend three months in Osorno next year. I'm going to do some research at the Universidad de Los Lagos. I don't know anything about Chile. Can you give me some information about the region?

Thanks

Brian Williams
Melbourne, Australia

Re: Osorno information request

Hi Brian

Osorno is about 920km south of the capital, Santiago. Osorno is in a region called the Lake District. It is one of most beautiful regions in the country. There are lovely old forests, blue nice lakes and amazing waterfalls. The forests are more than 2000 years old – some of the older forests in the world. Our region is famous for its snow-capped volcanoes, many of them more than 3000 metres high. Our winters are cold and wet, but there's good snow for skiing in the mountains. Our summers are quite heat, with temperatures around 25°.

Here's a photo of Osorno Volcano. I get the photo from the internet.

I hope this information is helpful to you.

Best wishes
Elvira Pardo
University relations officer

2 Correct the grammar mistakes in Elvira's email. There's a mistake in each line marked.

3 Read Elvira's email again. and complete these notes about Osorno.

	Osorno, Chile	my home town: _____, _____
location	about 920km _____, of the capital, S_____	
name of region	_____	
scenery	forests, l_____, w_____, v_____	
weather	winters = _____ summers = _____	

B Get ideas to write about

4 Write notes about your home town in the table in exercise 3.

5 Look at the things you wrote for scenery in your region. Add one or two adjectives to each one.
Example   cathedrals
                    fine old cathedrals

6 Elvira Pardo says the forests in her region are *some of the oldest in the world*. Write some superlatives about your region. Use *some of* and *one of*.
Example   It's the largest town in Albania.
                    We have some of the best beaches in France.
                    It's one of the oldest churches in Argentina.

7 Elvira Pardo says her region is *famous for its snow-capped volcanoes*. Write a sentence about what your region is famous for.
Example   Our region is famous for its red wine.

AB Put it all together

8 A person from another country is coming to your region (or another region you know) for three months. Write a description to send to them.

9 Read your partner's text and answer the questions.
   – How many interesting things does it say about the region?
   – Check the grammar of your partner's text.

I can write a description of a region.
Tick ✓ the line.   with a lot of help   with some help   on my own   very easily

Unit 2 Review

A Grammar

1 Adjective order Put the sentences in order.

1 white are There lovely beaches some
There are some lovely white beaches.

2 nice like We'd a holiday long
We'd like a nice long holiday.

3 little lots There horrible insects are of
There are lots of horrible little insects.

4 old I church a beautiful saw
I saw a beautiful old church.

5 lots islands are pretty There of green
There are lots pretty of green island.

6 castle a old We visited fine
We visited a fine old castle.

7 lovely Look water! the at blue
Look at the lovely blue water.

2 Comparative and superlative adjectives Complete the text with these words. Use the comparative or superlative forms of the adjectives.

adjectives
light extreme hot heavy cold
cloudy high sunny uncomfortable

other words
the than
more most

I'm from Sydney, Australia. The rain in Sydney is
¹ *heavier than* in London. London is ² *cloudier than* Sydney but the rain is ³ *lighter*. In summer, Sydney is ⁴ *sunnier* and ⁵ *hotter than* London and the temperature is ⁶ *more extreme*. The temperature is often ⁷ *highest than* 40°. ⁸ *The most uncomfortable* months are January and February. I left Australia in February and arrived in London on ⁹ *most coldest* day of winter. It was minus 2°.

3 Past simple Find ten sentences.

1 Where	did	2 My	brother	3 My	sister	bought
4 I	you	5 Did	went	to	6 When	me
lived	buy	he	buy	Malta.	did	a
in	your	shoes?	you	7 We	you	poster.
Mexico	for	8 Who	a	didn't	arrive	home?
9 Did	a	did	present?	buy	10 Where	did
you	year.	you	go	any	souvenirs.	she
enjoy	the	holiday?	on	holiday	with?	go?

B Vocabulary

4 Tourist attractions Label the map.

a	*island*	e	*village*	i	*mountains*
b	*lantern*	f	*church*	j	*train*
c	*castle*	g	*forest*	k	*beath*
d		h	*lake*	l	*river*

5 Day trips Write the words in the poster.

~~return~~ way adult fare journey round distance

FERRY to PEDDY ISLAND

1 *Return* 3 *fare* £14
2 *Adult* Children £10
4 *Distance* Five miles
5 *Journey* One ⁶ *way* 20 mins
time ⁷ *round* trip 40 mins

6 Weather Write the words.

1 opposite of wet = *d r y*
2 opposite of cold = *hot*
3 opposite of heavy = *light*
4 adjective of fog = *foggy*
5 cold, but not very = *warm*
6 opposite of low = *high*
7 noun of hot = *heat*
8 opposite of + = *minus*
9 adjective of sun = *sunny*
10 rain falls from these = *clouds*

Adventure sports

skiing   waterskiing   snowboarding   surfing   windsurfing   skating
roller skating   climbing   ice climbing   diving   scuba-diving   skydiving

Personality Test
Are you a daredevil or a chicken?

ice climbing   *roller skating*   *scuba-diving*

skydiving   *snowboarding*   *waterskiing*

Choose the option, a, b, or c, which is nearest to your point of view.

1
a ☐ I don't like deep water.
b ☐ I prefer swimming in the sea to swimming in the pool.
c ☑ I'd like to try scuba-diving.

2
a ☐ I hate flying.
b ☑ I like planes, but I don't think I'd like to jump out of one!
c ☐ I'd love to try skydiving.

3
a ☐ Surfing's great to watch, but I think it could be dangerous.
b ☑ I can't surf but I'd love to learn.
c ☐ I'd love to surf on some really big waves, like in Hawaii.

Count your score and find your place on this scale.
a=-1   b=0   c=1

4
a ☐ I don't think I'd enjoy skating, but it's quite nice to watch on TV.
b ☐ I'd like to skate, but not on a lake – the ice could break.
c ☐ Skating's boring in the ice-rink. I'd like to skate outdoors.

5
a ☐ I can't understand why people do dangerous sports.
b ☐ I like skiing, but ski jumping? No way!
c ☐ I'd love to try ski jumping. I bet it's a great feeling.

6
a ☐ Mountain climbing's not for me. I prefer more relaxing activities.
b ☑ I like walking up mountains, but I don't think I'd enjoy rock climbing.
c ☐ I'd like to climb the highest mountain on each continent.

7
a ☐ Sunbathing's relaxing.
b ☑ Sunbathing's all right for a couple of hours.
c ☐ Sunbathing's boring. I prefer doing things.

-7 -6 -5 -4 -3 -2 -1 0 1 2 3 4 5 6 7

Did you know?

❀ On average, men score more than women on a daredevil scale.

❀ People's highest daredevil score is usually in their late teens or early twenties. After that, their score usually goes down.

How to talk about likes and dislikes

G *like doing; would like to do* v adventure sports p words beginning *sn-, sp-, sk-*

A Vocabulary adventure sports

1 Look at **Adventure sports** opposite. Guess or find the names of the sports in the photos. Do you do any of these sports? Would you like to? Why? / Why not?

2 Where do the adventure sports happen? Work with a partner and match the sports with these phrases. There may be more than one answer.

on ice   on rock   on water   on snow
under the water   from a plane   on the street
on skis   on a board   on waves   with the wind

B Pronunciation consonant clusters

3 **3A.1▶** Listen and repeat.

A	B
Paul skis.	Paula's keys.
The ski school.	The skier's cool.
She skates.	She's a skater.
Snowboard.	A snowboarder.
Spanish sport.	A Spanish supporter.

4 **3A.2▶** Listen again and say A or B. Test a partner.
Example A Paula's keys. B B!

C Read and do a personality test

5 Do the **Personality Test** opposite with a partner. Find your score. Compare your score with others.

6 Read **Did you know?** opposite. Are you surprised? Why? / Why not?

7 Work with a partner. <u>Underline</u> any vocabulary you don't understand in the texts. Choose three words and find them in a dictionary.

D Grammar *like doing; would like to do*

8 Match sentences 1 and 4 in the grammar box with meanings a and b below.

+	1 I like climbing.	4 I'd like to climb Mount Everest.
–	2 I don't like climbing.	5 I wouldn't like to climb Mount Everest.
?	3 Do you like climbing?	6 Would you like to climb Mount Everest?
	Yes, I do. / No I don't.	Yes, I would. / No I wouldn't.

a I want to do this in the future.
b I do / feel this now.

9 Write eight true sentences with these beginnings.

I like ...   I'd like to go ...
I don't like ...   I wouldn't like to go ...

Example   I like swimming.
           I wouldn't like to go ice climbing.

10 Tell your partner what you like doing. Ask your partner questions. Do you like similar things?
More practice? **Grammar Bank** >> p.138.

E Listen and follow

11 **3A.3▶** Listen to the conversations and follow the conversation maps.

Conversation 1

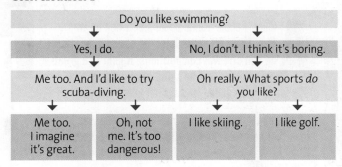

Conversation 2

12 Work with a partner. Say each conversation.

13 Change partners. Talk about a different activity.

ABCDE Put it all together

14 Write five things that:
  – you like doing
  – you'd like to do this weekend

15 Talk to other students in the class. Find the person with the most similar interests to you.

I can talk about likes and dislikes.

Tick ✓ the line.   with a lot of help   with some help   on my own   very easily

Abilities

do crosswords, puzzles, jigsaws
make dinner, clothes, a fire
play the guitar, golf, table tennis, chess

read a map, Arabic, music
ride a bike, a horse, a motorbike
use a sewing /'səʊɪŋ/ machine, a computer

Rabbit Kekai
the 85-year-old beach boy
WAIKIKI BEACH, HAWAII

Albert 'Rabbit' Kekai could surf when he was five. Now, 80 years later, he can still surf and he can still win competitions. Rabbit is a great-grandfather, but he's still physically fit. 'The water is so good,' he says. 'It keeps me young.'

Albert got the nickname 'Rabbit' because he was fast. He says that he could run the 100 metres in 9.6 seconds. When he was six, he could already ride the big waves with the older boys. In those days, the surfboards were very long and heavy, compared with today, but Rabbit was able to control the board with his quick footwork. Today's best surfers can't use those heavy old surfboards. 'They look like beginners,' says Rabbit.

In 80 years of surfing, you see a lot of different things. Rabbit was out on his board in World War Two when the first bombs fell on Pearl Harbour in 1941. 'We could see all the smoke,' he says. During the war, Rabbit worked as a scuba diver in the US army. In 1945, he returned home and started surfing again.

He taught many of Hollywood's most famous actors to surf – stars such as Gary Cooper and Kirk Douglas. More recently, he taught Kirk's son, Michael Douglas. Rabbit says Michael learned quickly. He could surf after just four lessons.

Now, Rabbit Kekai still surfs every day and he still gives lessons. He travels a lot to competitions around the world, and his wife Lynn often goes with him. With his fashionable sunglasses and Bermuda shorts, he looks like a real beach boy. He's 85 years old but he doesn't plan to stop surfing. 'I'm still looking for 100,' he says.

How to **talk about your abilities**

G ability   V abilities   P stressing the negative

A   Vocabulary abilities

1   Look at the **Abilities** phrases opposite and tick ✓ the ones you can do. Ask about your partner's skills.

– Can you do crosswords?   – No, I can't.

2   Which verbs can you use with these things?
Chinese   a camel   a digital camera
a Sudoku puzzle   tennis   a cheese sandwich

3   Add more words to the lists for the six verbs.

B   Read a magazine article

4   Work with a partner. Look at the photos opposite. What do you think the text is about?

5   Read **Rabbit Kekai** opposite and check.

6   The author's main point is that …
a   Rabbit is 85 years old.
b   an 85-year-old can still surf.
c   some famous film stars have had surf lessons.
d   modern surfers can't use the heavy old boards.

7   What do we learn about Rabbit Kekai? Write *true*, *false*, or *doesn't say*.
1   He's over 80 and he can still surf. *True*
2   He's got great-grandchildren. T
3   He was able to surf when he was five. T
4   Surfers today use very long and heavy surfboards. F
5   He could see the smoke from the bombs in Pearl Harbour. T
6   Kirk Douglas learned surfing quickly. F

C   Grammar ability

8   <u>Underline</u> examples of *can*, *could*, and *able to* in the text.

9   Complete the grammar rule below.
Use <u>can</u> to talk about ability in the present.
Use <u>could</u> to talk about ability in the past.
You can also use *be able to* to talk about ability, but it is less common than *can*.

10   Complete the text with *can*, *can't*, *could*, or *couldn't*.
When I was five
I was able to dive
I ¹ <u>could</u> swim really well
But I ² <u>couldn't</u> drive

Now, I ³ <u>can</u> cook
And I'm able to drive
I ⁴ <u>can</u> swim quite well
But now I ⁵ <u>can't</u> dive

11   **3B.1▶** Listen and check.

12   Pronunciation Listen again. Are the words *can*, *can't*, *could*, and *couldn't* stressed? Complete the rule and practise saying the text.
_____ and _____ are stressed.
_____ and _____ are not stressed.

13   Tell your partner about your abilities now and in the past. Use these ideas to help you.
cooking   sports   computers   games   languages
Example   When I was five, I could make a milkshake but I couldn't make a cake.

More practice? **Grammar Bank ▸▸ p.138.**

D   Listen for specific information

14   **3B.2▶** Listen to Ben and Sarah. Who likes mountain sports?

15   Listen again. Complete the table with these activities.
ski   windsurf   climbing
read maps   surf   mountain walking

	can do it	can't do it
Sarah	windsurf	surf, read maps.
Ben	swim, ski, climb, mountain walking	surf.

16   Work with a partner. Why do Ben and Sarah say these things? Match the sentences and reasons.
1   Windsurfing? I didn't know you were a windsurfer. b
2   Really? d
3   What about you? Do you do any water sports? c
4   What, like climbing? a

a   to ask for clarification
b   to ask for more information
c   to change the focus to the other person
d   to show surprise

17   Read the audio script on ▸▸ p.151. Act the conversation with a partner.

ABCD   Put it all together

18   Write notes to complete the table with your abilities in the past and now. Then tell a partner why these things are/were important to you. Is your partner similar to you?

at age	things you could do	things you couldn't do
	things you can do	things you can't do
NOW		

Example   **A**   When I was 10, I could play football quite well.
B   Really? Can you play now?

I can talk about my abilities.

Tick ✓ the line.   with a lot of help   with some help   on my own   very easily

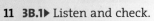

29

Nothing to do

The **carp**et's **green**
The **sof**a's **blue**
The **TV**'s **bor**ing
And **you** are **too**

I could **go** to **town**
And **meet** some **friends**
But **no** one goes **out**
Ex**cept** at week**ends**

We could **switch** it **off**
And **go** to the **park**
But there's **noth**ing to **do**
In the **park** in the **dark**

This **pro**gramme's so **bor**ing
Oh, **what** shall we **do**?
Let's change the **chan**nel
And **find** something **new**

Nowhere to **go**
Nothing to **do**
Watching TV
On the **sof**a with **you**

Jessica

Jack

TV Guide

TVC1	TVC2	Channel 3
18.00 News and weather	**18.00** Cartoon The Simpsons	**18.00** Series Belfort Road There's a surprise for Greg when Martha comes to visit.
18.30 The South Tonight Local news, weather and sports update	**18.20 Golf** Highlights of the US Open Championship.	**18.30** Comedy Three's a Crowd
19.00 National Geographic 'Going to Extremes' Nick Middleton travels to Siberia.	**19.20 Perspective** 'Climate change documentary'	**19.00 News** **19.20 Sports Week**
19.55 Poem for the Day A Walt Whitman reading		
20.00 Comedy **Mad House** More fun and games from the Mad House team.		**20.00 National Lottery**
20.30 Film **Anaconda!** Big snakes attack!	**20.30 Regional news** **20.50 National news**	**20.30 Big Brother** Who's going to leave the house today?
	**21.20 Home improvements** More practical ideas to make your house look better.	**21.15** Quiz Show **Win a Million!** Celebrity guests raise money for charity.
	22.00 The Money Programme What's it Worth? Buying foreign currency: Where to go for the best exchange rates.	**22.00** Film **Psycho** Hitchcock season – a classic thriller
22.45 Police Action Series **Crime Scene** Lost documents help police solve this week's crime.	**22.30 Change your Husband!**	

How to suggest what to do

G *could* (possibility)   V making suggestions   P intonation in suggestions

A Read and find

1 Look at the picture of **Jessica** and **Jack** opposite. What are they thinking? Tell a partner.

2 **3C.1▶** Listen and read **Nothing to do** opposite. Find the opposites of these words in the poem.
old   light   switch on   interesting   something to do
stay at home   somewhere to go
Example old – new

(handwritten: dark, switch off, boring, nothing to do, Roobut, nowhere to go)

3 Practise saying the poem. Stress the bold syllables.

4 Read the **TV Guide** opposite. With a partner, choose three programmes to watch together.

B Listen for specific information

5 **3C.2▶** Listen to two conversations. Which programmes from the TV guide do they talk about?
a Conversation 1   b Conversation 2

6 Answer the questions. Give reasons.
Conversation 1
1 Does the woman want to watch the film?
2 Does the man want to watch the film? What does the woman suggest?

Conversation 2
3 Does the boy want to watch the lottery?
4 Does the boy want to watch the film?

C Vocabulary making suggestions

7 Match the beginnings and ends of the sentences.
1 ☐ What shall we ...   a off the TV.
2 ☐ Shall we watch ...   b playing a game?
3 ☐ How about ...   c watch?
4 ☐ Let's switch ...   d go out.
5 ☐ We could ...   e the news?

8 **3C.3▶ Pronunciation** Listen and check. Listen again and repeat.

9 Put the conversation in order with a partner.
☐ Let's see. We could watch *Sports Week*.
☐ OK. What's on?
☐1☐ What shall we do?
☐ No, let's watch the *National Geographic* programme.
☐ OK. Good idea!
☐2☐ Shall we just stay at home and watch TV?

10 **3C.4▶** Listen and check. Say the conversation with a partner, but change the names of the programmes.

11 Have similar conversations with your books closed.

D Grammar *could* (possibility)

12 Read the grammar box and decide if the sentences below it are about ability or possibility.

could = ability in the past	*could* = possibility in the present
She could sing well as a child.	We could watch *The Simpsons*.
He could play the guitar when he was three.	We could go out tonight.

1 I could swim when I was four.   *Ability*
2 We could stay at home and watch TV if you want. P
3 We could watch *Sports Week*. P
4 Tom could play chess very well when he was younger. A
5 We could have a game of tennis. P
6 They could speak French when they were children. A
7 She could run very fast when she was young. A
8 We could go to the cinema after dinner. P

13 Work with a partner. Talk about three or more things you could do tonight.
Example   **A** We could watch the news.
            B Oh no. Let's ...

More practice? **Grammar Bank** ≫ p.138.

ABCD Put it all together

14 Imagine that you're planning a night out with other students in your class. With a partner, write some ideas about:
– where to meet
– places to go
– things to do
– how much to spend
– what to eat and drink
– how to get there

15 Work in small groups and suggest things you could do.
Example   **A** What shall we do?
            B We could go to a restaurant.
            C Yes, good idea. Or we could ...

16 Tell the class about your suggestions. Which suggestion is the best?

I can suggest what to do.

Tick ✓ the line.   with a lot of help   with some help   on my own   very easily

MOVIE MAGAZINE

QUIZ OF THE MONTH Classic film moments from the 20th century

1 True or false: Stan Laurel's going to fall. F

2 Do you know the name of the other character in this comedy?
Slapstick

3 Someone's going to bite that girl's neck. What's his name? *Dracula*

4 This 1931 horror movie was based on a novel. Who wrote it?
a   Mary Shelley
b   Bram Stoker
c   Arthur Conan Doyle

5 What's the name of this 1939 epic film?
a   *Gone With The River*
b   *Gone With The Money*
c   *Gone With The Wind*

6 What are they going to do?
a   Kiss   b   Cry   c   Fight

7 The character in the middle's going to die. What's his name? *Julius Cezar*

8 This 1953 epic was based on a play. Who wrote it?
a   Oscar Wilde
b   Agatha Christie
c   William Shakespeare

9 Who was the director of the 1960 thriller *Psycho*?
a   Steven Spielberg
b   Alfred Hitchcock
c   Martin Scorcese

10 In this scene, a character's going to kill somebody in the shower. What's the character's name?
a   Norman Bates
b   Frankenstein
c   Jack the Ripper

Daniel Craig

11 Sean Connery played James Bond in the 1962 spy movie *Dr No*. Name two more Bond actors. *Roger Moore* *Pierce Brosnan.*

12 What's going to happen in this scene? Say *true* or *false*.
a   The spider's going to walk up Bond's arm. T
b   The spider's going to bite Bond. F
c   Bond's going to kill the spider. T

13 *Blade Runner* is a 1982 science fiction movie set in the future. Here we see Harrison Ford in a difficult moment. What's going to happen? Say *true* or *false*.
a   He's going to fall.
b   He's going to climb up.
c   Somebody's going to help him.

14 We all know what's going to happen to the ship, *The Titanic*. But what's going to happen to these two young lovers in this 1997 romance?
a   The boy's going to die.
b   The girl's going to die.
c   They're both going to die.

How to talk about what's going to happen

G *going to* (predictions) **V** types of story; films **P** the letter *r*

A Read and do a quiz

1 What types of films do you like? Tell a partner.

2 Look at the photos opposite with a partner. Do you know these films?

3 Read **Movie Magazine** opposite and do the quiz.

4 Are there any words you don't understand? <u>Underline</u> them.

5 Choose three of your <u>underlined</u> words. Guess the meanings. Think about these questions:

  1 Can I find the meaning in the pictures?

  2 Can I guess the meaning of the word from the sentence it's in?

  3 Is the word similar to a word in my language?

6 Check the meaning of your three words in a dictionary.

B Vocabulary types of story; films

7 Look at **Types of story** opposite. Find the words in **Movie Magazine** and match them with these meanings.

word	meaning
1 *an epic*	a long story about a time in history
2 *a horror movie*	a very frightening story, about vampires, for example
3 *thriller*	an exciting story about crime, for example
4 *an action film*	a film with a lot of fast action
5 *a comedy*	a funny story
6 *a romance*	a love story
7 *a play*	a story for the theatre
8 *science fiction*	a book with a fictional story

8 Find one example of each type of story in the quiz. Try to think of more examples of your own.

9 Work with a partner. Think of three films. Write the titles and some true or false statements.

Example   The Da Vinci Code

1 This is a comedy.

2 It's set in Paris.

3 It's based on a novel by Dan Brown.

4 The main actors are Tom Hanks and Audrey Tatou.

5 Alfred Hitchcock directed it.

10 Read your statements to a new partner. Can they guess if they are true or false?

11 Test a partner. Actor, director, or character?

Example   **A** Tom Hanks.

         B Actor!

C Grammar *going to* (predictions)

12 Complete the grammar box.

	I	he / she / it	you / we / they
+	I'm going *to be* late.	He's going to fall.	They're *going to kiss*.
−	I'm not going to be late.	He's *not going to fall*.	They *are* not *going to kiss*.
?	Am I going to be late?	*Is* he *going to fall*?	Are they going to kiss?

Use *going to* to predict the future based on what you can see.

Example   He's going to fall.

13 Look at **Movie Magazine** again. <u>Underline</u> examples of *going to* in the quiz.

14 Work with a partner. Make sentences with *going to* about the other pictures in the movie quiz.

Example Vivian Leigh and Clark Gable are going to kiss. Harrison Ford isn't going to fall.

More practice? **Grammar Bank** » p.138.

D Pronunciation the letter *r*

15 **3D.1▶** Listen to a British speaker say these words. Which letters *r* are not pronounced? <u>Underline</u> them.

acto<u>r</u> sta<u>r</u> sto<u>r</u>y crime directo<u>r</u> thrille<u>r</u> characte<u>r</u> horro<u>r</u> Harrison Fo<u>r</u>d Laurel and Hardy Harry Potte<u>r</u> Star Wars

16 Tick ✓ the correct ending to the rule.

In British English, you only pronounce the letter *r* …

a at the end of a word.

b before a vowel sound.

c after a vowel sound.

ABCD Put it all together

17 Work with a partner and find the differences between the film studios.

Student A Look at the picture of a film studio on » p.126 and say what's going to happen.

Student B Look at the picture of a film studio on » p.133 and say what's going to happen.

Writing An invitation

A Read for information

1 Read these three invitations. Which one would you like to get?

1

Hi Marek

Italy are playing Germany in the World Cup tonight. If you're free, we could watch it together. It's on *Sky Sports*. I haven't got satellite TV, but we could watch the match in *The Castle*. It starts at 8.00. What do you think?

Niko

2

Hi Marek

'Angels and Demons' is coming out at the weekend. Shall we go and see it on Saturday? It's on at the *Odeon* in Hope Lane. We could meet at *Tapas Time* at 7.30? What do you think?

Manon

3

Hi Marek

They say the weather's going to be good on Saturday. Anni and I are thinking of going rock climbing in Snowdonia. Can you climb (or would you like to try!)? The bus leaves at 9.30. We could meet for a quick breakfast at *The Coffee Pot* at 9.00. Phone or send me a quick email, OK?

Zofia

2 Find names of these places and things in the emails.
1 a cinema *The Odeon*   4 a wine bar   7 a TV channel SS
2 a café CP   5 a street HL   8 a football team G/It
3 a pub TC   6 a movie A&D   9 a national park S

3 Do you think Marek knows the places and things in the emails? Why?

4 Find the parts of the message for emails 2 and 3.

parts of the message	email 1	email 2	email 3
to	Marek	Marek	Marek
activity	football match	watch a film	rock climbing
invitation	watch it together	see it together	
time and place	tonight, *The Castle*, 8.00	Saturday, TT, 7.30	TCP, saturday, CP, 9
request for answer	What do you think?	What do you think	phone, send email
from	Niko	Manon	Zofia

B Check for missing information

5 What parts of the message are missing in these emails? Use the table in exercise 4 to help you.

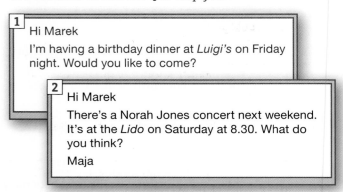

1

Hi Marek

I'm having a birthday dinner at *Luigi's* on Friday night. Would you like to come?

2

Hi Marek

There's a Norah Jones concert next weekend. It's at the *Lido* on Saturday at 8.30. What do you think?

Maja

C Put the information into a message

6 Work with a partner. Read the information and complete Marek's email.

Information: Marek has got two tickets to see *The Phantom of the Opera* at the *Palladium*. It's at 7.00 on Thursday evening. He wants to invite Zofia. There's a wine bar near the theatre called *Esperanto's*. It's a good place to meet.

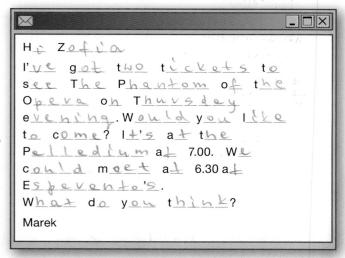

Hi Zofia
I've got two tickets to see The Phantom of the Opera on Thursday evening. Would you like to come? It's at the Palladium at 7.00. We could meet at 6.30 at Esperanto's.
What do you think?

Marek

7 3E.1▶ Listen and check.

ABC Put it all together

8 Think of an activity you would like to do next weekend. Write an email to invite another person in the class.

9 Check for missing information and give it to the person.

I can write an invitation.

Tick ✓ the line.   with a lot of help   with some help   on my own   very easily

Unit 3 Review

A Grammar

1 *like doing*; *would like to do* Complete A's problems with *'d like* or *like*. Then make B's suggestions with *could*.

1 **A** I'd like_____ to go to France, but I don't like flying.
   B *You could go by train*_____.
2 **A** I_____ to go out, but I haven't got any money.
   B _____.
3 **A** I_____ skiing, but it's summer and there isn't any snow.
   B _____.
4 **A** I_____ to learn Russian, but I can't find a teacher.
   B _____.
5 **A** I_____ climbing mountains, but there are no mountains near my home.
   B _____.
6 **A** I_____ to read, but it's too dark.
   B _____.

2 *can/could* (ability) Complete the conversation with *can*, *can't*, *could*, or *couldn't*.

A There are lots of things I couldn't do when I was young, but I ¹_____ do now. For example, play golf. What about you?
B When I was small, I ²_____ drive, but I can now.
A And when I was small, I could sing, but I ³_____ sing now!
B I ⁴_____ play football when I was young.
A And now?
B No, I can't.

3 *going to* (predictions) Write sentences with *going to* for these situations.

What's going to happen?

1 I can see big dark clouds.   *It's going to rain.*
2 Jack's putting some orange juice into a glass.
3 Jessica's opening a book.
4 Jessica's putting a DVD in the DVD player.
5 Jack's putting a CD in the CD player.

What isn't going to happen?

6 The traffic light is red but Bond's car is going very fast.
7 Jack's watching a comedy film on television.
8 Jessica's watching a horror film at the cinema.
9 Three men are trying to kill James Bond.

B Vocabulary

4 Prepositions of time Complete the sentences with *in*, *on*, or *at*.

1 The James Bond film *Dr No* was first shown _____ 1962.
2 The football's on *Sky Sports* _____ 8 o'clock.
3 Let's go to the cinema _____ Saturday.
4 We could meet at the tapas bar _____ 9.00.
5 I'm having a party _____ Friday night.
6 The final *Harry Potter* book was published _____ 2007.

5 Abilities Underline the correct verb.

1 My friend can't use/do/make a computer.
2 He could play/ride/use a horse when he was 12.
3 'Rabbit' can't make/do/play football, but he can surf.
4 I can read/make/do Arabic.
5 My sister could do/play/make the guitar when she was 15.

6 Types of story; film Do this film crossword.

Across

1 The film *The Da Vinci Code* is _____ in Paris.
2 The film *Lord of the Rings* is _____ on a book by Tolkien.
4 This is a long film about a time in history.
6 This is a frightening film.
9 A story in moving pictures. Watch it at the cinema or on DVD.
10 This is a fast, exciting film – it's an _____ film.
11 Another word for 'film'.

Down

1 This is a short piece of a film set in one place.
3 The most important actor in the film is the _____.
5 This is a funny film or TV programme. People laugh when they watch it.
7 This is a love story.
8 This is a story written for the theatre.

Hotel rooms

blanket glass lamp remote control pillow ashtray shampoo
sheet soap mini-bar tap towel toilet roll floor

Who steals hotel towels?

Have you ever stolen a hotel towel? One in five Americans has stolen one. Hotels across the U.S. lose $51 million a year in stolen towels.

But hotel guests don't just take towels. The most popular 'souvenirs' are soap, toilet rolls, and mini bottles of shampoo. In fact, most people don't think this is really stealing. But what about glasses and ashtrays? Or bigger things like blankets, sheets, and pillows? And hotel guests sometimes walk away with stranger things – toilet seats, TV remote controls, lamps, and in one case, even the hotel owner's dog.

Hotels sometimes charge for stolen items, such as drinks from the mini-bar, on the guest's credit card. But some guests have found solutions to this problem. For example, they drink the mineral water and then fill the bottle with tap water.

Perhaps the strangest hotel theft is from a hotel near Exeter, England. A couple left the hotel with the shower from their hotel room. Hotel owner Liz Hodges said the stolen shower was worth £300.

The Receptionist

c Here's your key. It's room 224 on the second floor.

b Can I help you?

d It's €80 a night, breakfast included.

a Breakfast's from 7.30 to 10.00 a.m.

e Just for one night?

f Could I see your passport, please?

The Guest

g Can I have an alarm call at 7.30 a.m., please?

h Could I have a cup of coffee, please?

i The TV doesn't work. Could you send someone to look at it, please?

j Can you give me an outside line, please?

How to ask for things in a hotel

G *can / could* (requests) v hotel words and phrases p guessing words from phonemic transcription

A Vocabulary hotel words and phrases

1 When did you last stay in a hotel? Did you like it? Tell a partner.

2 With a partner, write a list of all the things you normally find in a hotel room.
   Example a bed, a shower

3 Look at **Hotel rooms** opposite. Match the words with the things in the picture.
   Example blanket – 14

4 Pronunciation Complete the song about a bad hotel. Use the phonemic spellings to help you.

The ¹ *bed*   's too hard /bed/
The ² blanket 's old /'blæŋkɪt/
The ³ pillow 's small /'pɪləʊ/
The ⁴ sheet s are cold /ʃiːts/
The ⁵ towel 's wet /'taʊəl/
The ⁶ floor is too /flɔːr/
The ⁷   taps don't work /tæps/
There's no ⁸ szampoo /ʃæm'puː/
The ⁹ lamp s don't work /læmps/
The room's too hot
The ¹⁰ ashtray 's full /'æʃtreɪ/
And the mini-bar's not
No glass, no ¹¹ soap /səʊp/
No toilet roll
And someone stole
The remote ¹² control! /kən'trəʊl/

5 4A.1▶ Listen and check. Practise saying the song.

B Read for specific information

6 What things do you think people steal from hotels? Make a list with a partner.

7 Read **Who steals hotel towels?** opposite. Were you right?

8 Read it again. What things do people take from hotels? Write them on this line, from the cheapest to the most expensive.

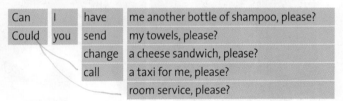
mineral water
cheap   expensive

9 Are the sentences *true* or *false*?
   1 Most people think taking the shampoo is OK. *True*
   2 One guest took the hotel owner's dog. T
   3 Some guests leave their credit cards in the mini-bar. F
   4 Some guests steal tap water. F
   5 One couple took the shower from their hotel room. T

10 What do you think? Is it OK to take towels from hotels? What about other things? Tell a partner.

C Listen and understand a receptionist

11 Look at **The Receptionist** opposite. Guess the order of the sentences. Compare with a partner.
   1 [b] 2 [e] 3 [f] 4 [d] 5 [a] 6 [c]

12 4A.2▶ Listen to the conversation and check your answers.

13 Look at the audio script on ≫ p.152 and act the conversation with a partner.

D Grammar *can / could* (requests)

14 4A.3▶ Listen to **The Guest** opposite and fill the gaps. Listen again and repeat.

15 Underline the correct words.
   Both *can* and *could* are used for making requests, but *can / could* is more polite. Use *could* if your request is small / big.

16 Work with a partner.
   Student A Make requests using sentences from the box.
   Student B Respond to the requests. Then change roles.

Can	I	have	me another bottle of shampoo, please?
Could	you	send	my towels, please?
		change	a cheese sandwich, please?
		call	a taxi for me, please?
			room service, please?

Example Can I have room service, please?
          Yes, of course. / I'm sorry, but …

More practice? **Grammar Bank** ≫ p.139.

ABCD Put it all together

17 Work with a partner. Do a hotel role play. Take turns to be A and B. Have a conversation at the reception desk, and then two or three phone conversations.

Student A Look at this role card.

You are a hotel receptionist. Look at the ideas below to help you. Decide what you can offer your guest.

receptionist – think about
– a single room = how much?
– a double room = how much?
– only one room available (room 336) and it's a double room.
– is breakfast included?
– is there room service?

Student B Look at the role card on ≫ p.133.

I can ask for things in a hotel.

Tick ✓ the line. with a lot of help with some help on my own very easily

Accidents at home

verb	past	past participle	verb	past	past participle
drop	dropped	dropped /drɒpt/	fall	fell	fallen
happen	happened	happened /ˈhæpənd/	cut	cut	cut
do	did	done	put	put	put
break	broke	broken	burn	burnt	burnt

Bingo!

Bingo rules

1 Choose a block of six photos. Draw a line around them.

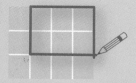

2 Listen to the conversations and tick the pictures.

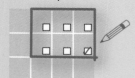

3 When all of your six squares have a tick, say 'Bingo!'.

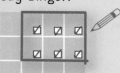

4 The first player to shout **Bingo!** is the winner.

How to say what's happened

G present perfect for recent events   **V** accidents at home   **P** short form of *have*

A Vocabulary accidents at home

1 Look at the **Bingo!** photos opposite with a partner. What can you see?

Example   There's a knife in picture d.

2 Match 1–6 with a–f. There may be more than one correct answer.

1 drop *a, c, d*   a your toast
2 break   b your finger
3 fall   c a cup
4 cut   d an egg
5 put   e salt in your coffee
6 burn   f off the shelf

3 Look at the photos again. Make sentences and say which picture or pictures they are describing.

Example   He's broken his glasses – picture f

1 He's broken   an egg.
2 He's dropped   her finger with a knife.
3 She's cut   his glasses.
4 He's put   his shirt.
5 He's burnt   salt in his coffee.

B Grammar present perfect for recent events

4 Look at the grammar box and complete the examples.

past action	present result
He's dropped an egg.	(I can see an egg on the floor)

Use the present perfect to talk about a past action when you are interested in the present result.

Examples

	past action	present result
1	She's *cut her finger*.	(I can see blood on her finger.)
2	He's *put* salt *in my coffee*.	(The coffee is horrible.)
3	She's *dropped a cup*.	(I can see a cup on the floor.)
4	She's *dropped a bowl of cereals*.	(There is milk all over the floor.)
5	The bottles have ____.	(They're on the floor.)
6	He's *burnt a toast*.	(The toast is black.)

5 Look at the grammar box. Underline the correct words in the rule below.

subject	have	past participle	object
I / You / We / They	've (have)	broken	a cup
He / She / It	's (has)	dropped	an egg

The past participle is **always / not always** the same as the past simple form.

6 Look at **Accidents at home** opposite. Decide which group A–D each verb is in.

A regular (+*ed*)		
drop – dropped – dropped		

B irregular	C irregular	D irregular
all three forms are the same	past simple = past participle	past participle is different from past simple
cut – cut – cut	burn – burnt – burnt	break – broke – broken

7 Look at **Bingo!** opposite. Work with a partner.
  A Say sentences about the photos.
  B Say the photo.

Example   **A** He's dropped the sugar.   **B** i!

More practice? **Grammar Bank** » p.139.

C Listen and play a game

8 **4B.1▶** Listen and read this conversation. Tick ✓ the picture.
  M Oh no!
  W What's happened? What have you done?
  M I've burnt the toast.
  W Yeah, I can smell it!

9 How did you know which picture to tick? Underline the key words in the conversation.

10 Read and follow **Bingo rules** opposite.

11 **4B.2▶** Play the **Bingo!** game. You will hear conversations. Listen for key words and tick ✓ the pictures.

D Pronunciation short form of *have*

12 Match the contractions and the phonemic spelling.
you've he's ~~I've~~ she's

1 /aɪv/   *I've*   cut my hand.
2 /jəv/   *you've*   burnt the toast.
3 /ʃiz/   *She's*   dropped an egg.
4 /hɪz/   *He's*   broken a glass.

13 **4B.3▶** Listen and repeat the sentences in exercise 12.

14 Look at audio script 4B.2 on » p.152. Choose five of the conversations. Act them with a partner.

ABCD Put it all together

15 Work with a partner and describe your picture. Find the differences.
  Student A Look at the picture of the kitchen on » p.127.
  Student B Look at the picture of the kitchen on » p.133.

I can say what's happened.
Tick ✓ the line.   with a lot of help   with some help   on my own   very easily   **39**

Around the house

cup   plate

knife   **in the
kitchen**   glass

fork   sink
spoon

water   heating

services

electricity   gas

How to say what you've done

A Vocabulary things around the house

1 Look at **Around the house** opposite. Work with a partner. Match the words and photos.
Example knife – picture 3

2 Work with a partner. How many endings can you think of for each sentence?
1 I've turned on *the gas.*   4 I've done
2 I've washed   5 I've fed
3 I've cleaned   6 I've watered

B Read for detail

3 Read **Home Alone** opposite. Where are Lisa's parents? What do you think is going to happen? Tell a partner.

4 Look at pictures a–k opposite. Underline the correct words.
1 Lisa's fed / hasn't fed the dog.
2 She's taken / hasn't taken the dog for a walk.
3 She's watered / hasn't watered the cactus.
4 She's kept / hasn't kept the house clean.
5 She's invited / hasn't invited all her friends for a party.

5 **4C.1▶** Listen. Lisa's mum asks two extra questions not in the picture story. Write them down.

C Grammar present perfect ⊕⊟⁇

6 Complete the grammar boxes and answer the questions.

+	I've cleaned the floor.	She's washed up.	They have fed the dog.
–	I haven't cleaned the floor.	She has washed up.	They haven't fed the dog.
?	Have you cleaned the floor?	Has she washed up?	Have they fed the dog?

short answers	+	Yes, I have.	Yes, she has.
	–	No, I haven't.	No, they haven't.

'She's washed up.'
1 Has she finished the washing up?
2 Does the sentence tell us when the action happened?

7 Read **Home Alone** again. Underline examples of the present perfect.

8 Look at **Lisa's house** on ≫ p.127 for one minute. Can you remember what she has and hasn't done? Write sentences.
Example She's washed the plates.

9 Test a partner.
A Has she washed the plates?   B Yes, she has.

More practice? **Grammar Bank** ≫ p.139.

D Pronunciation when to stress *have*

10 **4C.2▶** Listen and read the text. Then write *true* or *false* after the rules.
What have you **done** this **morn**ing?
What have you **done** to**day**?
Have you **cleaned** the **floors**?
Have you **cleaned** the **doors**?
What have you **done** to**day**?
I **haven't washed** the **sheets**
I **haven't made** the **bed**
I've **cleaned** the **floors**
I've **cleaned** the **doors**
But I **haven't bought** the **bread**
Rules
Stress the auxiliary *have*:
1 in affirmative sentences. *False*
2 in negative sentences.
3 in questions.

11 Listen again and repeat.

12 Act the conversation in **Home Alone** with a partner.

E Listen for detail

13 **4C.3▶** You will hear Frank talking on the phone. Underline the correct word.
1 Frank's speaking to his friend / mum / dad.
2 Frank has / hasn't finished cleaning.
3 Frank is / isn't busy at work.

14 Listen again. What housework has Frank done? Put ✓ or ✗ after the jobs.

cleaned the fridge	✗	made the bed	☐
washed the towels	☐	cleaned the bathroom	☐
cleaned the cooker	☐	cleaned the floors	☐
washed the sheets	☐		

15 Read the audio script on ≫ p.152 and check your answers.

ABCDE Put it all together

16 Write a list of ten jobs (big or small) you've done (at home) this week.
Example cleaned the house, put CDs in boxes, made a cup of coffee, taken the dog for a walk, washed the car, been to the supermarket

17 Stand up. Find other students in the class who have done the same jobs as you.
– Have you cleaned the house this week?
– Yes, I have.
– Me too. *or* Oh. I haven't.

I can say what I've done.

HOW **INDEPENDENT** ARE YOU?

There was a time when young people didn't leave their family home until they got married. In fact, in some languages, the word *married* comes from the word *house*. For example, in Turkish, the word for *house* is *ev* and the word for *married* is *evli*, meaning *with house*. In Spanish, the word for *house* is *casa* and the word for *married* is *casado*.

But times have changed. These days, young people often want to marry later. In Europe, getting married at 29 or 30 is normal. So what do they do before that? Do they stay in the family home or do they become independent? Well, the answer is some people are more independent than others. How independent are young people in your country?

Do this test – choose the best answers for yourself.*

*or for a typical young person in your country

1 Have you ever lived …
a alone? Yes
b in another town? Yes
c abroad? Yes

2 Have you ever paid …
a for the shopping? Yes, I've
b an electricity, phone, or gas bill? Yes
c rent? Yes

3 Have you ever bought …
a a towel? Yes
b knives, forks, and spoons? Yes
c a fridge? Yes

4 Have you ever had …
a your own room? Yes
b your own house keys? Yes
c your own home? Yes

5 Have you ever turned on …
a the cooker? y
b the heating? y
c the electricity? y

6 Have you ever cooked a meal …
a for yourself? y
b for your family? y
c for guests? y

7 Have you ever put …
a a battery in a remote control? y
b soap in a washing machine? y
c a shelf on the wall? y

KEY

Count your *yes* answers.
Each *yes* = 1 point.

Age
Under 18? =
Add 10 points.
Between 18 and 22? =
Add 5 points.
Over 22? =
Don't add any points.

Mark your score on the line.

0	VERY DEPENDENT
8	DEPENDENT
16	INDEPENDENT
24	
31	VERY INDEPENDENT

GLOSSARY
1 a*broad* = in another country
2 r_____ = money you pay to the owner of your home
3 h_____ = this is what makes your house warm
4 g_____ = vistors
5 r_____ c_____ = you use this to change the TV channel

How to talk about experiences

G present perfect with *ever*; past simple

A Read a questionnaire and respond

1 Work in small groups. Complete the sentences below and compare your answers.
Example In my country, most people ...

  1 leave school at about _____ (age).
  2 leave home at about _____ .
  3 rent or buy their first home at about _____ .
  4 get married at about _____ .
  5 have children at about _____ .

2 Read the first paragraph of **How Independent Are You?** opposite. What's the topic?
  a foreign languages b leaving home c the family

3 Read and complete the **Glossary** opposite.

4 Do the test with a partner and count your score.

5 **4D.1▶** Listen to Callum's answers to questions 1–7 opposite. Is he more or less independent than you?

B Grammar present perfect with *ever*; past simple

6 Match these pictures with the sentences.

  1 Have you broken your arm?
  2 Have you ever broken your arm?
  (In this question, *ever* means 'at any time in your life before now'.)

7 Write *Have you ever ... ?* questions with these words.
  1 sleep / boat *Have you ever slept on a boat?*
  2 steal / hotel towel
  3 lose / your house keys
  4 pay a bill / credit card
  5 buy something / Internet

8 Ask your questions to a partner. Answer your partner's questions. Use the expressions from the box below.

Yes,	I have.	No,	I haven't.
	once.		never.
	twice.		
	a few times.		
	lots of times.		

meet

Example Have you ever slept on a boat?
  Yes, a few times.

9 Read the grammar box and answer the questions below.

present perfect	past simple
I've broken my arm once (before now).	I broke my arm last summer.
before now (unfinished time)	last summer (finished time)

unfinished times	finished times
before now today	last summer yesterday
this week in my life	last week in 2001
this month this year	when I was five

  1 'I've broken my arm.' Do we know when?
  2 'I broke my arm last summer.' Do we know when?
  3 'I've had a coffee today.' Is today finished?
  4 'I had a coffee yesterday.' Is yesterday finished?
  5 For unfinished times, what tense do we use?

10 Underline the correct words.
  1 I've lost / lost my car keys last week.
  2 I've had / had the flu three times this year.
  3 She hasn't drunk / didn't drink any coffee today.
  4 Have / Did you ever lived / live in another country?
  5 Have / Did you watched / watch TV last night?

More practice? **Grammar Bank ≫ p.139.**

C Listen and follow a conversation

11 **4D.2▶** Listen to a short conversation between Alice and James and answer the questions.
  1 Who has broken their arm - Alice or James?
  2 When did it happen?
  3 How did it happen?

12 Follow the conversation in exercise 11 on this conversation map. Listen again to check.

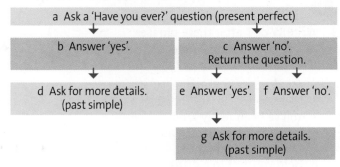

13 Practise the conversation with a partner.

ABC Put it all together

14 Work in groups. Play the *Liar!* game on ≫ p.127.

I can talk about experiences.

Tick ✓ the line. with a lot of help with some help on my own very easily

Writing A thank you note

A Read and understand the writer's aim

1 Read the note and answer the questions.
   1 Where is it?
   2 Who wrote it?
   3 Why did she write it?

Hi Ana!

Sorry I'm not here to welcome you!

Make yourself at home.

Help yourself to anything in the fridge.

There's tea and coffee in the cupboard above the cooker.

I've made the bed for you in the end room.

Feel free to have a shower and turn the heating on.

Back from work @ 6.30.

Phillipa

2 Detective work. What can you guess from the note? Write *yes*, *no* or *perhaps*.
   1 Ana is a guest in Phillipa's house. *Yes*
   2 Ana got the key from Phillipa's neighbour.
   3 Phillipa's at work.
   4 The weather's hot.
   5 There's milk in the fridge.
   6 Ana's going to stay for the night.

B Vocabulary welcome and thanking phrases

3 Write *W* or *T* after these phrases.
   W = from a welcome note
   T = from a thank you note

   1 Make yourself at home. *W*
   2 Feel free to use the phone.
   3 You've been really kind.
   4 I'm sorry I broke the plate.
   5 Thanks for everything.
   6 Help yourself to a drink.
   7 I've had a great time.

C Imagine your reader's questions

4 Read the situation. Work with a partner and write Ana's thank you note.
   Situation
   It's two days later, and Ana's leaving Phillipa's flat. Phillipa is at work again. Ana writes a thank you note to Phillipa. She imagines Phillipa's possible questions:

   Did Ana have a good time?
   Did Ana feed the cat?
   Where are the keys?
   Why is there a new box of eggs in the fridge?
   Where's Ana's towel?

Hi Phillipa

I've had a great time!

I've fed . . .

5 4E.1▶ Listen. How is this text different from your thank you note?

6 Read the audio script on ▶▶ p.152 and check.

ABC Put it all together

7 Work with a partner. Imagine you have stayed for a weekend in a friend's home while he or she was away. You've had lots of small accidents. Write a list.
   broken a glass   dropped an egg
   cut your hand   burnt a hole

8 Imagine your friend's questions when he/she comes home.
   Why is there a black hole in the sofa?
   Why is the bin full of broken glass?

9 Write a thank you note. Answer the questions you imagined in exercise 8.

I can write a thank you note.

Tick ✓ the line.   with a lot of help   with some help   on my own   very easily

Unit 4 Review

A Grammar

1 *can / could* (requests) You are staying at a hotel. Write requests with *can* or *could*.

1 You want a taxi.
   Could you call a taxi for me, please?

2 You want a cup of tea.
   _____

3 You want new towels.
   _____

4 You want an alarm call at seven.
   _____

5 It's hot and you don't know how to turn the heating off.
   _____

2 Present perfect for recent events Write four more sentences about little Steven.

Little Steven is five years old. He's standing in the kitchen and there is a jam sandwich on the floor. There is a carton of milk on the floor. There is toast in the toaster and it's black and smoking. There are pieces of broken plate on the floor. There's a cut on his hand and he's crying.

1 *He's dropped a jam sandwich* .
2 _____ .
3 _____ .
4 _____ .
5 _____ .

3 Present perfect for recent events Find nine sentences about Lisa.

1 Lisa	2 Has	3 Lisa	has	invited	her
hasn't	she	cleaned	4 Has	she	friends
watered	the	the	floor?	washed	for
5 Lisa	plants.	6 Lisa	has	up?	a
has	7 Lisa	hasn't	dropped	food	party.
turned	8 Her	kept	the	on	the
on	parents	have	kitchen	clean.	floor.
the	heating.	decided	to	come	home
9 Has	she	fed	the	dog?	early.

4 Present perfect questions with *ever* Write questions and Callum's answers.

Callum's 24 years old and he's never lived alone. He's paid for the shopping but he's never paid rent. He's cooked for his family but he's never cooked for guests. He's put soap in the washing machine but he's never put a shelf on the wall.

You Have you ever lived alone, Callum?
Callum No, I haven't.
You Have you ever …

B Vocabulary

5 Hotels Complete the conversation with these words.

with ~~help~~ included key may
night passport room second

A Can I [1] *help* you?
B Yes, I'd like a [2] _____ please.
A Just for one [3] _____ ?
B Yes. How much is it?
A It's €80, [4] _____ breakfast [5] _____ .
   [6] _____ I see your [7] _____ , please?
B Yes, here you are.
A Thanks. Here's your [8] _____ . It's room 224 on the
   [9] _____ floor.

6 Around the house Find the words in these anagrams.

On the bed
1 these   *sheet*
2 kneblat   _____
3 wipoll   _____

In the living room
8 rasthay   _____
9 plam   _____

In the bathroom
4 pat   _____
5 paso   _____
6 wetol   _____
7 littoe lorl _____

Services
10 gethain   _____
11 sag   _____
12 cletticeriy _____

7 Irregular past participles Find the past participles of these verbs. Some letters are used twice.

~~break~~ burn buy cut do fall
keep pay put see steal take

B	U	R	N	T	T	P
R	O	C	E	N	S	A
O	P	U	T	E	P	I
K	S	T	G	D	I	D
E	E	T	T	H	L	T
N	E	P	O	E	T	A
K	N	O	T	L	N	K
E	L	D	O	N	E	E
N	F	A	L	L	E	N

1 *broken*
2 _____
3 _____
4 _____
5 _____
6 _____
7 _____
8 _____
9 _____
10 _____
11 _____
12 _____

8 Time phrases Complete the conversations with these words.

~~ever~~ last never once this times twice

1 **A** Have you *ever* broken your leg?
  B No, I've _____ broken my leg, but I broke my arm _____ .

2 I broke a glass _____ night and I cut my foot on a piece of it _____ morning.

3 **A** How many _____ have you been in hospital?
  B Only _____ – once when I was five and again two years ago.

Clothes

dress sandals shorts socks
suit /suːt/ sweatshirt tights /taɪts/
top tracksuit trainers underwear

How to talk about clothes

G adverbs of degree   v clothes   P intonation in opinions

A Vocabulary clothes

1 With a partner, make a list of words for clothes.
Example   T-shirt, jeans ...

2 Look at **Clothes** opposite. Match the words and the photos.
Example   dress = 11

3 Answer the questions.
  1 Which are women's clothes? Which are men's clothes?
  2 Which clothes are smart and which are casual? Which are sportswear?
  3 Which words for clothes are plural and which are singular?
  4 What are you wearing now?

4 Which clothes can you describe with these adjectives?
  big casual comfortable long nice
  small short smart tight warm
  Example   a long dress, some comfortable sandals

B Listen for key words

5 Look at **Window Shopping** opposite. Name all the clothes you can find in the pictures with a partner.

6 **5A.1▶** Cover the opposite page. Listen to the conversation. Tick ✓ the clothes words that you hear.
  ☐ jacket ☐ sandals ☐ shirt ✓ suit
  ☐ sweatshirt ☐ tights ☐ top ☐ trainers
  ☐ trousers

7 Read **Window Shopping** opposite. Why does Gavin like Jeff's suit? Compare with a partner.

8 Read the story again and find sentences with the same meaning as the sentences below.
  1 The jacket is exactly your size. *The jacket's a really good fit.*
  2 It looks very good on you.
  3 Do you like the shirt?
  4 The woman who's wearing a red top.
  5 I'm not wearing anything.

C Pronunciation intonation in opinions

9 **5A.2▶** Listen and repeat. Copy the intonation. Note how the intonation goes down on the positive opinions and up on the negative opinions.

  😊 positive opinion   😠 negative opinion

  It's **really ni**ce.   They're **quite sh**ort ...

  It **real**ly **suits** you.   The **col**our's a bit **bright**, per**haps** ...

10 Act the **Window Shopping** conversation with a partner.

D Grammar adverbs of degree

11 Look at the grammar box. <u>Underline</u> more examples of adverbs of degree in **Window Shopping**.

	less	more
😐 neutral	They're quite dark.	They're very dark. They're really dark.
🙁 negative	They're a bit dark. They're a little dark.	They're too dark.

Note: The opposite of *too* is *enough*.
Example   They aren't dark enough.

12 Match the rules with the examples.
  Rules
  1 Put *enough* after the adjective.
  2 Put the other adverbs of degree before the adjective.
  3 Don't use the 🙁 adverbs with 😊 adjectives:
     good nice cheap clean new comfortable

  Examples
  a It's very small. ✓
  b They're a bit nice. ✗
  c It's big enough. ✓

13 <u>Underline</u> the correct word.
  1 I love your shirt. It's <u>really</u> / too / quite nice.
  2 These trainers are a bit / quite / too comfortable.
  3 The coat's a little / too / enough small, but I can wear it.
  4 These jeans are very / too / enough tight, but I like them.
  5 It isn't warm too / quite / enough to wear shorts.
  6 It's quite / very / too hot to wear a sweater today.
  7 I can't put this hat on – it's very / too / really small.
  8 I very / really / too like your new jacket.

  More practice? **Grammar Bank** >> p.140.

ABCD Put it all together

14 Work with a partner. Ask your partner questions to match the people with their names.
  Student A look at the photo on >> p.127.
  Student B look at the photo on >> p.133.

  Example   A What's Maria wearing?
         B She's wearing a blue cardigan ...

15 Tell your partner the clothes you like and dislike.
  Example   I don't like that dress. The colour's too bright.

I can talk about clothes. ▄▄▄▄▄▄▄▄▄▄▄▄▄▄▄▄▄▄

Style Factory
CLOTHES AND ACCESSORIES

Our promise to you:

* You won't find lower prices anywhere else. If you find the same product for less in another shop, let us know. We will lower our price to match.

* We sell only the best quality products. If you are not happy with your purchase, we will give you your money back.

* Don't be afraid to ask. Our trained staff will be happy to answer all your questions and give you friendly, honest advice.

* All our products come with a guarantee. We will replace any faulty or damaged products immediately.

* Don't worry if you can't find time to visit one of our shops. We will deliver anywhere in the country absolutely free.

* Register on-line and we will send you the latest catalogues. We will keep your personal details strictly private.

You'll look like a star in our fashions — without spending like one!

Sadie and Vic Go Shopping

a

b

c

d

How to make promises and offers

G *will* (promises and offers)   V favours   P stress in sentences with *will*, *won't*, and *shall*

A Read an advertising leaflet

1 Work with a partner. Answer the questions.
1 Where and how often do you buy clothes?
2 Do you have any favourite shops?
3 What do you look for? Style? Quality? Price? Service?

2 Read **Style Factory** opposite. Who is this text for?

3 Tick ✓ the promises the leaflet makes.
a cheap prices ✓
b the best designers
c good quality
d good service
e free tea and coffee
f your money back if you're not happy
g cheap delivery
h online shopping

4 Match the highlighted words with these meanings.
1 broken, not perfect *damaged*
2 something you bought
3 add your name to the list
4 something we made
5 a promise to repair any problems

5 How did you do exercise 4? Compare with a partner.
1 I thought about the meaning of the sentence.
2 I decided if the word was a noun, a verb, an adjective, an adverb, etc.
3 I thought about similar words in my language.
4 I guessed and checked in a dictionary.
5 I knew the word already.

B Listen and identify what people are talking about

6 **5B.1▶** Look at **Sadie and Vic Go Shopping** opposite. Guess the correct order of the pictures. Then listen and check.

7 Here are some phrases from the conversations. Listen again and answer the questions about the phrases.
1 'I'll be *there* in fifteen minutes.' Where?
2 'I'll pay for it.' Pay for what?
3 'Shall I carry one ...' One what?
4 'I'll lend you five pounds.' Why?
5 'I'll hold your bag ...' Why?
6 'Shall I wrap it for you?' Wrap what?

8 Look at audio script 5B.1 on >> p.153. What's the difference in meaning between these verbs?
1 wear – wrap
2 borrow – lend
3 pay – pay back
4 carry – hold

C Grammar *will* for promises and offers

9 Look at the grammar box and write *P* or *O*.
P = promises   O = offers

will / 'll		*won't*	
P	We'll call you later.		I won't forget.
O	I'll hold your umbrella.		You won't be sorry.
O	I'll lend you my jacket.	*Shall ... ?*	
P	I'll pay you back.		Shall I carry it?
			Shall I pay for you?

10 Underline the promises in the **Style Factory** leaflet opposite.

11 Underline the offers in audio script 5B.1 on >> p.153.

12 Complete these promises and offers with *'ll*, *won't*, or *shall*.
1 _____ I open the door for you?
2 We _____ replace any broken parts.
3 I _____ tell anybody your secret!
4 You _____ find better shoes in any other shop!
5 _____ I put these in a bag for you?
6 I _____ pay you back tomorrow, I promise!

More practice? **Grammar Bank** >> p.140.

D Pronunciation stress in sentences with *will*, *won't*, and *shall*

13 **5B.2▶** Listen and read these sentences. Copy the stress with *will*, *won't*, and *shall*.
We'll call you later.   I won't forget.   Shall I carry it?

Work with a partner. Say the offers and promises in exercise 7 and reply.

Examples **A** I'll be there in fifteen minutes.
B OK. See you soon.

A Shall I carry one?
B Yes, please. / No, that's OK.

14 **5B.3▶** Listen and repeat the sentences in the grammar box in exercise 9. Copy the stress.

15 Which word is always stressed – *'ll*, *won't*, or *shall*?

16 Look at audio script 5B.1 on >> p.153 again. Practise the conversation with a partner.

ABCD Put it all together

17 Work with a partner. Look at the **shopping maze** on >> p.127. Choose a way from start to finish. Decide what you will say in each situation. Look at audio script 5B.1 on >> p.153 for ideas.

18 Act your role play for another pair. Listen to the other pair's role play and follow their route in the maze.

I can make promises and offers.
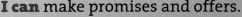
Tick ✓ the line.   with a lot of help   with some help   on my own   very easily

49

The Story of Jeans

The first jeans came from Genoa in Italy. The name *jeans* comes from the French name for Genoa, *Gênes*. Sailors in the Genoese navy wore jeans because they're strong and you can wear them wet or dry. The sailors washed their jeans by putting them in a large bag and dropping them in the sea.

Modern jeans were invented by Levi Strauss. Strauss moved to America from Germany, and he started making jeans in the 1870s. He originally made them for miners in California. He made them blue so they wouldn't look dirty.

In the 1950s, pop and movie stars like James Dean and Elvis Presley wore jeans, and they became fashionable with teenagers and young adults. At that time, wearing jeans was a symbol of independence for young people. However, in the 60s and 70s, jeans became a fashion for all ages. Today, the average American person owns seven pairs of jeans.

Dean's jeans!

Clean jeans, neat jeans
Sitting on your seat jeans
Dear jeans, cheap jeans
Wear them on the beach jeans
Wear them with a sweater
Great in any weather
Dirty jeans, clean jeans
The trousers of your dreams
Dean's jeans!

Buying Jeans

Shop assistant Do you like these ones?
Customer Yes. How much are they?
S £54.99.

C I'm not sure.
S OK, try this pair on. The changing room's over there.

S How would you like to pay?
C I'll pay in cash.

S What do you think?
C Yes, they're fine. I'll take them.

S How are they?
C They're a bit small.

S OK, try the next size. Here you are.
C Thanks.

S Can I help you?
C Yes, I'm looking for a pair of jeans.

C Can I try a pair on?
S Yes, of course. What size are you?

How to ask for things in shops

G phrasal verbs with *on* and *off*   V shopping phrases   P sounds spelt with *ea*

A   Think about the topic before you read

1   Work in small groups. Ask and answer the questions.
1   How many people in the class are wearing jeans?
2   Have you got many pairs of jeans?
3   When do you wear them?
4   What colour jeans do you prefer?
5   Have you got a favourite pair of jeans?

2   Guess the correct answers.
1   Who first wore jeans?
   a   American cowboys
   b   Italian sailors
   c   Chinese miners
2   Where does the word *jeans* come from?
   a   the French name for the city Genoa
   b   a short form of the name James Dean
   c   an Arabic word meaning *trousers*
3   Who invented modern jeans?
   a   Lee Wrangler   b   Elvis Presley   c   Levi Strauss

3   Now read **The Story of Jeans** opposite. Check your answers in exercise 2.

4   Work with a partner. Read four sentences from the text and respond.
   Example   **A**   The first jeans came from Genoa in Italy.
               B   I didn't know that / I knew that already / That's really interesting.

B   Pronunciation sounds spelt with *ea*

5   **5C.1▶** Listen to the **Dean's Jeans** advert opposite. Notice the pronunciation of *ea*. Then write the *ea* words from the advert in the box.

ea /iː/ *most common*	ea /e/ *also common*	ea /eɪ/	ear /ɪər/	ear /eər/
teach	head	break	near	bear

6   Can you add any more words to the spelling box?
7   Practise saying the advert.

C   Vocabulary shopping phrases

8   **5C.2▶** Listen to a conversation in a jeans shop, and answer the questions.
1   How much are the jeans?
2   Does the customer know his size?
3   How many pairs does the customer try on?
4   Does the customer pay in cash or by credit card?

9   Look at **Buying Jeans** opposite. Put the pictures in order.
   Example   1 = g

10   Listen again and check.
11   Work with a partner. This time the customer is buying a sweater, not jeans. Change the phrases in orange.
   Example   Do you like these ones? *Do you like this one?*

12   **5C.3▶** Listen and check.
13   Act the **Buying Jeans** conversation with a partner.

D   Grammar phrasal verbs with *on* and *off*

14   Look at this dictionary entry. What do you think *sth* means?

> **PHRASAL VERBS** **try sth on** felpróbál: *Can I try these jeans on, please?*

Extract from *Oxford Wordpower: angol-magyar szótár nyelvtanulóknak*

15   Look at the example sentences and complete the rules with *can* or *can't*.

| Try these **jeans** on. ✓ | Try on these **jeans**. ✓ |
| Try **them** on. ✓ | Try on **them**. ✗ |

1   You _can_ put a noun between *try* and *on*.
2   You _can_ put a pronoun between *try* and *on*.
3   You _can_ put a noun after *on*.
4   You _can't_ put a pronoun after *on*.

16   Which sentences are correct? Write ✓ or ✗. Correct the mistakes.
1   I like these jeans, but ~~I tried on them~~ and they were too small. ✗ *I tried them on*
2   I'm hot. Can you turn the heating off?
3   It's dark. Can you turn on the light? ✓
4   This sweater's too warm. I'm going to take off it.
5   Put your coat on before you go outside.
6   Those sunglasses are too dark. Take off them.
7   You can't wear shoes in here. Please take them off.
8   If you like this shirt, why don't you try on it?

17   Work with a partner. Take turns to be A and B.
   A   Say a problem.
   B   Make a suggestion with a phrasal verb.
1   I'm a bit cold. *Turn the heating on.*
2   It's too hot in here.
3   These shoes are uncomfortable.
4   It's too dark in here.
5   I like this shirt but I don't know if it's my size.

   More practice? **Grammar Bank** >> p.140.

ABCD   Put it all together

18   Act the conversation in **Buying Jeans** with a partner, but for a shirt, not jeans. Take turns to be **A** and **B**.

19   Close your book. Work with a different partner. Role play a conversation in a clothes shop.

I can ask for things in shops.
Tick ✓ the line.   with a lot of help   with some help   on my own   very easily

Signs

a — Please keep off the grass

b — Skateboards Bicycles and Rollerblades **PROHIBITED**

c — NO HOODIES NO BASEBALL CAPS THANKYOU

d — LOUNGE NO ADMISSION TO PERSONS WEARING WET SHOES OR WET CLOTHING

Welsh mall says NO to wheels in heels

A new kind of training shoe, with wheels in the heel, are in fashion in Wales. Many teenagers asked for them at Christmas. But the manager of the St Elli Shopping Centre in Llanelli says the shoes, called 'Heelies', are dangerous. He says kids in 'Heelies' can't enter the mall. They must take them off and walk around in their socks.

The manager, Gilmour Jones, thinks there is a safety problem. Teenagers with these shoes could break a shop window or knock down an older customer. Mr Jones says that the rule against wheels is not new. 'For many years we have had rules against using rollerblades or skateboards in the centre.'

Many other malls also have specific dress rules for teenagers. In the USA, some malls have rules about wearing baseball caps. You mustn't wear your cap to the side – the cap must be straight, and you mustn't wear it low over your face. Many shops in Britain now have rules about tops with hoods, or 'hoodies'. You mustn't enter the shop with the hood up. The security camera must be able to see your face.

Many of these rules are to stop big groups of teenagers getting in the way of shoppers. Groups of kids sometimes stand on the stairs or in doors and customers can't pass. Some shoppers are afraid of large groups of noisy teenagers. One mall manager said, 'We are here to sell. If you don't want to buy, we don't want you here.' However, the problem with 'Heely' shoes is not just the feelings of the other shoppers. There is a real safety problem – these shoes can be dangerous. The company that makes them tells users not to wear them in crowded places.

1

2 — baseball cap, hoodie

3 — hood, 4 — rollerblade, wheel

How to talk about rules (1)

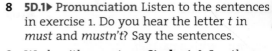

A Read a news article

1 Look at the **Signs** opposite. Match signs a–d with these meanings.
1 You mustn't cycle here. *b.*
2 You must walk on the path. *a*
3 You mustn't enter in your swimming costume. *d*
4 You must take off your cap or hood before you enter. *c*

2 Look at the article and photos 1–4 opposite. What do you think the text will be about? Tell a partner.

3 Read **Welsh mall says no …** opposite. Choose a topic for each paragraph. Compare with a partner. Which words helped you decide?
a Other dress rules in other malls.
b Why are wheels dangerous?
c New fashion is a problem in the mall.
d Who are mall dress rules for?

4 Look at these rules about the mall and shops in the article and say *true* or *false*.
1 Teenagers mustn't enter the mall in new trainers. *False*
2 People mustn't use skateboards in the mall. *V*
3 Teenagers must wear socks in the mall. *F*
4 People must wear baseball caps. *F*
5 You mustn't enter the shop with your hood up. *V*
6 You mustn't stand on the stairs. *V*

B Grammar *must, mustn't*

5 Look at the sentence and choose the best meaning.
You mustn't use rollerblades in the centre.
a This is just a suggestion for visitors.
b This is a rule in the mall.
c This is the opinion of the person who wrote the sentence.

6 Look at the sentences in exercise 1 and answer the questions.
1 What is the negative of *must*?
2 What is the form of the verb after *must*?
    a the infinitive (for example *to go*)
    b the *-ing* form (for example *going*)
    c the infinitive without *to* (for example *go*)

7 Write *must* or *mustn't* in the sentences below.

> ### BANK CARD SECURITY
> 1 You _must_ sign your card immediately.
> 2 You *must* keep your card in a safe place.
> 3 You *mustn't* give your card to another person to use.
> 4 You *must* be careful not to lose your card.
> 5 You *mustn't* keep your PIN* number with your card.
> 6 You *mustn't* give your PIN number to anyone.
> * PIN = Personal Identification Number

8 **5D.1▶** Pronunciation Listen to the sentences in exercise 1. Do you hear the letter *t* in *must* and *mustn't*? Say the sentences.

9 Work with a partner. **Student A** Say the meaning of one of the signs. **Student B** Say which sign your partner is describing.
Example
A You mustn't play football here.
B Sign 5.

More practice? **Grammar Bank** >> p.140.

C Listen to a conversation about rules

10 You will hear Simon telling Judy about the rules in a gym. Judy is a new member. Work with a partner. Guess what he tells her about these topics.
1 her membership card
2 what to wear in the machines area
3 what to wear in the pool area *Y*
4 what (not) to do on the exercise machines
5 what to do if you want to join a class

11 **5D.2▶** Listen. Were any of your guesses correct?

12 Find these phrases in the audio script on >> p.153. Why does the speaker use them? Match the words in green with meanings a–e.
1 OK, so these are the machines. *c*
2 Sorry?
3 Ehm, let's see …
4 Oh, there's a pool.
5 Right, OK.

a Can you repeat that?
b Give me a moment to think.
c Moving on to the next point.
d I understand.
e I didn't know that before.

ABC Put it all together

13 Work with a partner. Agree a list of rules for two of these places and topics.
Places – sports club; library; school; park; social club; youth hostel; *your ideas*
Topics – dress; behaviour; documents; equipment; food/drink; closing time; *your ideas*

14 Change partners and do a role play. Look at the **Rules** role cards on >> p.127. Take turns to be A and B. Do you think your partner's rules are good ones? Which would you like to change?

I can talk about rules.
Tick ✓ the line.   with a lot of help   with some help   on my own   very easily

Writing Tips for visitors from abroad

A Read and respond

1 Read the text. Work with a partner.
If you are Chinese Do you agree with the advice?
If you are not Chinese What differences can you find between your country and China?

2 Imagine you are going to visit China and you want to take a gift from your country. Answer the questions.
1 What will you take?
2 How many will you take?
3 How will you wrap your gift?

3 Imagine you visit China and you haven't read the text above. What mistakes could you make?
Example   You could offer a gift with one hand.

B Think about cultural differences

4 Work with a partner. Answer the questions.
1 Do you see any tourists where you live? Do they make any mistakes?
2 Have you ever gone abroad and made a mistake?

5 What mistakes are connected to these things?
Example   Some people wear shorts or hats in churches.
1 Religion.
2 Clothing.
3 Eating and drinking.

6 Match the titles in A with the subtitles in B.
Advice for visitors to your town or country

A	B
1 Shopping tips	a Good souvenirs to buy in my country
2 Clothing tips	b How not to dress for men / women
3 Packing tips	c Useful things to bring
	d What clothes to bring in summer / winter
	e What to wear in religious places
	f Where to find the best shops
	g What to wear in school or work
	h Good things to bring as gifts
	i Shop and bank opening times

AB Put it all together

7 Imagine somebody is going to visit your country. Choose a title from exercise 6. Write tips about your country that will help the visitor.

GIVING GIFTS IN CHINA

GIVING GIFTS
~ Offer and take gifts with two hands.
~ Chinese people usually refuse a gift three times. Offer the gift again and again. If somebody offers you a gift, you must do the same.
~ Don't unwrap the gift in front of the giver. Put it away and open it later.

CHOOSING GIFTS
~ Typical things from your home country are good gifts. You mustn't give clocks – they are connected with dying.
~ Eight is a lucky number, but four is unlucky. You mustn't give four of anything.
~ Wrap your gift, but don't wrap it in white, black, or blue. Red is a good colour.

GIFTS FOR SPECIAL OCCASIONS
~ If somebody invites you to their home, take a gift. For example, take sweets, biscuits, fruit or whisky.
~ At Chinese New Year, people often give money to children in a red envelope. Give an even number of new notes.

I can write tips for visitors from abroad. ▬▬▬▬▬▬
Tick ✓ the line.   with a lot of help   with some help   on my own   very easily

Unit 5 Review

R5

A Grammar

1 Adverbs of degree Put the best word in each gap.

too   enough   a bit   ~~really~~

1 I love your suit. It's _really_ nice.
2 I hate white chocolate. It's _____ sweet.
3 The shirt's _____ big, but it's not a problem.
4 These shoes aren't big _____. They don't fit.

quite   enough   too   a little

5 I can't see anything – it's _____ dark.
6 This shirt's _____ nice, but I prefer the other one.
7 The colour's _____ bright, but I like bright clothes.
8 This coat isn't warm _____ in winter.

2 *will* (offers and promises) Complete these promises and offers with *'ll*, *won't* or *shall*.

1 _____ I put these in a bag for you?
2 I _____ lend you five pounds.
3 I _____ tell anybody your secret.
4 I _____ pay you back tomorrow, I promise!
5 _____ I open the door for you?
6 You _____ find better prices anywhere.
7 We _____ replace any broken parts.
8 I _____ forget.

3 Phrasal verbs with *on* and *off* Write the word in the sentence. There may be two possible places.

1 Turn the computer and go to bed! (off)
2 I like this shirt. Can I try it? (on)
3 Put your coat, it's cold outside. (on)
4 You must take your shoes when you go into the house. (off)
5 It's dark. Can you turn the lights, please? (on)
6 These lights use a lot of electricity. Turn them. (off)

4 *must* and *mustn't* Complete the sentences with *must* or *mustn't* and one of these verbs.

take   smoke   arrive   ~~keep~~   leave   tell

Tips for travellers
1 You _must keep_ your money in a safe place.
2 If anything is stolen, you _____ the police.
3 You _____ bags on the plane for strangers.
4 You _____ cameras, phones, or money in your hotel room.
5 You _____ at the airport 2 hours before your flight.
6 You _____ on the plane.

B Vocabulary

5 Clothes Do this crossword.

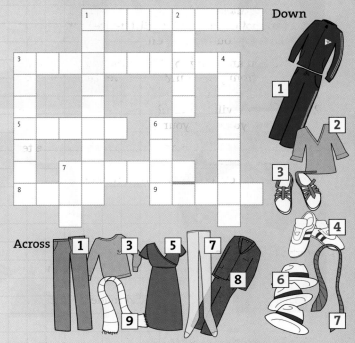

Down

Across

6 Shopping phrases Complete the conversation in a shoe shop with these words.

fine   cash   ones   size   pay   ~~help~~   take   try

A Can I [1] _help_ you?
B Yes, I'm looking for some trainers.
A Do you like these [2] _____?
B Yes. Can I [3] _____ a pair on?
A Of course. What [4] _____ are you?
B 38 … They're [5] _____. How much are they?
A €35.
B OK, I'll [6] _____ them.
A How would you like to [7] _____?
B I'll pay in [8] _____.

7 Favours Read about your friend's holiday problems. Write six offers with these verbs.

~~take~~   pay   water   feed   lend (x2)   meet

Your friend is going away on holiday.
1 She's got heavy bags and she hasn't got a car to go to the airport.
2 Who's going to pay her telephone bill?
3 What about her plants and her cat?
4 She wants to take photos but she hasn't got a camera.
5 She's going to a cold place but she hasn't got a warm coat.
6 She's going to arrive back at the airport really late next Sunday night and she thinks there won't be any taxis.
Help her!

Example   1 I'll take you to the airport.

Paola phones the college

Automated Message

Sometimes when you phone a bank or a big company, you speak to a machine, not a person. These are some of the things you hear ...

Thank you for calling, hold the line
Please press **1** and we'll waste your time
Press **2** and we'll put ¹ _you_
² _through_ up, you're in a queue
Hello, my name's Caroline
Please press **3** and hold ³ _the line_
If you want some music, just press **4**
Then press **5** and hear some more

Press **6** to speak to an operator
Sorry, she's ⁴ _busy_ , ⁵ _call back_ later
Press **7** for an answer-phone
And leave ⁶ _messages_ after the tone
Press **8** and wait and then press **9**
If no one answers, just hold the line
If you're calling from abroad, press **10**
Get ⁷ _cut_ off and dial again

How to talk on the phone

v telephone phrases   p stress in corrections

 Read and follow a conversation

1 Ask and answer these questions with a partner.
   1 How many phone calls do you make a day?
   2 How much time do you spend on the phone?
   3 Which do you use most: a mobile or a landline?

2 **6A.1▶** Read and listen to **Paola phones the college** opposite. How many phone calls does Paola make?

3 Read again and answer the questions.
   1 What three phone problems does Paola have?
   2 Where does Mr Hardy work? *Mr. Hardy work at college.*
   3 Does Mr Hardy know Paola? *Yes, he does. Paola*

 Vocabulary telephone phrases

4 Cover the phone conversations opposite. Try to complete the phrases in the box.

telephone phrases	
caller	answerer
Can I ¹ *speak to* Mr. Hardy	Who's calling?
Sorry, wrong ² number !	Just a moment.
I called a moment ago.	He's ⁵ busy at the moment.
I got ³ cut off.	Would you like to ⁶ leave a message?
I'll call ⁴ back later.	Hold the ⁷ line .
Is that Mike Hardy	Don't ⁸ hang up.
This is Paola Moore speaking.	I'll ⁹ put you through. (I'll connect you).

5 **6A.2▶** Read and check. Then listen and repeat.

6 **6A.3▶** Look at **Automated Message** opposite and complete it with words and phrases from the box in exercise 4. Then listen and check.

7 Work with a partner. Find words in **Automated Message** with these meanings.
   1 a line of people who are waiting   *queue*
   2 a telephonist   *an operator*
   3 a machine that takes messages   *an answer-phone*
   4 the sound you hear before leaving a message   *the tone*
   5 in a foreign country   *press to abroad*
   6 push buttons to call a phone number

8 Are these sentences from a person or an automated message on a machine? Write *P* or *M*.
   1 Please leave a message after the tone. *M*
   2 Hello, this is Mike Hardy speaking. *P*
   3 I'm sorry, there's no one here to take your call at the moment. *M*
   4 Would you like to leave a message? *P*
   5 Just a moment. I'll put you through. *P*
   6 Hello, this is Jeff's house. I'm afraid I'm out just now. *M*
   7 If you would like to make a reservation, please press 3. *M*

C **Listen and follow phone calls**

9 **6A.4▶** Listen to three phone calls. Who do the callers want to speak to?
   Ms Perry   Mr Mills   Frank
   call 1 _____   call 2 _____   call 3 *She's busy.*

10 Listen again. What is the problem with each call?
   a The person isn't available. *3*
   b It isn't the right number. *1*
   c The caller says the name incorrectly. *2*

11 Read the audio script on **>> p.154**. In which conversations do the speakers do these things? Underline the phrases they use and practise the conversation.
   1 Ask a question to check that they heard correctly. *Did you say Mr Perry?*
   2 Check some information by repeating it. *Four thirty*
   3 Spell the letters of a word or name. *Ms Perry,*
   4 Say the information in another way to make it easier to understand. *half past five.*
   5 Stress a corrected word.

D **Pronunciation** stress in corrections

12 **6A.5▶** Can you hear the difference? Listen to the corrections and say *A* or *B*.

	A	B
1	No, **five** one five.	No, five one **five**.
2	No, Mr **Ardwick**.	No, **Mr** Ardwick.
3	No, seven **fifteen**.	No, **seven** fifteen.

13 Work with a partner. Match the answers in exercise 12 with these questions and ask a partner.
   1 Did you say five one nine? [B]
      Did you say nine one five? [A]
   2 Did you say Mr Hardwick? [ ]
      Did you say Mrs Ardwick? [ ]
   3 Did you say eleven fifteen? [ ]
      Did you say seven fifty? [ ]

ABCD **Put it all together**

14 Do this role play. Work with a partner and look at the **role cards** on **>> p.128**. Take turns to be caller and answerer.
   Example   A Hello, can I speak to Ms Breen, please?
             B Just a moment. Ms Green, you say?
             A No, **Breen**. B-R-E-E-N.
             B Sorry, there's no Ms Breen here. I think you've got the wrong number.

I can talk on the phone.
Tick ✓ the line.   with a lot of help   with some help   on my own   very easily

Road Rules Quiz!

What do you know about the rules of the road? Do this test and find out!
Answer true, false, or maybe. If you think the answer is maybe, explain why!

1 You have to stop at red lights.

2 You have to be over 18 to drive.

3 You mustn't drive on the left-hand side of the road.

↑ 🚗
🚙 ↓
DRIVE ON LEFT IN AUSTRALIA

4 You don't have to pay to drive on a motorway.

5 You have to switch the lights on when you're driving.

6 Learners have to put a sign on their car.

7 Cyclists don't have to wear a helmet.

8 Passengers don't have to wear seat-belts.

9 Everybody has to stop at a pedestrian crossing.

10 You mustn't use your mobile while driving.

11 You have to wait for the police after an accident.

12 If you have an old car, you don't have to have number plates.

13 You have to carry a spare wheel in case you get a flat tyre.

14 You mustn't start the engine in a petrol station.

How to talk about obligations

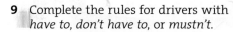

A Read and answer quiz questions

1 Work with a partner. What words do you know for parts of a car?

Example   door, lights …

2 Look at **Road Rules Quiz!** opposite. Match these words with things a–j in the photos.

accident   cyclist   helmet   number plate
motorway   pavement   pedestrian crossing
seat-belt   traffic lights   tyre

Example   accident = i

3 Work with a partner and answer the quiz questions about the country where you are now.

4 Change partners and compare your answers.

B Grammar *have to, don't have to, mustn't*

5 Look at the sentences and choose the best answers to the questions.

You have to stop at red lights.
Passengers don't have to wear seat-belts.

What does *have to* mean?
a You can do this or not – you can choose.
b This is an obligation – you can't choose.

What does *don't have to* mean?
c You can do this or not – you can choose.
d Don't do this – it's against the rules.

6 Make sentences with *have to* and *don't have to* for these people: a driver, a cyclist, a pedestrian. Use these words. Tell a partner.

wear a helmet   use lights at night   pass a driving test
wear a seat-belt   buy petrol   *your ideas*

Example   A driver doesn't have to wear a helmet.

7 Match this sentence with one of the meanings a–d in exercise 5. Does it express an obligation?

You mustn't use your mobile while driving.

What's the difference between *don't have to* and *mustn't*?

8 Underline the correct word.

I prefer driving to cycling. You ¹mustn't / don't have to go out in the rain. You ²mustn't / don't have to wear a helmet. And you ³mustn't / don't have to work so hard with your legs! But there are problems with driving too. You ⁴mustn't / don't have to drive after drinking alcohol. You ⁵have to / don't have to buy petrol. You ⁶have to / don't have to pass a driving test. And in big cities, there are a lot of places where you ⁷mustn't / don't have to park.

9 Complete the rules for drivers with *have to, don't have to,* or *mustn't.*

1 You _have to_ wear a seat-belt.
2 You _mustn't_ drive through a red light.
3 You _don't have to_ wear a helmet.
4 You _mustn't_ park on the motorway.
5 You _have to_ drive on the right in most countries.
6 You _have to_ wear training shoes.

More practice? **Grammar Bank** >> p.141.

10 6B.1▶ Pronunciation Listen and compare the pronunciation of *have to* and *have two*. Repeat the two sentences.

They have two clean windows. /hæv tu:/
They have to clean windows. /hæf tə/

11 6B.2▶ Listen and repeat the answers to exercise 9.

C Listen to a radio interview

12 You will hear a radio interview with Robert Ellis, a traffic police officer. What do you think he will answer to these questions? Tell a partner.

1 What's it like being a traffic policeman?
2 What qualities do you need?
3 Do you have to follow the rules of the road?

13 6B.3▶ Listen to the interview. Were your guesses correct?

14 Complete the table about Robert's obligations. Write the numbers of these things in the correct places.

He has to …	He doesn't have to …	He mustn't …
1 2 3 4 6 8	9 (10) 11	5 7

1 start work at four in the morning
2 be a good driver
3 get an advanced driving licence
4 be good with people
5 get angry
6 stay calm
7 panic
8 be fit and healthy
9 be an athlete
10 wear a seat-belt
11 keep to the speed limit

ABC Put it all together

15 Work with a partner. Use the notes on >> p.128 to compare different forms of transport.

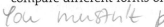

Bank and post office

account number   cash   cash machine
cashier   envelope   cheque   credit card
ID   stamp   traveller's cheque   post code

TRUE CRIMES

1

BARRY LYN STOLLER of Kent, Washington, opened his mail one morning and got a nice surprise. He found a cheque for $98,002. He put the cheque in his bank account. Eight days later, he took out all the money in cash, closed his account and quickly left town.

The money was the result of a computer error. A few weeks before, Mr Stoller, a 38-year-old builder, went to a pharmacy and bought a box of *Ex-Lax* laxative pills for $1.99. The pills didn't work so he wrote to Sandoz, the makers of *Ex-Lax*, and asked for his money back. The company sent Stoller a cheque, but not for $1.99. The company's computer printed 98,002 instead – Mr Stoller's post code!

So Mr Stoller took the money and ran. He left no contact address. The company's private detective couldn't find him, and the police only caught Mr Stoller three years later.

2

GENNIFER ROBINSON, 20, is a cashier at the *Sav-A-Center* grocery store. One day in April, she drove to her friend's house in Matairie, Louisiana, and parked the car. When she was in the house, somebody broke into her car and stole her purse, cheque book, and driving licence.

Five days later, she was at work. She came back after the coffee break and her first customer wrote a cheque for $259.17. Ms Robinson asked to see some ID, and the customer gave her a driving licence. Ms Robinson saw her own name and photo on the licence! She told the customer to wait – she had to make a phone call 'to the manager'. The customer, 20-year-old Ashlie Williams of New Orleans, was still waiting when the police arrived.

How to tell a story

G past of irregular verbs **V** bank and post office **P** *-ought / -aught* /ɔːt/

A Vocabulary bank and post office

1 Look at **Bank and post office** opposite. Match the pictures and words.
Example account number = b

2 Match the beginnings and ends of the sentences.
Example I bought a stamp.

1	d	I bought	a £100 in cash.
2	e	I changed	b an account.
3	b	I'd like to open	c cheque.
4	h	I sent	d a stamp.
5	a	I took out	e a traveller's cheque.
6	c	I wrote a	f credit card.
7	h	I wrote to	g me for some ID.
8	f	Someone stole my	h him a letter.
9	g	The cashier asked	i the company.

3 6C.1 Listen and check. Then listen again and repeat.

B Read two true crime stories

4 Which do you use most – cheques, credit cards, or cash? When? Why? Tell a partner.

5 Read **True Crimes** opposite. Choose a good title for each story.

Ex-Lax pills   Kent man closes his account
Money by mistake   Shopping in New Orleans
Woman loses purse   Cashier checks cheque

6 Work with a partner. Answer these questions about the people in the stories.
1 How old is he / she?
2 Where is he / she from?
3 What does he / she do?

7 Match the names and the questions.
Stoller Sandoz Robinson Williams
Who ...
1 asked for ID?   *Robinson*
2 sent a cheque? the company Sandoz
3 asked for money? Mr Stoller
4 wrote a cheque? the company's computer
5 printed a cheque?
6 called the police? Ms Robinson
7 worked in a shop?
8 broke into a car? somebody Williams

8 Which words do you think describe the stories?
sad amazing strange funny frightening

C Pronunciation *-ought / -aught* /ɔːt/

9 Guess the order of the poem.

4	And it caught a rat
3	She brought it back
5	So I guess she bought a cat
1	My neighbour's daughter Pat
2	Thought she bought a hat

10 6C.2▶ Listen and check.
6C.3▶ Now listen and repeat.

D Grammar past of irregular verbs

11 Look at these two verbs in the dictionary and answer the questions.

ask /ɑːsk; *AE* æsk/ *Verb* **1** ask (sb) (about sb/sth) (jdn) (nach jdm/etw) fragen **Did you ask Sarah about the bike? Hast du Sarah wegen des Fahrrades gefragt?**

buy[1] /baɪ/ *Verb* (**bought, bought** /bɔːt/) kaufen **Can I buy you a coffee? Kann ich Sie zu einer Tasse Kaffee einladen?**

Extract from *Das Oxford Schulwörterbuch*

1 Which entry gives the past form of the verb?
2 Why doesn't the other entry give the past form?

12 Underline the irregular past verbs in **True Crimes**. Write them next to the verbs below.

break	*broke*	give	gave	send	sent
buy	bought	go	WENT	steal	stole
catch	caught	have	had	take	took
come	came	leave	left	tell	told
drive	drove	put	put	write	wrote
find	found	run	ran		
get	GOT	see	saw		

More practice? **Grammar Bank** >> p.141.

13 Test a partner.
Example **A** Catch. **B** Caught!

ABCD Put it all together

14 Work with a partner.
Student A Look at the picture story on >> p.128.
Student B Look at the picture story on >> p.134.

Give names to the people and decide where they are in the world. Think of extra details (what was in the handbag, etc.). Make notes to tell your story.

15 Tell your story to your partner. Listen to your partner's story and think of a good title for it.

I can tell a story.
Tick ✓ the line.   with a lot of help   with some help   on my own   very easily

Terror on Dock Street

1

MR BASSET
I was driving along Dock Street and he ran in front of me. I put my foot on the brake, and the car behind crashed into me. I called the police immediately.

2

MISS SETTER
I was standing in front of the post office. I was waiting for the number 94 bus.

3

Then he ran past and knocked me down. He didn't help or say sorry.

4

MRS SAMOYED
I was standing in a queue in the butcher's and he came in. He didn't say anything. He just went to the front of the queue and he took something from the counter - I think it was a leg of lamb. Then he ran out without paying!

5

MR COLLIE
I was at the National Bank cash machine on Dock Street. I was taking some money out of the machine and I heard a noise. I looked round and I saw him. He was running towards me, and I saw blood on his face. He had something in his mouth. I think it was red meat. He was like a ... a wild animal!

6

Judge: Quiet, please!

7

MRS BEAGLE
It was a nice, sunny day, and I was sitting in my garden, and the children were playing. They were making a castle out of old boxes. Then he came into the garden and he knocked it down. The children started crying, and he just ran away.

8

P.C. SHEPHERD
When we were putting him into the police car, he bit me!!

9

Judge: Do you have anything to say?

to be continued ...

How to say what was happening

G past continuous   P is / are or was / were

A Read for detail

1 Look at the pictures in **Terror on Dock Street** opposite. What do you think happened? Tell a partner.

2 Read the text. Were you right?

3 Read **Terror on Dock Street** again. Write the names.
1 She wasn't outside.   *Mrs Samoyed*
2 She wasn't standing. *Mrs. Beagle.*
3 He wasn't driving. *Mr. Collie.*
4 She was standing outside. *M. Setter*
5 He wasn't at the cash machine. *Mr. Basset*

4 Work with a partner. Complete the notes.

	where	doing what?	what happened?
Mr Basset	Dock Street	was driving	he ran in front
Miss Setter	post office	was standing	he knocked her down
Mrs Samoyed	queue in the butcher's	standing in queue	he ran out without paying.
Mr Collie	bank	was taking money	saw blood on face
Mrs Beagle	garden	was sitting	knocked the castle down
PC Shepherd	police car	putting him in car	he bit her hand

5 **6D.1▶** Listen. Who is *he*?

B Grammar past continuous

6 Complete the grammar box.

	I / he / she		you / we / they
+	He was driving.	You	___ .
−	He wasn't driving.	We	___ .
?	Was ___ ?	Were you driving?

7 Underline examples of the past continuous in **Terror on Dock Street**.

8 Look at the diagram and complete the rule.

I was driving along Dock Street (longer action)

and he ran in front of me (shorter action)

If two things happen in the past at the same time,
– use past continuous for the shorter / longer action.
– use past simple for the shorter / longer action.

9 Complete the sentences with verbs in the past simple or continuous.
1 She *was waiting* when the police *arrived* . wait / arrive
2 He was sitting at the bus stop when it started raining. sit / start
3 I saw a car crash when I was waiting for the bus. see / wait
4 We were having lunch when the phone rang. have / ring
More practice? **Grammar Bank** ≫ p.141.

C Pronunciation
is / are or was / were

10 **6D.2▶** Listen and repeat. Keep the ●●●● rhythm.
Present *is* /ɪz/ *are* /ə/   Past *was* /wəz/ *were* /wə/

The **bus** is **com**ing.   The **bus** was **com**ing.
The **boss** is **watch**ing.   The **boss** was **watch**ing.
The **boys** are **play**ing.   The **boys** were **play**ing.
The **birds** are **sing**ing.   The **birds** were **sing**ing.

11 **6D.3▶** Listen and say *present* or *past*. Now test a partner.
Example   **A** The bus was coming. **B** Past!

12 Ask and answer with a partner.
Student A Look at **What were they doing?** on ≫ p.128.
Student B Look at **What were they doing?** on ≫ p.134.

D Listen for key words

13 **6D.4▶** Listen to Nick, Sarah, and Tom talking about what they were doing when they heard some important news. Write *N* (Nick), *S* (Sarah), or *T* (Tom) next to these words.
☐ bed ☐ bus ☐ friend ☐ phone ☐ sister
☐ switch on ☐ window ☐ teacher
☐ text message ☐☐ TV ☐ shop

14 Listen again. Write notes in the box.

	Where was he / she?	What was he / she doing?
Nick	on the bus	
Sarah		
Tom		

15 Look at the audio script on ≫ p.154 and check your answers. Practise the conversation with a partner.

ABCD Put it all together

16 Work with a partner. Make a list of the ten most important international events in your lifetime.

17 Choose one event. When did it happen, where were you, and what were you doing? Write notes like in exercise 4.

18 Tell other students in the class about it. Which story is the most interesting?

I can say what was happening.
Tick ✓ the line.   with a lot of help   with some help   on my own   very easily

Writing An insurance claim

A Read and order

1 Here are some sentences from insurance claim forms. Which ones are funniest? Tell a partner.

'I was trying to kill a fly and drove into a phone box.'
'I thought my window was down, but found it was up when I put my head through it.'
'I was leaving the car park when a parked lorry crashed into me.'
'The cause of the accident was a small man in a small car with a big mouth.'
'I was coming to a red light when the car in front stopped.'

2 Put this story in order.

- [3] I turned to the left and I crashed into a traffic light.
- [4] I told the police immediately. I was wearing a seat-belt, but I hurt my neck. I had to go to hospital.
- [1] I was driving home. I was on Wellington Road. It was half past eleven at night.
- [2] I was passing the sports centre when a young man ran in front of me.

3 **6E.1▶** Listen and check.

4 Complete the insurance form for the man in exercise 2.

Insurance Claim Form

Part 3 Accident Details

A Context

What were you doing? *(please tick)*
- [ ] walking
- [✓] driving
- [ ] sitting in a car
- [ ] riding

When did the accident happen?

11.30 pm.

Where did the accident happen?

the Sports Centre on Wellington Road.

B Event

What happened? *(two sentences please)*

A young men ran in front of car. He turned and he crashed into a traffic light.

C Result

Did you tell the police? *(please tick)*
- [✓] yes
- [ ] no

Were you hurt? *(please tick)*
- [✓] yes
- [ ] no

Did you go to hospital? *(please tick)*
- [✓] yes
- [ ] no

B Check the story is complete

5 Put these phrases from the story in the correct column.

at night   crashed into   ~~driving home~~   half past 11.00   hurt my neck   ran in front of   turned to   was passing   Wellington Road   went to hospital   young man

context	event	result
driving home ran in front of was passing	at night half past 11.00	crashed into hurt my neck went to Hospital

6 Which questions on the claim form in exercise 4 don't these people answer?

1 I was walking along Dock Street when I saw an accident. It was about 9 o'clock on Monday evening in front of the post office. I ran to the phone box and called the police. Nobody was hurt.

2 A cow walked into the middle of the road. I crashed into it. The cow was hurt. The farmer had to kill it. I was wearing a seat-belt and I was fine.

3 I was riding my bike along the side of the river. It was early on Sunday morning. A big dog ran towards me. I fell into the river.

7 Work with a partner. Choose one of the stories in exercise 6 and invent the missing information.

C Join sentences

8 You can join sentences with *when*. Look at the examples. Then join the sentences below with *when*.

He hit his head when he was getting out of the car.
When he was getting out of his car, he hit his head.

1 I was driving to work. I saw an accident.
2 I crashed into a parked car. I was turning the corner.
3 I was waiting at the lights. A man knocked on my car window.
4 My car stopped. I was driving in the mountains.

ABC Put it all together

9 Think of an accident you've had or heard about (or choose one of the accidents in exercise 1). Write notes. Answer all the questions in the insurance claim form.

Example [✓] driving
When: 10.00 a.m.
Where: New Street

10 Use your notes and write the story of your accident. Try to join a few sentences with *when*.

11 Read other students' stories. Do they have a context, event and result?

I can write a story.

Tick ✓ the line.   with a lot of help   with some help   on my own   very easily

Unit 6 Review

A Grammar

1 *have to, don't have to, mustn't* Complete the sentences with *have to, don't have to* or *mustn't*.

1 Drivers in Britain _have to_ have insurance.
2 Cyclists _____ wear bright coloured clothes, but it's a good idea.
3 Pedestrians _____ cross the road when the red light is on.
4 If you take the bus, you _____ worry about parking your car.
5 When you're travelling by train, you sometimes _____ show your ticket.
6 You _____ use your mobile phone when you're driving.
7 Students _____ pay the full train fare – there is a special students' fare.

2 **Past of irregular verbs** Find the past forms of 16 more verbs. Some letters are used twice.

T	O	O	K	T	O	L	D
C	F	O	U	N	D	O	S
A	A	P	S	A	W	S	T
M	B	U	G	N	E	T	O
E	R	T	G	O	N	W	L
B	O	U	G	H	T	R	E
H	K	S	E	N	T	O	G
R	E	N	L	E	F	T	E
A	R	D	R	O	V	E	T

3 **Past simple or continuous** Put the verb in the correct tense – past simple or past continuous.

I ¹ _saw_ (see) an accident when I ² _____ (walk) along Baker Street. A woman ³ _____ (cross) the road and a cyclist ⁴ _____ (knock) her down. I ⁵ _____ (go) to work and I was late, but I ⁶ _____ (stop) to help. The woman ⁷ _____ (lie) on the floor and blood ⁸ _____ (come) from a cut on her head. I ⁹ _____ (put) my coat under her head and then I ¹⁰ _____ (phone) an ambulance.

Later that day, when I ¹¹ _____ (leave) the office for lunch, a colleague ¹² _____ (say), 'Are you OK?' 'Yes', I said, 'Why?' 'Because there's blood on the back of your coat,' she said.

B Vocabulary

4 **Telephone phrases** Complete the telephone conversation.

Jim Hello, can I ¹*speak* to Mr Perez, please?
Lil Yes, who's ²c_____?
J It's his student, Jim. I called a moment ago but I got ³c_____ off.
L Hold the ⁴l_____ please. I'll put you ⁵t_____.
ring ring
L I'm sorry. Mr Perez is not in his office at the moment. Would you like to leave a ⁶m_____?
J Yes please, could you tell him Jim phoned and I'll call ⁷b_____ later? Thanks.
L OK. Thank you. Goodbye.

5 **On the road** Solve the anagrams at the end of the sentences to find the words.

1 You have to stop at these when they are on red.
   fftarci hglist   _traffic_ _lights_
2 You don't have to wear this if you are on a bicycle.
   melhet   h_____
3 Passengers don't have to wear these in some countries.
   teas-slebt   s_____-b_____
4 You have to wait for the police if you have one of these.
   tednccia   a_____
5 You mustn't drive your car on this - it's where people walk.
   nepavemt   p_____
6 You have to have one of these to drive a car.
   cliecen   l_____
7 In some countries, you have to pay to drive on one of these.
   towmayor   m_____
8 Everyone has to stop at these when people are walking across the road.
   destinaper grossinc   p_____ c_____

6 **Bank and post office** Complete the sentences with these words.

account bank card ~~cash~~ cheques credit details insurance ~~machine~~ traveller's

1 You can take money out of a _cash machine._
2 You can normally cash _____ _____ in banks and hotels.
3 You normally use a _____ _____ to buy things on the Internet.
4 If you have a crash, you have to give the other driver your _____ _____.
5 When you phone the bank, you have to tell them your _____ _____ number.

Job Advertisements

1 Wanted
Telephone sales staff
for a company selling holiday apartments on the Mediterranean coast

- Attractive salary plus commission
- Flexible working hours
- Excellent opportunity

Call 071 882 7720 for interview

2 Native Spanish & Italian teachers
wanted for city centre language school

- Evening classes
- 2 years' experience
- £10/hr
- 1-year contract

Fax CV to 071 883 2765 or email paul@newlang.com

3 POWER GYM
We are looking for fitness instructors

Must be fit and friendly
Evenings and weekends
Competitive salary

info@powergym.com
Contact Rob on 071 882 6653

4 Age Care
WANTED
Experienced, qualified nurses to visit old people in their homes

- Car provided
- Must have a valid driving licence
- Salary £1,000 /month

CALL 071 637 4463

5 Drivers wanted
for a luxury limousine company to meet VIPs at airport, etc.

- Clean driving licence
- Must have good appearance
- Uniform provided
- Flexible hours
- Good salary

Contact Stewart on 071 539 6209

6 ZedBeds
We are looking for bed testers

- No experience necessary
- Must enjoy sleeping
- Pyjamas provided
- Work hours: nights

Call 071 558 3865 for interview

7 Want to travel, have fun, and get paid for it?
We are looking for entertainers to work on cruise ships – musicians, actors, magicians, comedians

- **Must be fun, friendly, and work well in a team**
- **2 weeks on, 2 weeks off**
- **All expenses paid**
- **Attractive pay**

Call 081 773 6635 for interview

Dictionary

staff /stɑːf/ USA stæf/ *nombre, verbo*
▸ n [v sing o pl] personal, plantilla: *The staff are all working long hours.* Todo el personal está trabajando hasta tarde.

flexible /ˈfleksəbl/ *adj.* **1** hajlékony **2** rugalmas: *flexible working hours*

uniform /ˈjuːnɪfɔːm/ ▸ *agg* uniforme
▸ *s* divisa, uniforme **LOC** in uniform in divisa

salary /ˈsæləri/ *n* (*pl* -ies) salaire

magic /ˈmædʒɪk/ *s* magia: like ~ como que por magia ● *adj* mágico **magical** *adj* mágico /məˈdʒɪʃn/ *s* mágico/a

Extracts from *Diccionario Oxford Pocket para estudiantes de inglés, Oxford Wordpower: anglo-magyar szótár nyelvtanulóknak, Dictionnaire Oxford Poche pour apprendre l'anglais, Dizionario Oxford Study per studenti d'inglese, Oxford Pocket Dicionário Bilíngüe para brasileiros*

How to have a conversation about work

v using a dictionary; job conditions **P** contrastive stress

A Read for information

1 What information do you expect to find in a job advertisement? Compare with a partner.

- ☐ salary
- ☐ manager's name
- ☐ company address
- ☐ job title
- ☐ responsibilities
- ☐ company phone number
- ☐ size of company
- ☐ email address

2 Look at **Job Advertisements** opposite. One of the ads is a joke. Read and find it.

3 Work with a partner. Say which job ads.
  1 They give you a car. *4 and 5*
  2 You work with language students.
  3 You work on a boat.
  4 You have to sell things.
  5 You have to look smart.
  6 You have to work well with other people.
  7 You help people to exercise.
  8 They tell you how much you get paid.

4 Which job is best for you? Why? Tell a partner.

B Use a dictionary

5 Look at **Dictionary** opposite. Find the missing words in the **Job Advertisements** text.

6 How did you guess?
  1 From the pronunciation.
  2 From the translation.
  3 From the other connected words.
  4 From the example phrases or sentences.

7 Are there any other words you don't know in **Job Advertisements**? Work with a partner and try to guess their meaning.

8 Check in your dictionary.

C Pronunciation contrastive stress

9 **7A.1▶** Listen and read the conversation. Which jobs do Andy and Belén do?
  Andy What do you do?
  Belén I'm a Spanish teacher.
  A Oh yeah? Where do you work?
  B In a school called *Lingo City*.
  A Do you like it?
  B Yes, it's fun. What do YOU do?
  A I'm a limousine driver.
  B Oh. Interesting!

10 **7A.2▶** Andy starts the conversation (like a tennis player 'serving' the ball). Belén continues the conversation by returning the question (like a tennis player 'returning' the ball). Listen and repeat.

Serve

● ● ● ●

What do you **do**?

Return

● ● ● ●

What do **you** do?

11 **7A.3▶** Listen. Are they *serve* or *return* questions? Say **S** or **R**.

12 Act the conversation in exercise 9 with a partner.

D Listen for specific information

13 **7A.4▶** Listen. Which jobs do these two people do?

14 Listen again. Who says what about their job? Write *M*, *W*, or *X*.
  M = the man says it
  W = the woman says it
  X = nobody says it.
  Compare with a partner.
  1 I have to travel a lot. *M*
  2 I like the work.
  3 We have to wear a uniform.
  4 The hours are quite long.
  5 We have flexible hours.
  6 I get two weeks off.
  7 I work nights.
  8 I like working in a team.
  9 The money's not bad.
  10 I get a company car.
  11 All expenses are paid.

15 Look at the audio script on ≫ p.154 and check your answers together.

16 Choose a job from **Job Advertisements** opposite. Ask and answer using the ideas in exercise 14 to guess your partner's job.

ABCD Put it all together

17 Think about your job (or a job you would like to have). Tick ✓ the true sentences about your job in exercise 14.

18 Have conversations with other students in the class about their jobs (or a job they'd like to have). Remember to serve and return questions – it's a conversation, not an interview!

Have the conversation for just one minute and change partners. Which person has the most interesting job?

I can have a conversation about work.

Tick ✓ the line. with a lot of help with some help on my own very easily

A guided tour of my workplace

1

This is me, Kevin Taylor.

2

2

3

This is me with my form class.

4

4 d

5

This is the room where we sit in the breaks.

6

This is one of the computers which we use to prepare lessons. e

7

This is Lenny. He's the man who takes care of the building.
c

8

8

9

9 b

10

This is the room where the kids have IT lessons, and Andy, the school technician.

What are they saying?

a
3
What's the name of the man who wrote Hamlet?
William

b
What do you call the chemical that is in this bottle? Jackie?
9

c
This is the place where you put the battery.
7

d
4
What do you call a number which is less than zero? Yes, Martin?

e
6
What are the names of the people that started *Google*?

How to explain what you mean

G defining relative clauses   V jobs, workplaces, and tools

A Read for general meaning

1 Work with a partner. Think of a job. Now think of all the places and tools connected with it.

Example   Teacher – school, classroom, board ...
   Secretary – office, computer, telephone ...

2 Read **A guided tour of my workplace** opposite. Write these captions below the correct pictures.

   3 This is the place where the kids have lunch.
   2 This is the school where I work.
   1 This is Chris Walton, head of Maths.
   4 This is the lab where the kids have Chemistry lessons.

3 Read **What are they saying?** opposite and match each question with one of the people in the photographs.

B Listen for detail

4 **7B.1▶** Listen to Kevin describing the photos. Make notes on any extra information you hear.

Example   he teaches English literature

5 Write *true* or *false*. Listen again and check.
   1 Kevin is an English literature teacher.   *True*
   2 Chris Walton teaches in the classroom opposite.   F
   3 Linda is the school secretary.   T
   4 Josh is a history teacher.   F
   5 Maria Carmen is from Madrid.   T
   6 The woman in the canteen photo is called Moira.   T
   7 Kevin always eats in the canteen.   F
   8 Jack's going to leave work next year.   T
   9 The kids don't like the school technician.   F

C Grammar defining relative clauses

6 Look at the sentence and answer the question.
He's the man who takes care of the building.

The red part of the sentence is a relative clause.
What is it for?
a It asks a question about the man.
b It explains which man we're talking about.

7 Look at the sentences in **What are they saying?** The relative clauses begin with the words *who*, *which*, *that* or *where*. Complete the rules about when to use the words.
   1 Use WHERE for places.
   2 Use WHO for people.
   3 Use WHICH for things.
   4 Use THAT for people or things.

8 Complete the sentences with *who*, *which* or *where*. Answer the two questions.
   1 A caretaker is a person _who_ takes care of a building.
   2 The staff room is the place _where_ teachers sit in the breaks.
   3 This is the camera _which_ students use for projects.
   4 What do you call the place _where_ students have lunch?
   5 What do you call the person _who_ takes care of the electrical equipment?
   6 This is the computer _which_ we use to prepare lessons.

9 Complete these definitions with relative clauses.
   1 A playground is a place in a school where children play in the breaks.
   2 A photocopier is a machine _which we use to cope_
   3 A library is a place _where I borrow books_
   4 An English teacher is a person _who te_

More practice? **Grammar Bank** >> p.142.

which makes copies.

D Vocabulary jobs and workplaces

10 Work with a partner. Match the jobs and workplaces.

Jobs   artist cashier dentist mechanic nurse
   pilot receptionist scientist secretary

Workplaces   bank cockpit garage hospital hotel
   laboratory office studio surgery

11 Test a partner on the workplaces and jobs in exercise 10. Use the questions below.

Asking for the word when you know the meaning
A What do you call the place where an artist works?
B A studio.

Asking for the meaning when you know the word
A What's a studio?
B It's the place where an artist works.

12 Work in two small teams to play a quiz.
Team A look at **Jobs Quiz** on >> p.129.
Team B look at **Jobs Quiz** on >> p.134.

ABCD Put it all together

13 Use the instructions in **Describing a Job** on >> p.129 to write about a job and workplace.

14 Tell a partner about the job and workplace from exercise 13. Listen to your partner and ask for explanations.
Example   **A** I'm a motorcycle courier.
   B What's that?

Office Life

Episode two

1 Holly Boss-alarm!

2 Anna Justin, this is Joan. She's new. Can you show her around and tell her the office rules?

3 Justin OK, let's start with coffee. The rules say you can't have more than four cups a day. So I've started drinking tea.

4 Justin This is the smoking room. Nobody can go in there because smoking isn't allowed.
Joan So why is there a smoking room?

5 Justin Don't ask. Now, this is the office supplies cupboard. You can take anything you want, if you can find the key.

6 Joan Are there any dress rules?
Justin Yes, but they're quite flexible. You aren't allowed to wear jeans but you can wear any colour socks you want.

7 Joan Hmm. Can you send personal emails?
Justin Yes, but not before 6.00.
Joan But the office closes at 6.00!

8 Justin True. Now, we also have our own office rules. You can't arrive early, you can't leave late and you can't work in the lunch hour.

9 Justin And finally, this is the boss-alarm. If you see her coming, you have to ring this bell. That gives us time to start working.
Joan Ahem …

How to talk about rules (2)

G *can / can't* (permission) P short and long *o* /ɒ/ and /əʊ/

A Read a comedy sketch

1 Look at the people in **Office Life** opposite. What do you remember about them from lesson 1C?

2 Now read **Office Life** and choose a good title. Compare with a partner.
   a Office Rules
   b The Smoking Room
   c This is Joan
   d Not Before Six

3 Answer the questions.
   1 What are the rules about these things?
      coffee smoking office supplies dress emails
   2 Do you think Justin agrees with the rules? How do you know?

4 Work with a partner. Where do you think the **Office Life** audience will laugh? Write *L*.

5 7C.1▶ Listen and check.

6 Find phrases with the same meaning as these.
   1 You aren't allowed to drink more than four cups of coffee.
      You can't have more than four cups of coffee.
   2 You can't smoke.
   3 You can't wear jeans.
   4 You are allowed to wear any colour socks you want.
   5 Are you allowed to send personal emails?

7 Who is *you* in the sentences above?

B Grammar *can / can't* (permission)

8 Complete the grammar box

+	You can wear jeans.	You can leave early.
–	You can't wear jeans.	_____.
?	Can _____ ?	_____ ?

Remember We also use *can* to talk about ability.
I can draw quite well.

9 Underline *can* and *can't* for permission in **Office Life**.

10 Are these sentences about permission or ability?
   1 You can go home now, if you want.
   2 Parents can take time off work when they have a baby.
   3 I can run a kilometre in one minute.
   4 Can you speak any foreign languages?
   5 Can you wear jeans in your office?

11 Work with a partner. Find the differences between the rules in your offices.
   Student A Look at **Office** on ≫ p.129.
   Student B Look at **Office** on ≫ p.134.

   More practice? **Grammar Bank** ≫ p.142.

C Pronunciation
short and long *o* /ɒ/ and /əʊ/

12 7C.2▶ Listen and repeat.

short /ɒ/	This is John.	They want work.	They're not books.
long /əʊ/	This is Joan.	They won't work.	They're notebooks.

13 7C.3▶ Listen to these words from **Office Life**. Is the orange letter *o* short (S) or long (L)? Practise saying the words.

   boss *S*   closes   coffee   don't   go   not
   office   own   show   smoking   socks

D Listen for general meaning

14 7C.4▶ Listen to a girl and a boy talking about their schools. Answer the question.
   Which school has more rules?
   a The girl's school   b The boy's school

15 Listen again and write *he* or *she* in the gaps.
   1 *She* can wear trousers or a skirt.
   2 ____ isn't allowed to hit people.
   3 ____ can't eat in the classroom.
   4 ____ can miss lessons.
   5 ____ isn't allowed to wear jeans.
   6 ____ can't run in the corridor.

16 Look at the audio script on ≫ p.155 and listen again. Why do the speakers say 'erm'? Tick ✓ two reasons.
   a to get thinking time
   b to finish the sentence
   c to show they haven't finished speaking

17 Can you remember the school rules from the listening? Work with a partner and choose one school each. Tell your partner the rules.

ABCD Put it all together

18 Think of a place you know where there are a lot of rules. Use the ideas below and write notes.

   a library   your work   your school   an airport
   the cinema   a bus   a museum   *your ideas*

   Example   a library – no talking, no food …

19 Work in small groups. Tell the others about the rules in the place you chose. Listen to the rules. Are they good rules?

 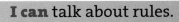

A day in the life of **a postman in India**

1 Rajendra gets on his _bicycle_ and starts _work_ .

2 Geeta gets a _postcard_ from her _cousin_ in Bangalore.

3 The news is _good_ so Geeta's _happy_ .

4 Today, Sua gets her _pension_

5 Sua can't _sign_ her name, so she gives her fingerprint. Rajendra has to _help_ her.

6 Rajendra _dials_ a number for Samundar.

7 At the _end_ of the day, Rajendra does the _paperwork_

Six mornings a week, Rajendra Prasad gets on his bicycle and starts work. He puts on his postman's uniform, and takes mail to the desert villages of Rajasthan. He wears a turban on his head because the desert sun is very hot. When he arrives in a village, he rings the bell on his bike and everybody runs out. They don't get many visitors so they're excited. Today, Rajendra's first stop is Geeta's house. She's got a postcard from her cousin in Bangalore. Rajendra has to read it out because Geeta can't read. The news is good, so she's happy.

Rajendra doesn't only take the mail. He also has to take the pension money for the old people. Today Sua gets her pension. She can't sign her name, so she has to give her fingerprint instead. Rajendra has to help her because she's very old. "I don't know how old I am," says Sua. "Maybe 50 or 60?" Her neighbours think she's about 75.

Rajendra also carries a telephone because many of the villages don't have phones. It's good for Rajendra because he can earn 1,000 rupees a month as commission from the telephone calls. His salary is only 3,000 rupees a month (under €50). Today, Samundar wants to make a call. She shows Rajendra the number in her notebook and he dials for her. She speaks to her son Vishnu. "I told him to come home because I need some money," she says.

At the end of the day, Rajendra does the paperwork and thinks about his job. He knows the problems well because he's been a postman for 22 years. The big problem is transport. Sometimes there are no roads. Sometimes he has problems with his bike so he has to push it. "But on the whole, it's a good job," he says.

Adapted from a text by Geeta Pandey on http://news.bbc.co.uk

How to describe a typical day

G *because, so*   P grouping words

A Read and identify the people

1 Look at the photos opposite but cover the text. Guess what the text will be about.

2 Work with a partner. Read **A day in the life of ...** opposite and complete the captions for photos 2–7.

3 Read the text again and name the people in the photos.
Example   1 = Rajendra

4 Match the pronouns in red with these people and things.
Rajendra Geeta Sua Samundar Vishnu
everybody in the village   the postcard

1 Why does he wear a turban? *he = Rajendra*
2 Why are they excited? *everybody in the village*
3 Why does he have to read it out? *Rajendra the postcard*
4 Why is she happy? *Geeta*
5 Why does she have to give her fingerprint? *Sua*
6 Why does he have to help her? *Rajendra Sua*
7 Why does he carry a telephone? *Rajendra*
8 Why did she tell him to come home? *Samundar Vishnu*
9 Why does he know the problems well? *Rajendra*

5 Now answer the questions in exercise 4 with a partner.
Example   1 because the desert sun is very hot.

B Grammar *because, so*

6 Read the grammar box and underline the correct word in the rule.

	result	
	She's happy	because the news is good.
The news is good so	she's happy.	

Rule *Because* comes **before** / **after** the result.
So comes **before** / **after** the result.

7 Work with a partner. Make sentences with *because* and *so*.
1 I can't open the cupboard. I haven't got the key.
I can't open the cupboard because I haven't got the key.
I haven't got the key so I can't open the cupboard.
2 I haven't got a computer. I can't send you an email.
3 He can't read the phone number. He hasn't got his glasses.
4 She's ill. She can't come to work today.
5 He had a job interview. He was wearing a suit and tie.
6 We came on the bus. Our car's broken down.

More practice? **Grammar Bank** ≫ p.142.

C Pronunciation grouping words

8 **7D.1▶** Listen and repeat. Pause where there is a full stop.
A He doesn't work at night. He sleeps.
B He doesn't work. At night he sleeps.

9 Test a partner. Listen and say **A** or **B**.
A He doesn't work. At night he sleeps.   B B!

10 **7D.2▶** Sometimes you hear a pause even without a full stop. Listen and mark the pause with /.
1 He wears a turban/because the desert sun's very hot.
2 They don't get many visitors/so they're excited.
3 Rajendra has to read it out/because she can't read.
4 The news is good/so she's happy.
5 Sometimes he has problems with his bike/so he has to push it.
6 I told him to come home/because I need some money.

11 Look at the last paragraph of **A day in the life of ...** Where are the best places to pause? Mark them with /.

12 Read the paragraph to a partner. Do you have pauses in the same places?

D Listen for specific information

13 You will hear a travel agent talking about his typical day. Guess the order of the following things that he does every day. Compare with a partner.

1 arrive at work	6	close the shop for lunch
2 check the emails	4	make a cup of coffee
7 close the shop	5	open the shop 9⁰⁰
8 do the paperwork	3	switch on the computer
9 go home		

14 **7D.3▶** Listen and check together.

15 Listen again and answer the questions.
1 How many days a week does he work? *6 days*
2 What time does he open the shop? *9⁰⁰*
3 How many people work in the shop now? *Just one.*
4 Why aren't there many customers now? *because they get internet*
5 What time does he go home? *7⁰⁰*

16 Read the audio script on ≫ p.155 and check your answers.

ABCD Put it all together

17 Think of ten things you do on a typical day at work, school, or university. Make notes.

18 Work with a partner. Take turns to be A or B.
Student A Describe your typical day.
Student B Listen to your partner's day. Ask three questions with 'why'.

I can describe a typical day.

Tick ✓ the line.   with a lot of help   with some help   on my own   very easily

Writing A job description

A Read a description of a job

1 Look at the photo and guess the answers to these questions.
1 Where is this man?
2 What does he do?
3 Where does he work?
4 Does he like his work?
5 Who is the girl with him?
6 How old is she?

2 Read the text and check your answers in exercise 1.

3 Make notes about Karol's job.

😊 good points	🙁 bad points
doesn't have to travel to work	

4 How is Karol's working life different from your daily life? Tell a partner.
Example Karol doesn't have to travel to work. I have to spend 20 minutes on the bus every morning.

B Think before you listen

5 You will hear Karol talking about his last job, when he worked in an office. What good and bad points do you think he will talk about? Make two lists with a partner.

6 **7E.1▶** Listen and tick ✓ the points you hear on your lists.

C Write a first draft

7 Copy the table in exercise 3 and make notes about <u>your</u> job or a job you know about. Then decide which points are the best and worst and <u>underline</u> them.

8 Use your notes from exercise 7 and write about the good and bad points of your job.

9 Read your partner's writing. Do you think your partner could give more explanations? Write *Why?* in the text.
Example

> I don't have to travel to work. ↙ Why?

ABC Put it all together

10 Write a second draft of your text. Give reasons with *because* and *so*.

11 You are going to read out your text to the class. Mark the pauses with /. Practise reading it out.

The WORLD of WORK

This week's article comes from an architect in Poland ...

❝ The best thing about my job is that I don't have to travel to work and I haven't got a boss because I'm self-employed. I don't have to wear a uniform because I work from home. Also, I've got flexible working hours so I don't have to get up early in the morning. I can work when I want and I can go on holiday at quiet times of the year, when tickets and hotels are cheap. I like working at home because I see a lot of my daughter, Renata, who is six.

The worst thing about my job is that I don't have a salary. I don't get paid every month and I don't get any holiday pay. Some months I earn a lot of money, but other months I don't earn anything! Also, I have to fill in my tax forms every three months so I have to spend hours with a calculator. I hate that! I could pay an accountant but I don't because it's expensive.

On the whole, there are more good things than bad things about my job. ❞

Karol *Architect, Gdansk, Poland.*

I can write a description of my job.

Tick ✓ the line. with a lot of help   with some help   on my own   very easily

Unit 7 Review

A Grammar

1 Defining relative clauses Add one missing word in each sentence, then answer the four questions.

1 A caretaker is a person who takes care of a building.
2 What do you call a shop you buy fruit and vegetables?
3 A chemist's is a shop you get medicines.
4 A vet is a doctor takes care of animals.
5 What do you call a person teaches history?
6 What do you call a place students have lunch?
7 A photocopier is a machine makes photocopies.
8 What do you call the place an artist works?

2 Defining relative clauses: *who, which, that, where*
Complete these sentences.

1 A taxi driver is _____ .
2 A book shop is _____ .
3 A guitarist is _____ .
4 An office worker is _____ .
5 A cinema is _____ .

3 can / can't (permission) Write sentences with *can* or *can't* for permission.

1   *You can't smoke here* _____ .

2   _____ .

3   _____ .

4   _____ .

5   _____ .

6 _____ .

4 because / so Complete the two endings for each sentence with *so* or *because*.

1 I haven't got a car ...
   a *so* _____ I can't take you to the airport.
   b *because* _____ I haven't got enough money.
2 Alex is ill ...
   a _____ he ate some bad food.
   b _____ he isn't at work today.
3 Jeanne's happy ...
   a _____ she's smiling.
   b _____ she passed her exams.

B Vocabulary

5 Job advertisements Put these words in the job advertisement.

expenses salary experience company
well ~~wanted~~ interview flexible staff

---

[1] *Wanted*

Travelling sales [2]_____

- attractive [3]_____
- a [5]_____ car
- [4]_____ hours
- all [6]_____ paid

Must ...
* have good appearance
* have sales [7]_____
* work [8]_____ in a team.

Call 8837727 for an [9]_____ .

---

6 Job conditions Complete the sentences.

1 You have to look s_____ in the office.
2 The hours are f_____; you can start late.
3 We have to wear a u_____ to work.
4 I get a c_____ car.
5 All e_____ are paid.
6 I get two w_____ off a year.
7 The money's not b_____ .
8 I like working with people in a t_____ .

7 Work and workplaces Write the word.

1 The pilot of a plane sits in the *cockpit* . pickoct
2 A person who takes care of the electrical equipment is a t_____ . haccientin
3 The room where a doctor works is called a s_____ . yesrurg
4 The room where an artist works is called a s_____ . oduist
5 A person who repairs cars in a garage is a m_____ . camichen
6 A person who gives and takes your money in a bank is a c_____ . sirache
7 A person who takes care of a building is a c_____ . atrackeer
8 A place where scientists work is called a l_____ . tarrybaloo
9 A person who works at the desk in a hotel lobby is called a r_____ . spottiniceer
10 A place where the students and staff eat in a school is called a c_____ . neatnec
11 A person who takes care of patients in hospital is a n_____ . suren
12 A photographer takes pictures with a c_____ . macare

Wi-fi thief says he's sorry

A Singapore teenager who used his neighbour's wi-fi Internet network will not be able to use the Internet for the next 18 months. The message for wi-fi users is clear: if it isn't yours, don't use it.

An online-game fan

Seventeen-year-old Garyl Tan Jia Luo was an online-game fan and played games at all hours of the day. He didn't have time to study and wasn't able to complete his course at the polytechnic. In the end, his parents were very worried and they disconnected their Internet access so Tan couldn't go online. However, this didn't stop him. He knew his neighbours had Internet access, so he used theirs. He was able to connect to their wireless Internet network, or 'wi-fi', and continue playing online games from his own home.

With many laptops, you can connect to any wi-fi network in your area, not just yours.

In Singapore, wi-fi thieves can go to prison for three years.

A crime in Singapore

The neighbours noticed Tan was using their wi-fi one night. They told him to stop, but he didn't, and so they called the police. Under Singapore's 'Computer Misuse Act', it's a crime to use a wi-fi network that isn't yours. In the end, the young wi-fi thief had to go to court. He is the first person to go to court for this crime in Singapore.

No Internet for 18 months

In court, Tan said he was very sorry. Judge Bala Reddy decided not to send him to prison. Instead, he sent Tan to a boys' hostel for nine months. At the hostel, he will do sports and other activities, but he won't be allowed to play video games. Furthermore, he won't be able to use the Internet for the next year and a half. However, the judge also gave Tan another choice – he could join the army and do his national service early instead of going to the hostel.

GLOSSARY	
wireless network	a computer network which works without cables
Internet access	a way of entering the Internet
court	a place where they decide what will happen to a criminal
judge	a person who decides what will happen to a criminal
army	a large group of people who fight for a country
national service	the time that young people must spend in the army in some countries

Sorry!

Tina Oh no!

Bill What's the matter?

T I'm so sorry, Bill, I've just deleted something by mistake.

B But why are you using mine?

T Well, mine's broken, and I wanted to send a quick email, so …

B Uh huh …

T So I used yours, and ehm … oh, I'm really sorry!

B Well, what did you delete?

T I don't know – just a file that was open. I thought it was mine. Sorry Bill!

B Oh, never mind, it wasn't important. Don't worry about it.

T Are you sure?

B Yeah, no problem.

T OK, thanks. I'm really sorry about that.

How to apologize and respond to apologies

A Read and understand a newspaper article

1 Work with a partner. How many words about computers do you know in English? Make a list.
Example   mouse, screen ...

2 Look at the photos and headings in **Wi-fi thief** opposite. What do you think the article is about?

3 Read the article quickly and check. Compare with a partner.

4 Read the article again. Look at the sentences below and write *true* or *false*.
   1 Tan's parents were unhappy about how long he played computer games. T
   2 Tan used his neighbours' computer in their house. F
   3 The neighbours talked to Tan. T
   4 Tan apologized to the judge. T
   5 The judge sent Tan to prison for nine months. F

5 Find these words in the article. Guess what they mean.
   disconnected   access   misuse   hostel

6 How did you guess? Choose one or more of these answers for each word.
   a I decided if the word is a noun, verb, adjective, etc.
   b There is a part of the word that I already know (for example -*use*).
   c There is a similar word in my language.
   d I thought about the meaning of the sentence.
   e Other ...

7 What do you think? Answer the questions with a partner.
   1 Do you think the judge was right?
   2 Do you think Tan was really sorry?
   3 Why do people apologize? Think of three reasons.

B Vocabulary apology phrases

8 **8A.1▶** Listen and read **Sorry!** opposite. Match the conversation with one of the photographs.

9 Answer the questions.
   1 What was Tina doing?
   2 What did she do by mistake?
   3 Is the computer hers?
   4 Why was she using it?

10 How does Tina apologize? Does Bill accept her apologies? How? Underline phrases in the conversation.

11 **8A.2▶** Pronunciation Listen and repeat. Copy the pronunciation.
   A **Sor**ry! I'm **sor**ry! I'm **sor**ry about **that**!
   B No **prob**lem. **Don't wor**ry.
   A **Sor**ry! I'm **sor**ry! I'm **real**ly **ver**y **sor**ry!
   B **That's** all **right**. Nev**er mind**.

C Grammar possessive pronouns

12 Read these phrases from **Sorry!** The words in green are possessive pronouns. Answer the questions.
   Why are you using mine?
   Well, mine's broken ... so I used yours.
   1 What are they talking about?
   2 Why don't they use the word *computer*?

13 Make the sentences shorter using these object pronouns.
   ours   ~~his~~   hers   theirs
   1 Her phone's broken so she used his phone. *Her phone is broken so she used his.*
   2 If your computer's broken, you can use our computer.
   3 My camera is the same as their camera.
   4 His Internet access doesn't work, so he's using her Internet access.

   More practice? **Grammar Bank** >> p.143.

D Predict before you listen

14 Look at photograph 3. The girl's name is Jess and she's talking to her brother Zach. Guess the answers to these questions with a partner.
   The problem ...
   1 What is Jess doing? Why?
   2 The phone isn't hers. Whose is it?

   The explanation ...
   3 Why wasn't she using her own phone?
   4 How did the phone get wet?

15 **8A.3▶** Listen and check your answers.

16 Can you remember how Zach responded to Jess's apology? Check in the audio script on >> p.155.

ABCD Put it all together

17 Answer the questions about a true or an imagined situation. Make notes. Then tell a partner.
   1 You used something that wasn't yours. What was it? (a computer, a phone, an umbrella, a camera, some sunglasses, *your ideas* ...)
   2 You damaged the thing by mistake. What happened? (you dropped it, you lost it, you spilt something on it, *your ideas* ...)
   3 What explanation can/did you give to the owner?

18 Do a role play with a partner. Take turns to be A and B.
   Student A The thing you used in exercise 17 belongs to B. Explain to B what happened, and apologize.
   Student B Listen to A's explanations and respond. Try to make A feel better about the mistake.

I can apologize and respond to apologies.

Material and shape

wood
metal
cloth *klof*
plastic
glass
cardboard
china

round round round round round
square square square square
long and thin
flat

fabric

Making pencils

6 [6] The pencil sandwich is cut into separate pencils.

2 [2] The blocks are cut into flat pieces.

[1] The wood is cut into square blocks.

9 [9] An eraser is fitted on the end of the pencil.

8 [8] The information about the pencil is printed on the side.

3 [3] Lines are cut in one side of each flat piece.

5 [5] A second flat piece is stuck on top of the first to make a pencil sandwich.

4 [4] The pencil leads are put in the cut lines. *(leds)*

7 [7] The pencils are shaped and painted.

block

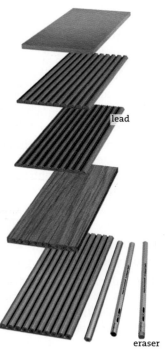

lead

eraser

PENCILS TRIVIA

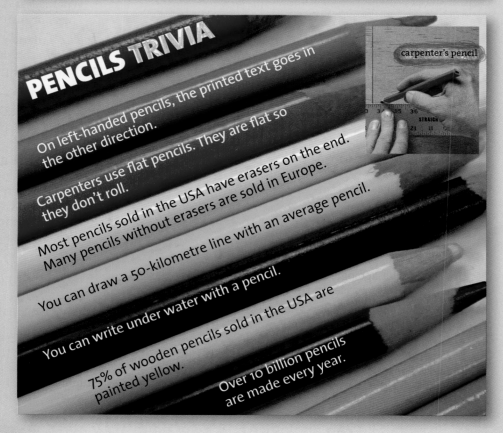

carpenter's pencil

On left-handed pencils, the printed text goes in the other direction.

Carpenters use flat pencils. They are flat so they don't roll.

Most pencils sold in the USA have erasers on the end. Many pencils without erasers are sold in Europe.

You can draw a 50-kilometre line with an average pencil.

You can write under water with a pencil.

75% of wooden pencils sold in the USA are painted yellow.

Over 10 billion pencils are made every year.

How to describe things

G present passive   V material and shape   P passive or active?

A Vocabulary material and shape

1 Look at **Material and shape** opposite. Match these descriptions with things in the photos.
   1 It's made of wood. It's long and thin. *Spoon*
   2 It's round and flat. It's made of china. *plate*
   3 It's made of metal. It's round and it's got a handle. *pan*
   4 The top is round and flat. It's made of glass and metal. *table*

2 Describe and guess the other things in the picture.
   Example **A** It's long and thin. It's made of plastic.
              B Toothbrush!

B Read for interest

3 Read **Making pencils** opposite. Put the text in order.

4 Read **Pencils trivia** opposite. What new information did you find out about pencils?

5 Work with a partner. Read the texts again. Now find a wooden pencil and answer these questions.
   1 Can you see that it is made of two pieces of wood?
   2 What information is printed on the side?
   3 Is there an eraser fitted on the end?
   4 Does it roll off your desk easily?
   5 Do you think it is a left-handed pencil?
   6 How many kilometres are left in it?
   7 Is it painted the same colour as most American pencils?

C Grammar present passive

6 Here are two possible alternative titles for the **Making pencils** text. Which one do you think is best? Why?
   1 The people who make pencils
   2 How pencils are made

7 Why is sentence b better for **Making pencils**? What is more important, the person or the wood?
   a **active**   A person cuts the wood into square blocks.
   b **passive** The wood is cut into square blocks.

8 Look at the grammar box and answer the questions.

	subject	verb	object
active	A person	cuts	the wood ...
passive	The wood	is cut ...	

   To make the passive:
   1 Which words are taken out of the sentence?
   2 Which words are moved?
   3 How does the verb change?

9 Underline the examples of verbs in the passive in **Making pencils**.

10 Make these sentences passive.
   1 People sell CDs in plastic boxes.
      CDs are sold in plastic boxes.
   2 A person paints the pencils yellow.
   3 People sell tuna fish in cans.
   4 A person washes the plates and puts them away.
   5 A person makes the ties from the best cloth.
   6 People make toothbrushes of plastic.

   More practice? **Grammar Bank** >> p.143.

D Pronunciation passive or active?

11 **8B.1▶** Listen and say active or passive. Then listen and repeat.

active	passive
He watched.	He's watched.
They painted.	They're painted.

12 Test a partner.
   Example **A** He's watched. **B** Passive!

E Listen for key words

13 **8B.2▶** Listen and guess the object.

14 Read the text. When did you first guess the object? Which words helped you? Underline them.
   It's made of plastic and metal, and ehm, it works by electricity. It's got a handle, and it's used for drying hair. It has two words, and the first word is *hair*, and the second word begins with the letter *d*. And the answer is ... It's a hair-dryer!

15 **8B.3▶** Listen and guess three more objects.

ABCDE Put it all together

16 Work in small groups. Look at the objects on >> p.129. Take turns to describe an object. Guess the object.
   Example It's made of metal. It's used for cutting things ...

ADULTS OF THE FUTURE

Britain's kids predict how lives will change in the next 1,000 years

'Mobile phones will be everywhere. Everyone will have one in their pocket. And they will be amazing. They will control everything – TV, car, even Mum! And everyone will eat food out of packets – plastic food or something like that.'
James Williams, 11, Bristol **1**

'We'll have time machines, so instead of going on holiday to Spain we'll go to another time. But we won't go to the future because that will ruin everything. I'd like to go to the past and meet my great grandma.'
Jessica Potter, 8, Wallasey **2**

'All our pets will have computers so we can talk to them and understand them. They'll be able to talk to us, so they won't just be pets anymore they'll be more like friends. Perhaps they'll even be able to get jobs.'
Kelly Graham, 7, Liverpool **3**

'You won't have to get dressed. You'll just put this thing around your neck, press a button and your clothes will drop down. It'll save a lot of time in the morning and my mum won't shout at me so much.'
Nicholas Paolozzi, 9, Monkseaton, North Tyneside **4**

'We will live in tall buildings miles high.'

'Everybody will be dead in the next 1,000 years – or else they'll be really old. Most people will live in houses underground because they won't be able to live on top of the earth like we do now – the air and the land will be too horrible.'
Rachael Gadomski, 10, Newcastle **5**

'We will live in tall buildings miles high. But we won't have normal lifts. We will go up big tubes, but nobody will do any work because they will have too much fun going up and down the tubes.'
Rosie Smith, 7, Wirral **6**

'There will be lots of robots everywhere and they'll get really angry and eat us all – or most of us, anyway. Only a few people will live, and we'll be able to beat the robots in the end.'
Joseph Taylor, 7, Merseyside **7**

'We'll have houses made of chocolate because it's easy to work with, and if you get hungry you can eat it. You won't eat the floor though because you've walked on it.'
Paul Ashworth, 8, Anfield **8**

How to make predictions

G *will (predictions)*   P pronoun + *'ll*

A Read for general meaning

1   Read **Adults of the future** opposite quickly. Match the texts with these topics.

☒ Chocolate houses   ☐ Clothes   ☐ Environment
☐ Mobile phones   ☐ Pets   ☐ Robots
☐ Tall buildings   ☐ Time travel

2   Most of the children are optimists 😊. Read the texts again and find the pessimist(s) 😟. Underline the words that helped you. Compare with a partner.

3   What do you think of the texts? Answer these questions and tell your partner.
1   Do you agree with any of the predictions?
2   Which text is funniest?
3   Which text has the most interesting ideas?

B Grammar *will* (predictions)

4   Read the sentence and answer the questions.
'We will live in tall buildings miles high.' (Rosie Smith)
1   Is Rosie talking about the past, present, or future?
2   Does Rosie know this is true, or is she guessing?
3   Does Rosie want this to happen?
    a yes   b no   c doesn't say

5   Complete the table.

+	We'll live underground.	Robots _____ _____ all the work.	Our pets _____ _____ to talk.
–	We _____ underground.	Robots won't do all the work.	Our pets _____ _____ to talk.
?	Will we live underground?	_____ robots _____ all the work?	Will our pets be able to talk?

6   Underline examples of *will* for prediction in **Adults of the future**.
More practice? **Grammar Bank** >> p.143.

7   Ask and answer with a partner.
Example
A Do you think Italy will win the next World Cup?
B I hope so!

question	answer
Do you think Italy will win the next World Cup?	Yes, I think so.
Do you think the world will run out of oil?	No, I don't think so.
Do you think we will have flying cars?	I hope so!*
Do you think ... *add your own questions!*	I hope not!
	I've no idea!

*I hope so. = I want this to happen.
 I hope not. = I don't want this to happen.

C Pronunciation
pronoun + *'ll*

8   **8C.1▶** Listen and match the words and their pronunciations.
I'll   ~~you'll~~   he'll   she'll   it'll   we'll   they'll
1 / juːl /   *you'll*   5 / hiːl / _____
2 / ʃiːl /   _____   6 / aɪl /   _____
3 / ðeɪl /   _____   7 / ɪtl /   _____
4 / wiːl /   _____

9   **8C.2▶** Listen, check and repeat.

10 **8C.3▶** Listen and repeat.

present	future
We go to Spain.	We'll go to Spain.
They live in boxes.	They'll live in boxes.
I have lunch at 2.00.	I'll have lunch at 2.00.
They talk to us.	They'll talk to us.

11 **8C.4▶** Listen and say *present* or *future*.

12 Test a partner.
Example   A We'll go to Spain.   B Future!

D Listen for general meaning

13 **8C.5▶** Listen to Jon (age 12) talking about the future. Which topic is he talking about?
TV travel weather telephones education
food world politics science

14 Listen again. Do you agree with Jon's prediction? Tell a partner and say why or why not.

ABCD Put it all together

15 Work with a partner. Talk about the topics in exercise 13. How do you think these things will change in the future?
Example   A I think TVs will be bigger.
            B Yes, and there will be thousands of channels.

16 Compare your ideas in small groups. Who is the most optimistic? And the most pessimistic?

I can make predictions.   ▬▬▬▬▬▬▬
Tick ✓ the line.   with a lot of help   with some help   on my own   very easily

It's your lucky day!

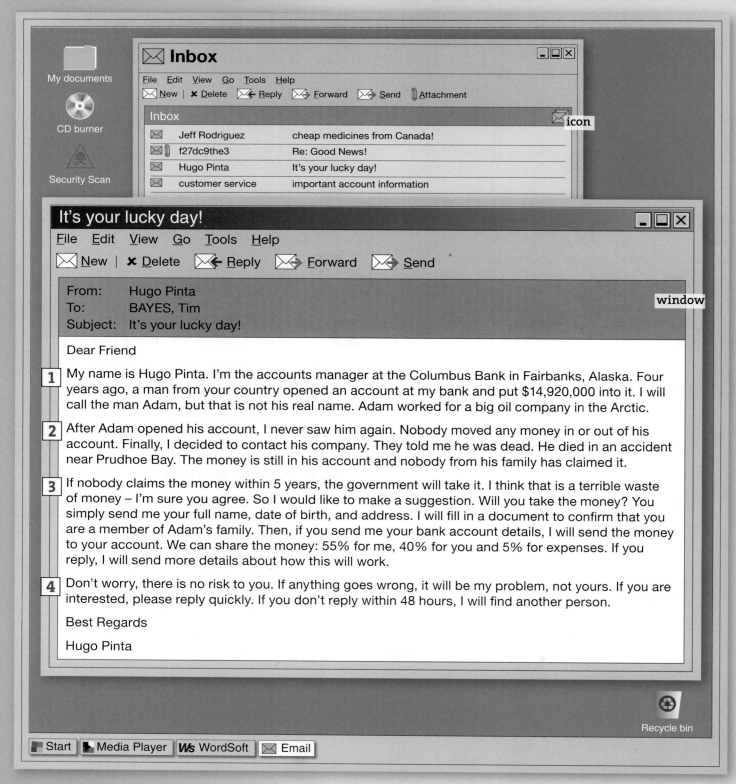

Inbox

File   Edit   View   Go   Tools   Help

New | ✕ Delete   Reply   Forward   Send   Attachment

Inbox   icon

✉	Jeff Rodriguez	cheap medicines from Canada!
✉	f27dc9the3	Re: Good News!
✉	Hugo Pinta	It's your lucky day!
✉	customer service	important account information

It's your lucky day!

File   Edit   View   Go   Tools   Help

New | ✕ Delete   Reply   Forward   Send

From: Hugo Pinta
To: BAYES, Tim   window
Subject: It's your lucky day!

Dear Friend

1 My name is Hugo Pinta. I'm the accounts manager at the Columbus Bank in Fairbanks, Alaska. Four years ago, a man from your country opened an account at my bank and put $14,920,000 into it. I will call the man Adam, but that is not his real name. Adam worked for a big oil company in the Arctic.

2 After Adam opened his account, I never saw him again. Nobody moved any money in or out of his account. Finally, I decided to contact his company. They told me he was dead. He died in an accident near Prudhoe Bay. The money is still in his account and nobody from his family has claimed it.

3 If nobody claims the money within 5 years, the government will take it. I think that is a terrible waste of money – I'm sure you agree. So I would like to make a suggestion. Will you take the money? You simply send me your full name, date of birth, and address. I will fill in a document to confirm that you are a member of Adam's family. Then, if you send me your bank account details, I will send the money to your account. We can share the money: 55% for me, 40% for you and 5% for expenses. If you reply, I will send more details about how this will work.

4 Don't worry, there is no risk to you. If anything goes wrong, it will be my problem, not yours. If you are interested, please reply quickly. If you don't reply within 48 hours, I will find another person.

Best Regards

Hugo Pinta

Start   Media Player   WS WordSoft   Email

Recycle bin

How to talk about results of future actions

G 1st conditional V email P intonation of conditionals

A Vocabulary email

1 Work with a partner. Make a list of English words you know connected with email, Internet, and computers.

2 Look at **Computer words** opposite. Which ones are nouns and which ones are verbs? Check in your dictionary.

3 <u>Underline</u> the correct word.

Receiving emails

If you ¹<u>double-click</u>/send on the *Email* ²click/icon, the email Inbox will open. Now ³delete/click on the *Send and Receive* button to ⁴download/delete your messages. If it's junk mail, highlight it and click on the ⁵*Send*/*Delete* button. Be careful – if the message has an ⁶icon/attachment, don't open it. It could be a virus.

Sending emails

If you click on the *New Message* button, an email ⁷window/icon will open. Write the email address and the ⁸attachment/subject at the top. Write your message and click on the ⁹*Send*/*Delete* button. The message will go the next time you are ¹⁰online/send.

4 **8D.1▶** Listen and check.

B Read and interpret

5 Work with a partner. Answer these questions together.
1 Have you ever had a computer virus?
2 What is junk email? Is it a problem for you?
3 Do you ever buy things online?

6 Read **It's your lucky day!** opposite. Why did Hugo Pinta write it?
a to steal money from the reader
b to give the reader some money

7 Read the email again and answer the questions.
1 Where do you think Hugo lives?
2 Is Hugo his real name?
3 What does Hugo say will happen to Adam's money?
4 What does Hugo want?
5 Is any part of the story true?

C Grammar 1st conditional

8 Read the sentence and answer the questions.
'If you send your bank details, Hugo Pinta will steal your money.'
1 What are the two possible future actions?
You send your bank details or ...
2 Imagine you send your details. What will happen?
3 Imagine you don't send your details. What will happen?
4 Will Hugo Pinta steal your money? *Yes, but only if ...*

9 Complete the grammar box with the correct form of these verbs.

claim reply get (x2) open look take (x2)

Use present simple tense for the possible future action. Use *will* + infinitive for the future result.

possible future action	future result
1 If Hugo *gets* your bank details,	he'*ll take* money from your account.
2 If you _____ that attachment,	you _____ a virus.
3 If nobody _____ the money,	the government _____ it.
4 If you don't _____,	Hugo _____ for another person.

If you put the future result first, you don't need a comma:
He'll take money from your account if you send your bank details.

10 Write sentences.
1 you open the attachment / you get a virus
If you open the attachment, you'll get a virus.
2 you click on this icon / new window open
3 you give them your address / you get lots of junk mail
4 we not open the attachment / we not get the virus
5 you not watch your bag / somebody steal it
6 Hugo get your bank details / steal your money
7 you not want the money / I give it to someone else

11 **8D.2▶ Pronunciation** The intonation goes up at the end of the *action* part and down at the end of the *result* part. Listen and repeat the sentences from exercise 10.

If you open the at^tach_me^nt, you'll get a ^virus.

More practice? **Grammar Bank** ≫ p.143.

ABC Put it all together

12 Work with a partner. Look at **Options** on ≫ p.129. Think about the good and bad points of the different options.

13 Change partner and do a role play.
Student A Choose one of the options and tell your partner.
Student B Give your partner advice about which option to choose.
Example **A** I want a new computer – maybe a laptop, but I can't decide.
B Well, if you get a desktop, it'll be cheaper ...

I can talk about results of future actions. ████████████
Tick ✓ the line. with a lot of help with some help on my own very easily

83

Writing A message of apology

A Read for the main idea

1 Which is the worst mistake? Decide with a partner. Compare with the class.
1 I forgot to reply to your last email.
2 I forgot to send you a message on your birthday.
3 I sent you a virus by mistake.
4 I thought your email was junk mail and I deleted it.
5 I wrote an email to someone else and I sent it to you by mistake.

2 Read this email. How well does Paul know Jen?

> Hi Jen, I'm sorry but I think I've sent you a virus by mistake. because I opened an email this morning, and I didn't know who sent it but the subject was just 'Good News!', and It had an attachment called 'Message from a Friend' and I opened it without thinking and It was a virus and I think it went into my address book and sent an email to all my contacts so if you got an email from me, DON'T open the attachment because If the virus gets into your computer, it will go to all the people in your address book and I'm really sorry about this, all the best from Paul. : (

3 When we apologize, we often give details to explain what happened. What details does Paul give?

4 Work with a partner. How would you apologize for the other mistakes in exercise 1?

B Check the style

5 8E.1▶ Read the email again and listen. Answer the questions.
1 Is it easy to understand? Why? / Why not?
2 How many sentences are there?
3 How could you make it better?

6 Use these symbols to edit the email, and change the punctuation if you want.
  // new line
  / new sentence
  ~~and~~ delete word

Example Hi Jen,// I'm sorry but I think I've sent you a virus by mistake.**.**/ ~~because~~ I opened an ...

7 8E.2▶ Listen. Does the speaker pause in the same places where you put // and /? Now check the audio script on ≫ p.156.

C Organizing an apology message

8 Put this email in order.
a ☐ All the best, Jen
b ☐ Could you send it again?
c ☐ 1 Hi Paul
d ☐ It came together with a lot of junk emails and I deleted them all.
e ☐ Sorry, I've deleted the email you just sent by mistake.
f ☐ Sorry about that!
g ☐ Then I remembered there was a message from you, but it was too late.

9 Match parts of the message with the sentences in exercise 8.
1 Greeting = ☐ c
2 Why I am sorry. = ☐
3 What happened. = ☐ and ☐
4 What to do (or not to do) next. = ☐
5 Final apology. = ☐
6 Goodbye. = ☐

10 Work with a partner. Find the same parts of the message in Paul's email in exercise 2.

ABC Put it all together

11 Think of a situation where you did something bad to someone by mistake. Answer the questions.
1 What did you do?
2 Why did you do it?
3 What did the other person do / say?

12 Write an email message to apologize. Remember to include the parts of the message in exercise 9.

13 Check your partner's message.
Are the sentences too long?
Do they give details to explain what happened?

I can write a message of apology.
Tick ✓ the line. with a lot of help with some help on my own very easily

Unit 8 Review

A Grammar

1 Possessive pronouns Write sentences with possessive pronouns.

1 Is this your bag?   *Is this yours* ?
2 Which is my seat?   _____ ?
3 That's our camera!   _____ !
4 Is that her bike?   _____ ?
5 It isn't their car.   _____ .
6 Are these his glasses?   _____ ?

2 Present passive Write the sentences in the passive.

1 First, a person cuts the trees down.
  First, the trees are cut down .
2 Then, a person puts the trees on a lorry.
  _____.
3 A person takes the wood to a factory.
  _____.
4 A person cuts the wood into flat pieces.
  _____.
5 A person makes the flat pieces into doors.
  _____.
6 A person paints the doors.
  _____.
7 Finally, a person sells them.
  _____.

3 will (prediction) Correct the conversation. Eight of the verbs are in the present simple when they should be in the *will* form.

1 **A** What do you think life ~~is~~ will be like in the future?
2 **B** I think people live longer. More people live to be 100.
3 **A** Do you think you see your 100th birthday?
4 **B** I hope not! I don't want to be really old!
5 **A** Yes, but maybe there are new body parts – a new
6   heart, new eyes …
7 **B** Yuk! I don't think so. Do you think you live to be
8   100?
9 **A** I hope so. I leave work at 60 and then I have a 40
10   year holiday!

4 1st conditional Put these verbs in the correct tense in the sentences.

steal   call   ~~win~~   leave (x2)   get   be (x2)   rain   drink

1 If he _wins_ this race, he _'ll be_ the world champion!
2 If you _leave_ your telephone number, she _will call_ you back later.
3 You _get_ wet if it _will be rain_.
4 Someone _will steal_ your car if you _leave_ the door open.
5 If she _drinks_ any more coffee, she _will be_ awake all night.

B Vocabulary

5 Apology phrases Complete the conversation with these words.

mistake   mind   really   all right   ~~sorry~~   worry

A I'm 1 _sorry_ . I took your bag by 2 _mistake_ .
B That's 3 _all right_ . Don't 4 _worry_ about it.
A I'm 5 _really_ sorry. My bag is very similar, you see.
B Never 6 _mind_ . It's an easy mistake to make.

6 Material and shape Describe these things. Use *material* and *shape* words.

1 A CD
  It's flat and round.
  It's made of plastic.

4 A pan
  _____
  _____

2 A cereal packet
  _____
  _____

5 A mirror
  _____
  _____

3 A brush handle
  _____
  _____

6 A towel
  _____
  _____

7 Email Solve these computer anagrams.

1 nilone   Connected to the Internet.   *online*
2 noic   A small picture.
3 themactant   A file sent with an email.
4 njuk alim   Mail you don't want and didn't ask for.
5 totbun   You press this.
6 ruvis   This is dangerous for your computer.
7 ilkcc   You do this with the mouse.
8 tdeele   To cut and remove a file.

Prepared food

a baked potato   some frozen peas   some grated cheese   a boiled egg
some grilled fish   some mashed potato   a fried egg   some scrambled egg
a roast chicken   some sliced bread

Healthy, tasty, or easy?

Do you like your food healthy, tasty, or easy? Do this quiz and find out!

1 Which of these is most important to you?
  a Vitamin pills.
  b My recipe books.
  c The microwave.

2 What's the most difficult part of a meal?
  a Choosing what to have.
  b Opening the tin or packet.
  c Washing the vegetables.

3 How do you usually eat potatoes?
  a In a bag of crisps.
  b Boiled.
  c Baked.

4 How do you like your bread?
  a Fresh.
  b Wholemeal.
  c Sliced.

5 Which question do you ask most often?
  a What's in it?
  b How long does it take to make?
  c How do you make it?

6 Which sounds best to you?
  a Healthy!
  b Delicious!
  c Ready to eat!

7 In a competition, you win one of these free for a year. Which do you choose?
  a Takeaway pizzas.
  b Meals in a good restaurant.
  c Fresh farm vegetables.

8 You read about a man who lived for a year eating only hot dogs. What do you say?
  a That's so boring!
  b That's so bad for his health!
  c I think I'll try it!

9 You buy a cheese sandwich and it's a bit dry. What do you say?
  a Oh well, it will fill me up!
  b Oh well, it won't kill me.
  c I can't eat that!

10 You're eating fish in a restaurant and you send it back. Why?
  a It isn't fresh.
  b It's overcooked.
  c It's got bones in it.

Now check your score on page 135.

How to talk about food

G countable / uncountable **V** prepared food **P** linking consonant-vowel

A Vocabulary prepared food

1 Do you like cooking? Why? / Why not? What type of food do you ususally cook? Tell a partner.

cabbage carrot egg fish fruit meat peas

2 Look at **Prepared food** opposite. Match the phrases with photos a–j.

Example a = a fried egg

3 Choose three adjectives from **Prepared food**. Answer the questions.

1 Can you find this adjective in the dictionary?
2 Can you find a similar verb in the dictionary?
3 Can you guess the meaning of the adjective from the meaning of the verb?

4 ~~Cross out~~ the wrong word.

1 some grated carrot / ~~orange~~ / apple
2 some boiled bread / cabbage / rice
3 some sliced tomato / onion / yoghurt
4 some roast milk / beef / lamb
5 some fried onion / oil / rice
6 some grilled pork / tomatoes / ice-cream
7 some mashed soup / banana / potato

5 **9A.1▶ Pronunciation** Listen and complete the phrases. Then listen and repeat.

When a word ends with a consonant and the next word begins with a vowel, it often sounds like the consonant is part of the second word. For example:

these phrases	))) sound like ...
1 *an orange*	'a_norange'
2 _____	'a slice_tapple'
3 _____	'a boil_degg'
4 _____	'some grill_donion'
5 _____	'some scramble_degg'
6 _____	'a_nuncook_tegg'

B Grammar countable / uncountable

6 Which foods in photos a–j opposite are countable? Which are uncountable? Complete the table. What do you notice about *egg* and *potato*?

countable	uncountable
a _baked_ potato	some _____ potato
a _____ egg	some _____ egg
a _____ egg	some _____ cheese
some _____ peas	some _____
a _____	some _____

More practice? **Grammar Bank** >> p.144.

C Read and respond

7 Look at **Healthy, tasty, or easy?** opposite. Where do you think the text is from?

a a text book for students of medicine
b a general interest magazine
c a public health poster

8 Read the text again but don't answer the questions. Find words with these meanings.

1 An adjective for something which has a nice taste. *tasty*
2 A book which tells you how to cook different meals.
3 A natural, brown bread.
4 An adjective meaning the opposite of *old*, for food.
5 An adjective meaning *cooked too much*.

9 Work with a partner. Read the quiz and choose the best answers for you. Count and compare your scores on page 135. Do you think your scores are correct?

D Listen for detail

10 **9A.2▶** You will hear two friends, Jon and Kate, having one of these conversations. Read the questions. Then listen and decide if it is conversation A or B.

Conversation A
1 What are your favourite dishes?
2 What's in them? / How are they prepared?
3 Are there any foods you really hate or can't eat?
4 Is there anything you've never tried?

Conversation B
1 Can you recommend any good restaurants?
2 What country or region does the cooking come from?
3 What did you have last time you went there?
4 Describe some of the other dishes they serve.

11 Listen again to Jon and Kate. What do they like?.

Jon likes	Kate likes ...
	pizza

 olives   sushi   fish   pie

ABCD Put it all together

12 Look at the conversations in exercise 10. Think about your answers to the questions. Have the conversations with two or three other students. Who would you most like to have dinner with?

Example **A** What are your favourite dishes?
B Well, I really like moussaka ...

I can talk about food.

Tick ✓ the line. with a lot of help with some help on my own very easily

Cooking verbs

barbecue boil chop fry grill
heat peel pour roast stir wash

Round the World
Al Fresco

1 a few fritters in Brazil

2 a little soup in the Himalayas

3 a lot of potatoes in a lake in Latvia

4 some water in Wales

5 a few chestnuts in China

6 a few sausages on a roof in Seattle

7 some corn in Croatia

8 a few mangoes in the Middle East

9 a lot of vegetables in Venezuela

10 a little tea near Timbuktu

11 some stew in South Africa

Recipe
Delicious beef and vegetable kebabs

You will need some ... beef, olive oil, yellow and green peppers, onions, tomatoes, herbs, garlic, pepper.

☐ After that, chop some yellow and green peppers.

☐ Then cut the beef into square pieces and put it into the bowl with the oil mix. Leave it for two hours.

☐ Grill the kebabs for 10–15 minutes, turning them until the meat is brown on all sides.

☐ Next, prepare the vegetables. First, peel a few onions and chop them into big pieces.

☐ Finally, serve the kebabs with a little salad and a cold drink!

☐ Then pour a little of the oil mix over the kebabs.

1 First of all, put some olive oil, a few herbs, and a little garlic into a bowl and stir it. Add some lemon juice and a little pepper.

☐ Now you're ready to make the kebabs. Put the meat and chopped vegetables onto a skewer with some small tomatoes.

How to explain how to cook something

G quantifiers V cooking; sequencers

A Vocabulary cooking

1 Look at the **Round the World *Al Fresco*** photos opposite and answer the questions with a partner.
1 Would you like to be in these places? Why? / Why not? Choose three places and tell a partner.
2 Do you ever cook 'al fresco' (outside)? What, where, and when do you eat outside?

2 What can you see in the pictures? Answer the questions and compare with a partner.
1 Is there any seafood in the photos?
2 Are there any vegetables?
3 Is there any meat?
4 Is there any fruit?
5 Which food would you like to try?

3 Look at the **Cooking verbs** opposite and match them with the photos. Write the *-ing* form of the verb at the beginnings of the captions.
Example Frying a few fritters in Brazil.

4 **9B.1▶** Listen, check, and repeat.

5 Match the **Cooking verbs** and definitions.
1 Cook food on or under a high heat.   *grill*
2 Clean something in water.
3 Make water very hot.
4 Make food hot.
5 Cut the skin off fruit and vegetables.
6 Cut food into pieces.
7 Use a spoon to move the food around the pot.
8 Cook food over a fire or in an oven.
9 Cook food in hot oil.
10 Put drinks into cups or glasses.
11 Cook on a frame over a fire.

B Grammar quantifiers

6 Match these words with the pictures.
~~a lot~~ a lot a little a few none

a lot _____ _____ _____ _____

7 Answer the questions about the photos with *a lot, a little, a few,* or *none*.
1 How many fritters are there?   *a few*
2 How much tea is there?
3 How much water is there?
4 How many sausages are there?
5 How many potatoes are there?
6 How much soup is there?

8 Write *countable* or *uncountable*. Then complete the example sentences using *sugar* or *sausages*.
1 much + _uncountable_ There isn't _much sugar_.
2 many + _____ There aren't _____ _____.
3 a few + _____ There are _____ _____ _____.
4 a little + _____ There's _____ _____ _____.

9 Ask a partner about their diet. Use *How much ... ?* and *How many ... ?*
Example **A** How much bread do you eat?
           B Not much.
           A How many cups of tea do you drink?
           B None, I hate tea.

More practice? **Grammar Bank** >> p.144.

C Read and put in order

10 Read **Recipe** opposite. Put the instructions in order.

11 Underline the words that helped you, for example *First of all, next*. Compare with a partner.

D Listen for key words

12 **9B.2▶** Listen to another recipe. Which of these salads does the man explain how to make?

13 Listen again and tick the words and phrases you hear.
☐ first ☐ then ☐ after that ☐ next ☐ finally

14 Explain to your partner how to make one of the salads. Listen to your partner's explanations and say which salad it is. Use these words to help you.
ham tuna lettuce olive oil
tomato egg vinegar olive onion
Example First of all, wash some lettuce. Next, ...

ABCD Put it all together

15 Work with a partner. Think of some food or drink you know how to prepare. Write a list of the things you need and make some notes about how to prepare it. Use your dictionary to help.

16 Explain your recipe to a different partner. Listen to your partner's recipe. Would you like to try the food? Why? / Why not?

I can explain how to cook something.
Tick ✓ the line.   with a lot of help   with some help   on my own   very easily

A The Original Food Guide Pyramid

Source: US Department of Agriculture

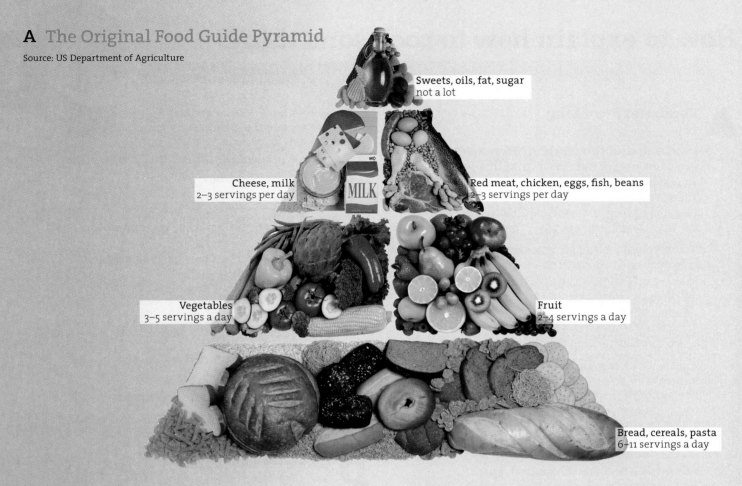

Sweets, oils, fat, sugar
not a lot

Cheese, milk
2–3 servings per day

Red meat, chicken, eggs, fish, beans
2–3 servings per day

Vegetables
3–5 servings a day

Fruit
2–4 servings a day

Bread, cereals, pasta
6–11 servings a day

B An Updated Food Guide Pyramid

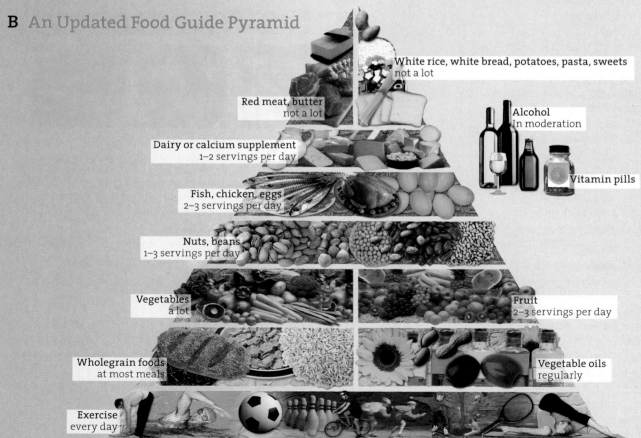

White rice, white bread, potatoes, pasta, sweets
not a lot

Red meat, butter
not a lot

Alcohol
In moderation

Dairy or calcium supplement
1–2 servings per day

Vitamin pills

Fish, chicken, eggs
2–3 servings per day

Nuts, beans
1–3 servings per day

Vegetables
a lot

Fruit
2–3 servings per day

Wholegrain foods
at most meals

Vegetable oils
regularly

Exercise
every day

How to give lifestyle advice

G *should*   V verb phrases with *make, do, have*   P *should, shouldn't*

A   Listen for detail

1   Look at the **Food Guide Pyramids** opposite. Work with a partner and name the foods in the pictures.

2   Match the sentences with pyramid A or B or both.
1   You shouldn't eat a lot of white bread. *B*
2   You should eat a lot of potatoes and pasta.
3   You should eat a lot of vegetable oils.
4   You should eat a lot of fruit and vegetables.
5   You should eat more chicken and fish than red meat.
6   You shouldn't put a lot of sugar in your drinks.

3   **9C.1▶** You will hear a doctor speaking on the radio. Which pyramid does she describe, A or B?

4   Listen again. Note the names of any foods she talks about which are <u>not</u> in the pyramid.
Example   Canned drinks

5   Compare your diet with pyramid B. Give yourself some advice and tell a partner.
Example   I should eat more fish.

B   Grammar *should*

6   Read the dialogue and answer the questions.
Jim   I want to be healthier.
Irene   Well, you should eat more fruit.

1   What is Irene doing?
a   explaining rules
b   saying what's best for Jim (giving him advice)
c   asking Jim to do something

2   What does Irene want to do?
a   complain about Jim's lifestyle
b   tell Jim to do something
c   help Jim

7   Complete the grammar box.

+	We should have fish.	She _____ _____ more fruit.
–	We _____ _____ fish.	She shouldn't eat more fruit.
?	Should we have fish?	_____ she _____ more fruit?

8   Match the advice with the people who gave it.
doctor   ~~teacher~~   parent   husband or wife   boss

1   You should do more homework and make an effort in class. *teacher*
2   You shouldn't eat a lot of salt. You should exercise.
3   You should be tidier and make your bed.
4   You should talk less and work more.
5   You should help more in the house and do more cleaning.

9   **9C.2▶** Pronunciation. Listen to the sentences from exercise 2 and answer the questions.
1   Which word does *should* /ʃʊd/ rhyme with?
a   cold   b   food   c   good
2   When do you hear the *t* in *shouldn't* /ʃʊdn(t)/?

10   Say the sentences.

11   Write sentences giving advice to these people. You can use *more* or *less*.
Example   Simon Sofa – You should do more exercise.

Simon Sofa

Laura Lonely

Michael Mess

Steven Stress

12   Read out your advice. Other students guess who it is for.
Example   **A** You should watch less TV.   **B** Simon Sofa!

More practice? **Grammar Bank** >> p.144.

C   Vocabulary verb phrases with *make, do, have*

13   Write the phrases in the correct boxes. Some can go in two boxes.

a break   a drink   a mess   a phone call   a shower
an appointment   an effort   dinner   some exercise
the shopping   a holiday   the washing up   your homework

make ...	do ...	have ...
your bed	the cleaning	a sleep

14   Work with a partner. Make sentences with *should* or *shouldn't* and the phrases from exercise 13.
Example   You should do your homework earlier.

ABC   Put it all together

15   Look at the **Lifestyle Pyramids** on >> p.130. With a partner, imagine who the people are, and give them advice.

16   Draw a lifestyle pyramid for you and give it to your partner. Look at your partner's pyramid and give him / her advice.

I can give lifestyle advice.

Tick ✓ the line.   with a lot of help   with some help   on my own   very easily

File Edit View Favourites Tools Help

Back Next Stop Refresh Home Search Favourites

Address http://www.etiquette-online/tablemannersmadeeasy

Table Manners Made Easy

Frequently Asked Questions (FAQs)

1 How should I set the table?
2 How should I use my knife and fork?
3 Should I use my hands?
4 When should I start eating?
5 Is it all right to talk during the meal?
6 Should I drink from the soup bowl?
7 Is it OK to put my knife in my mouth?
8 Should I serve myself?
9 Which knife and fork should I use?
10 What should I do if I don't like the food?
11 How should I leave my knife and fork at the end?
12 If the host offers more, is it OK to refuse?

How should I use my knife and fork?

Two styles

There are two ways to use a knife and fork, the *European style* and the *American style*.

The European style (two-handed): You should hold the knife in your right hand and the fork in your left hand. Use the knife to cut food. Use the fork to put the food in your mouth. You mustn't use your knife for this.

The American style (one-handed): You should hold the fork in your right hand and leave the knife on the plate. When you need to cut a piece of food, move the fork to the other hand, and cut with the knife in the right hand. Then put the knife down and put the fork in your right hand again.

Why the difference?

In the past, there were no forks. People ate with just a knife. The knife had a pointed end and you could use it to put the food in your mouth.

However, a pointed knife is dangerous. In 17th-century France, many people were killed with knives in fights, so in the end, pointed knives were forbidden.

pointed knife

After that, forks became more popular in Europe, and people started eating with a knife and a fork, using both hands. However, forks only arrived in America much later, and people continued to eat with a one-handed style. When the fork finally arrived, people continued eating with one hand.

So which style should I use?

Some people think you should use the European style in Europe and the American style in America. However, many Americans now use the European style because it's easier for some dishes. And many Europeans like the one-handed style. So really, it's your decision.

Can I use my hands?

Most people in the world use their hands. Next time you're dining in Khartoum or Kathmandu, don't expect to get a knife and fork. If you go to someone's home or a local restaurant, you must eat with your fingers like the locals.

And remember – your left hand mustn't touch the food. You must use your right hand. In Western countries, you can use your hands for some foods such as fruit, olives, party snacks, sandwiches and barbecued meat. You should also use your hands to break bread – you shouldn't use your knife and fork.

How to talk about table manners

G *should, must*

A   Think before you read

1   What table manners did your parents and other adults teach you as a child? Tell a partner.

Example   You shouldn't put your arms on the table.

2   What do you know about table manners? Say *true* or *false*.

1   The British and the Americans use forks the same way.
2   In the past people used knives, but not forks.
3   Europeans always use two hands to eat.
4   In many places, people eat with their fingers.

3   Read **Table Manners Made Easy** opposite and check.

4   Answer the questions.

1   Do you use the American or European style?
2   Which came first – the knife or the fork?
3   What was the problem with pointed knives?
4   Why didn't the Americans start using two hands like the Europeans?
5   Which hand must you use for eating in Khartoum or Kathmandu?
6   What foods can you eat with your hands in Western countries?

5   Answer these questions with a partner.

1   Which eating style do you prefer?
2   Do you ever use a pointed knife to eat?
3   When do you eat with your hands?

B   Grammar *should, must*

6   Read the sentences and answer the questions.

Sam   You shouldn't put your knife in your mouth.
Mike   You mustn't put your knife in your mouth.

1   Are both sentences correct?
2   Whose advice is stronger, Sam's or Mike's?
3   Do you agree with Sam or Mike? Why?

7   Underline the words that you think are correct.

Table manners in Nepal

In my country, you ¹mustn't / must touch food with your left hand. It's OK to hold your glass or a bottle with your left hand, but you ²should / shouldn't pass things to people with your left hand. You ³must / mustn't use your right hand to eat. You ⁴should / must wash it first. When you have started eating, you ⁵must / shouldn't offer your food, bread for example, to anyone else. It's fine to drink from a bottle, but your lips ⁶must / shouldn't touch the bottle.

8   **9D.1▶** Listen and check your answers.

9   Write notes about your country.

In my country, …	
1 it's polite to … (should)	*break bread with hands*
2 it isn't polite to … (shouldn't)	
3 it's very bad manners not to … (must)	
4 it's very bad manners to … (mustn't)	

10   Write table manners advice for visitors to your country. Use *should, shouldn't, must* and *mustn't*.

Example   You should break bread with your hands.

More practice? **Grammar Bank** ≫ p.144.

C   Think before you listen

11   Look at **Table Manners Made Easy** again. You will hear a British person answer the **Frequently Asked Questions** on the left. Can you predict what he will say?

12   **9D.2▶** Listen and check your predictions.

13   Are these table manners the same in your country? Tell a partner.

ABC   Put it all together

14   Do a role play with a different partner. Take turns to be A and B.

Student A   You are a visitor to Student B's country. Imagine you come from a country with very different table manners. Ask for advice about table manners in B's country.

Student B   Student A is a visitor to your country. Give advice about table manners.

Example   **A** Can you tell me about table manners in your country?
B Yes. You should hold the knife in your right hand and …

I can talk about table manners.
Tick ✓ the line.   with a lot of help   with some help   on my own   very easily

Writing A food and drink guide for visitors

A Read for information

1 Read the text and choose the best title.
a Where to eat in Cabo Verde
b Food and drink in my country
c A restaurant guide to my town
d My favourite food and drink

In my country, the traditional local dish is *cachupa*. There are two types: 'poor man's' *cachupa* is boiled maize, beans, herbs, and sweet potato. 'Rich man's' *cachupa* has chicken or other meat as well. My favourite is *cachupa grelhada* – everything you can find fried together. If you come to Cabo Verde, you should try the seafood. I recommend the grilled lobster – it's delicious! The fresh tuna is excellent too. And don't miss the octopus.

For dessert, we often have dried fruit with fresh goat's cheese. We also have fresh fruit like papaya, mango, and banana. You shouldn't drink water from the tap. You can buy bottled water easily. Buy it from a shop – it's quite expensive in hotels. The traditional local drink is *grogue*. This is an alcoholic drink and it's very strong, so you mustn't drink a lot! You can also get wine, beer, and soft drinks. Most of the wine comes from Portugal, but they make local wine on the island of Fogo.

Eugénio Barbosa
Praia, Cabo Verde

2 Write the words in the lists. Try to guess from the text.
~~banana~~   beans   lobster   maize   mango
octopus   papaya   sweet potato   tuna

1 Fruit *banana* , _____, and _____.
2 Sea food _____, _____, and _____.
3 Vegetables _____, _____, and _____.

3 Complete the information about Cabo Verde in the table.

	Cabo Verde	my country or region
Traditional local dish	*cachupa*	
I recommend ...		
For dessert ...		
Tap water?		
Drinks		

4 Complete the information for your country or region.

B Practise punctuation

5 Answer the questions
1 ... boiled maize, beans, herbs, and sweet potato.
   In a list, when do you use commas and when do you use *and*?
2 ... the traditional local dish is *cachupa*.
   Why does the writer use *italics* for the word 'cachupa'?
3 Underline these words in the text: *as well, also, too*.
   Which of these words do you find before a full stop?

6 What do you know about other countries? Make lists with your partner.
Example
In China, I think they eat a lot of rice, fish, and soy sauce.

7 Tell a different partner.

8 Read this text and add commas, inverted commas, and *and*.

In my country we eat a lot of dairy produce like milk goat's cheese yoghurt. We eat a lot of fish lamb. You can get fast food like pizza hamburgers hot dogs. For dessert we have a sweet pastry called *baklava*. We have ice cream fruit salad fresh fruit. The traditional local drink is *raki*. We have a yoghurt drink called *ayran*. We drink a lot of tea coffee.

9 Guess which country the text in exercise 8 is about.

10 Add *as well*, *too*, and *also* to the text in exercise 8. Compare your answers with a partner.

AB Put it all together

11 Write a paragraph about food and drink similar to the text in exercise 8. Write about your country or another country you know.

12 Give your text to a partner. Check your partner's punctuation. Do you think there is any information missing?

I can write about food and drink in my country.

Tick ✓ the line.   with a lot of help   with some help   on my own   very easily

Unit 9 Review

A Grammar

1 Quantifiers Match the questions and answers.

1 [c] Have we got any fruit?
2 [ ] Have we got any potatoes?
3 [ ] How much soup would you like?
4 [ ] How many chips would you like?
5 [ ] Would you like some pepper?
6 [ ] Would you like some peas?
7 [ ] Can I have some milk?
8 [ ] Can I have some carrots?

a I'm sorry, there aren't any.
b Yes please, but not too much.
c ~~Not much. Only two apples.~~
d Just a little, please.
e Not many. Only three.
f I'm sorry, there isn't any.
g Just a few, please.
h Yes please, but not too many.

2 should Complete the sentences using *should* or *shouldn't*.

1 You _____ do more homework.
2 _____ I do more exercise?
3 She's very untidy. She _____ make a mess.
4 How _____ I use my knife and fork?
5 They _____ watch less TV.
6 You _____ eat a lot of salt. It's bad for you.
7 What _____ I do if I don't like the food?

3 should and must Complete the sentences using *should*, *shouldn't*, *must* or *mustn't*.

Eating in other countries

When you're eating in Khartoum or Kathmandu, you don't get a knife and fork. If you go to someone's home or a local restaurant, you ¹_____ eat with your fingers like the locals. It's impolite not to. And remember – your left hand ²_____ touch the food. You ³_____ use your right hand.
In Western countries, you can use your hands for some foods such as fruit, olives, party snacks, sandwiches and barbecued meat. You ⁴_____ also use your hands to break bread. When you do use your knife and fork, you ⁵_____ hold the knife in your right hand and the fork in your left hand. Use the knife to cut food. Use the fork to put the food in your mouth. You ⁶_____ use your knife for this – it's extremely bad manners.

B Vocabulary

4 Prepared food Find ten cooking words starting with these letters. Some letters are used twice.

ba- bo- fr- (x2) gr- (x2) ma- ro- sc- sl-

B	F	G	R	A	T	E	D	G
A	O	R	F	G	F	B	F	R
K	S	I	O	R	R	F	A	A
E	O	L	L	Z	I	R	R	S
D	S	L	I	E	E	D	O	C
G	F	E	B	C	D	N	A	R
B	R	D	A	O	E	A	S	L
O	M	A	S	H	E	D	T	C
S	C	R	A	M	B	L	E	D

1 *grated*
2 _____
3 _____
4 _____
5 _____
6 _____
7 _____
8 _____
9 _____
10 _____

5 Cooking Write the words for these definitions

1 Cook food on or under a high heat. *grill*
2 Make water very hot. b_____
3 Make food hot. h_____
4 Cut the skin off fruit and vegetables. p_____
5 Cut food into pieces. c_____
6 Use a spoon to move the food around the pot. s_____
7 Cook food over a fire or in an oven. r_____
8 Cook food in hot oil. f_____
9 Put drinks into cups or glasses. p_____

6 Verb phrases Complete the text with *made*, *did*, or *had*.
Last Saturday, I got up and ¹ *had* a shower. Then I ²_____ my bed and ³_____ breakfast. In the morning, I ⁴_____ some exercise. Then I ⁵_____ a few phone calls. I phoned the dentist and ⁶_____ an appointment. In the afternoon, I ⁷_____ the shopping. I invited some friends to my house that evening. First we ⁸_____ a drink, then I ⁹_____ dinner for them. I ¹⁰_____ a mess in the kitchen. When my friends went home, I cleaned and ¹¹_____ the washing up.

7 Sequencers Complete the recipe.
Beef and vegetable kebabs
¹*First* , put some olive oil, a few herbs and a little garlic into a bowl and stir it. Add some lemon juice and a little pepper. Chop the beef into pieces and ²t_____ put them into the bowl with the oil mix. ³N_____, peel a few onions and chop them. ⁴A_____ that, chop some yellow and green peppers. Put the meat and chopped vegetables onto a skewer with some small tomatoes, and pour a little of the oil mix over the kebabs. ⁵F_____, grill the kebabs for 10–15 minutes.

Journey times

a short bus ride   a five-minute walk   not far   a thirty-minute drive   a half-hour flight
a two-day boat journey   four or five hours by car   six hours by train   five minutes on foot   a long way

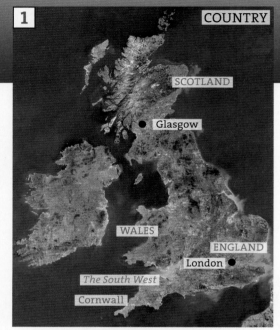

1   COUNTRY

SCOTLAND

Glasgow

WALES

ENGLAND

London

The South West

Cornwall

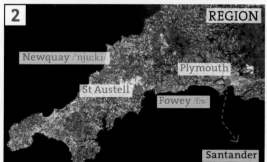

2   REGION

Newquay /ˈnjuːki/

Plymouth

St Austell

Fowey /fɔɪ/

Santander

Escape to Fowey!

Fowey is the perfect place to relax. You can explore the countryside or sit by the Fowey River and watch the boats.

Fowey is on Cornwall's south coast, near many of the area's top attractions. It's only a ten-minute walk from Readymoney Beach and a thirty-minute drive from the famous surfing beaches in Newquay. The village of Polruan is just a ten-minute ferry ride across the river. The Lost Gardens of Heligan and the Eden Project are both only a short bus ride away.

There's a lot for the visitor to do and see in Fowey. There are lovely walks along the cliffs, and good sailing on the river. Fowey was the home of the famous writer Daphne du Maurier, who wrote *Rebecca*, *Jamaica Inn*, and *The Birds*. There is a Daphne du Maurier festival every May. You can also visit the Lost Gardens of Heligan, with 80 acres of beautiful gardens which have over 400 years of history. At the Eden Project, you will find plants and trees from many different countries, and the biggest greenhouse in the world. The interesting thing about the greenhouse is that it has different types of environments, from tropical jungle to desert.

It's easy to reach Fowey. It's a four or five-hour drive from London. Or fly to Newquay, just a half-hour flight from London Gatwick. National rail and bus services stop in St Austell, a twenty-minute bus ride away. Ferry services from the continent (Roscoff and Santander) arrive in Plymouth just a forty-minute drive to the east. Plymouth also has an airport with services to London, Dublin, and Paris.

3   TOWN

Harbour /ˈhɑːbə(r)/

Place Road

Place House
Church

4

The King of
Prussia pub

5   MARKET STREET

ST AUSTELL ALES

THE KING OF PRUSSIA

How to ask and say where places are

v places; journey times

A Read a description in a brochure

1 Read **Escape to Fowey!** opposite. Answer the questions with a partner.
   1 How many places in the text have you heard of? What do you know about them?
   2 What kind of people would like Fowey? People who:
      ☐ like exciting nightlife?   ☐ like surfing?
      ☐ like going to quiet places? ☐ *others?*
   3 Would you like to visit Fowey? Why? / Why not?

2 How near are these places to Fowey? Number them: 1 = nearest, 5 = furthest away.
   ☐ London   ☐1☐ Polruan   ☐ Newquay
   ☐ St Austell ☐ Plymouth

3 Imagine you are planning a holiday in Fowey. Work with a partner. Decide how to get there from where you are now.
   Example   We could take a plane to …

B Vocabulary places; journey times

4 Look at the box and complete the sentences below.

in	a country, a region, a town, a village, mountains, a forest, a desert …
on	a river, a coast, a small island …

   1 I live _in_ a village ____ a small island ____ the south of Greece.
   2 I live ____ Darwin, a town ____ the north coast of Australia.
   3 I live ____ a small town ____ the desert ____ California.
   4 I live ____ a town ____ the Danube in Hungary.
   5 I live ____ a village ____ the Alps.

5 Read **Escape to Fowey!** again. Find phrases with these meanings.
   1 thirty minutes by air   3 a short journey on foot
      a half-hour flight   4 a short journey by bus
   2 half an hour by car   5 a few hours' drive

6 Look at **Journey times** opposite. Match them with the journeys in photos 2–4. Guess! There may be more than one correct answer. Compare with a partner.
   1 Fowey to Newquay   *a thirty-minute drive* or *half an hour by car*
   2 London to Newquay
   3 Place Road to the harbour
   4 Plymouth to Glasgow
   5 Plymouth to Santander
   6 St Austell to Fowey

7 Look at **Journey times** again. Make sentences about five places that are near you with the times.
   Examples   The train station is a short bus ride from here. The museum's twenty minutes by bus.
   Tell a partner. Do you agree?

C Listen for general meaning

8 Read this conversation. What do you think Nick will say next? Choose one option, a, b, or c.
   Nick Hi, I'm Nick.
   Wendy Hi Nick. I'm Wendy.
   N Where are you from, Wendy?
   W Cornwall.

   a OK, thanks. Goodbye.
   b Oh. I'm not from Cornwall.
   c Really? Whereabouts in Cornwall?

9 **10A.1▶** Listen to the start of the conversation and check.

10 **10A.2▶** You will hear Wendy telling three people where she's from. Match the three conversations with the people that Wendy's talking to.
   a someone from Cornwall, but not from Fowey
   b someone from another country, not from Britain
   c someone from a different part of Britain, not from Cornwall

11 Read the audio script on ≫ p.157. Answer the questions.
   1 How did you know the answers to exercise 10? Underline the important phrases.
   2 What's the difference between these two questions?
      a Whereabouts in Fowey?
      b Where's Fowey?
   Act the conversations with a partner.

ABC Put it all together

12 Think of three interesting places you know and make notes about them. Use these ideas to help you.
   The place
   a place in your local town
   another town or village in your area
   a place in your region
   a place in another part of your country
   a place in another country
   More information
   – Where? Whereabouts?
   – It's near / in / on …
   – Things to see and do

13 Ask and answer about your place with a partner.
   Example   **A** Have you ever been to Natal?
              B No. Where's that?

I can ask and say where places are.

Tick ✓ the line.   with a lot of help   with some help   on my own   very easily

Air travel

- [ ] board the plane
- [ ] collect your bags
- [ ] go through customs
- [ ] go to the departure gate
- [1] arrive at the airport
- [ ] go to the duty-free shop
- [ ] land
- [ ] leave the airport
- [ ] [ ] go through passport control
- [ ] take off
- [ ] check in your bags
- [ ] go through security

Ben's Journey Home

1 Airport

2 Lufthansa Quick Check-in

3 رابات المغادرة Departure Gates تدقيق الجوازات Passport Control

4

5 Curren Exchan

6 dutyfr

7 GE MORE FROM

8 Gates C3 C4

9 Departu

10 DELAYED

11 Gentlem

12 BOARDING DEPARTED ON TIME ON TIME ON TIME — Jumbo Jet

13 Arrivals Baggage reclaim Flight connections

14 CUSTOMS ANNEL & GREEN C ration - please re NOTHING declare

15 EXIT

16 WELCOME HOME — Ben — Jess

How to talk about stages of a journey

G present perfect with *yet*, *just*, and *already*   **V** air travel   **P** *yet* /j/ or *jet* /dʒ/

A Vocabulary air travel

1 What are the good and bad things about air travel? Tell a partner.

2 Look at **Air travel** opposite. Put the stages of a journey in order.

3 **10B.1** Listen, check, and repeat.

4 Look at **Ben's Journey Home** pictures opposite. Say *true* or *false*.

1 Ben changed some money before passport control. *False*
2 He read a newspaper before going to the departure gate.
3 His plane was late.
4 He went to the duty-free shop immediately after checking in.
5 He went to the toilet after boarding the plane.
6 Jess met him after he went through customs.

B Listen to a phone call

5 **10B.2▶** Listen to two phone conversations between Ben and Jess. Whereabouts in his journey is Ben?

6 Listen again and fill the gaps. Compare with a partner.
1 Have you checked _____ _____?
2 I've just come through _____ _____.
3 I've already bought your _____.
4 We've just _____.
5 Have you collected your _____ _____?
6 I haven't been through passport _____ _____.
7 I've already read the _____.

7 Look at the audio script on >> p.157. Check your answers.

8 Act the conversations with a partner.

C Grammar present perfect with *yet*, *just*, and *already*

9 Match the questions and responses.
1 ☑ *d* What have you done this morning?
2 ☐ Why don't you wash your hair?
3 ☐ Have you finished in the bathroom?
4 ☐ Why is your hair wet?
5 ☐ Have you had a shower yet?

a I've just washed it.
b No. I'll have one later.
c I've already washed it.
d ~~I've washed my hair.~~
e No. I haven't washed my hair yet.

10 Look at the sentences in exercise 9. Complete these rules with *yet*, *just*, and *already*.
1 Use _____ in questions and negative sentences.
2 Use _____ or _____ in positive sentences.
3 Use _____ to say the action is very recent.
4 If the other person thinks you haven't done something, use _____ to say that you <u>have</u> done it.
5 Use _____ if you haven't done something, but you plan to do it.

11 Complete this phone call with *just*, *already*, or *yet*.
Jess Have you arrived at the airport _____?
Ben Yes, but I haven't checked in _____.
J Don't forget to buy some postcards.
B I've _____ bought some. Oh no!
J What's happened?
B The handle on my bag has _____ broken!

12 Look again at **Ben's Journey Home**. Play a guessing game with a partner. Take turns to be A and B.
A Choose one of the pictures, but don't tell your partner.
B Ask *Have you ... yet?* questions and guess where your partner is.

Example
B Have you boarded the plane yet?
A Yes, I've already done that *or* No, I haven't done that yet.

More practice? **Grammar Bank** >> p.145.

D Pronunciation *yet* /j/ or *jet* /dʒ/

13 **10B.3▶** Listen to the difference.

A /j/	**B** /dʒ/
Have you been on a Jumbo yet?	Have you been on a Jumbo jet?
'Yes', said Jess.	Jess said 'yes'.
This film's good, but yours is better.	This film's good, but *Jaws* is better.

14 **10B.4▶** Listen and say A or B. Test a partner.

ABCD Put it all together

15 Work with a partner. Make a list of things you need to do when you are preparing for a trip to another country. **buy a guidebook, change money ...**

16 Do a role play. Imagine you are both going on a holiday to another country. Ask and answer about preparations. Decide if your partner is a *Type 1* or *Type 2* traveller.
Type 1 You leave things to the last minute.
Type 2 You like preparing a long time in advance.

Example A Have you bought your tickets yet?
B No, not yet. What about you?
A Yes, I've already bought my tickets.

I can talk about stages of a journey.

Tick ✓ the line.   with a lot of help   with some help   on my own   very easily

Flight Attendants

1. Oh – you have to tell them about the seat-belt signs again.

Sandra

Beth

It's your turn. I did it last time. Oh, and don't forget to switch off the intercom when you finish.

2. Ladies and Gentlemen, the captain has switched on the seat-belt signs. Please return to your seats and fasten your seat-belts. Please take a moment to look again at the emergency instructions in the seat pocket in front of you.

3. Very good. Very professional.

Thank you.

4. How long have you worked with this airline?

For about a month. This is my first job. What about you?

5. I've worked with them for three years, but I've been a flight attendant since 2002.

Do you like it?

6. Yes and no. I love travelling. I've loved flying since I was a child.

So what's bad about it?

7. Beth

The passengers. They're so stupid. The man in seat 3A, for example. He's asked three times where the toilets are. They don't move!

8. Ha ha, yes. And the woman in 10D – she's talking to her husband and he's been asleep for two hours!

9. And that man in 8E – It's been dark since five o'clock and he's still wearing his sunglasses. He thinks he's so cool! Ha ha ha!

10. Shh! Listen – why is everybody laughing?

HA! HA! HA! HA! HA!

Oh no! You forgot to switch off the intercom!

How to keep a conversation going

G present perfect with *for* and *since*   P *How long have you ... ?* questions and answers

A Read and study the language

1 What do flight attendants normally say on a plane journey? Compare with a partner.

2 Read **Flight Attendants** opposite. Choose the best title.
   a The Passengers   b A Funny Mistake   c A New Job

3 Answer the questions.
   1 Why does Beth want Sandra to tell the passengers about the seat-belt signs?
   2 Who has been a stewardess for longer?
   3 Why does Beth like her job?
   4 Why doesn't Beth like her job?

4 Find words and phrases in **Flight Attendants** with these meanings.
   1 two times   *twice*
   2 go back to
   3 a short period of time
   4 fashionable
   5 didn't remember

5 **10C.1▶** Listen to the conversation and underline six differences. Compare with a partner and read the audio script on ≫ p.157. to check your answers.

B Grammar present perfect with *for* and *since*

6 Look at the grammar box and answer the questions.

present perfect + *for* = for a period of time until now	
period of time ⌐ - - - - ⌐→ one month now	*Sandra's worked for this airline for a month.* *Examples* for three years; for two days; for three hours; for a long time
present perfect + *since* /sɪns/ = from a point in the past until now	
point in the past - - - * - - - - ⌐→ 2002 now	*Sandra's worked for this airline since last month.* *Examples* since last year; since 2002; since I left school; since four o'clock

   1 Does Sandra work for the airline now?
   2 Did she work for the company a week ago?
   3 Did she work for the company two months ago?

7 Underline examples of *for* and *since* in **Flight Attendants**.

8 Complete the sentences with *for* or *since*.
   1 She's been a flight attendant _____ 2002.
   2 He's been asleep _____ two hours.
   3 It's been dark _____ five o'clock.
   4 I've wanted to be a flight attendant _____ I was a child.

9 **10.C.2▶** Pronunciation
   Listen and repeat.
   Example   **Audio** How long have you lived there?

10 Write true answers to the questions. Use *since* and *for*.
   How long have you ...
   1 had a driving licence?
      For five years or *Since 2004* or *I haven't got one.*
   2 known your best friend?
   3 been a student at this school?
   4 been in this lesson today?
   5 lived in the place you live now?
   6 had this book?

11 Ask the questions to a partner.
   More practice? **Grammar Bank** ≫ p.145.

C Listen for specific information

12 Maria and Patrick are sitting together on a plane to Athens, Greece. Read the descriptions. What have Maria and Patrick got in common? Tell a partner.

   Maria
   She's travelling for work. She's a tour guide and she's going to work in Greece for a month. She works for a company called *Golden Holidays*. She's worked for them since 2006. Before that, she worked for *Sun Tours*. She's been a tour guide since 2002. She lives in Geneva, Switzerland. She's lived there for eight years.

   Patrick
   He's going to Greece on holiday. He's travelling with a company called *Sun Tours*. He's American and he's been in Europe for two weeks. He's visited France and Switzerland. Geneva was his favourite city. He works for *Trans-Atlantic Bank*. He's worked there since 2002. He lives in Philadelphia. He's lived there since he was born.

13 **10C.3▶** Listen to a conversation between Maria and Patrick. What do they tell each other? Underline the information in the descriptions in exercise 12.

14 How do you think the conversation will continue? Role play it with a partner.

ABC Put it all together

15 Work with a partner. Look at the **Flight to Athens** role cards on ≫ p.131. Each choose a different role card. Read your role card and write a few words to help you remember the main information.

16 Do a role play. Imagine you are on a flight to Athens together. Start a conversation. What have you got in common?

I can keep a conversation going.
Tick ✓ the line.   with a lot of help   with some help   on my own   very easily

The Silk Road

Take a journey through history. Follow the Silk Road from the old capital of the Chinese empire across the deserts and mountains of Central Asia to Samarkand.

1 A journey through history

The Silk Road used to be an important trading route in Central Asia. Travellers from the East took silk and other goods from China along this route to sell in the west. This tour follows their route from Xian through China into Central Asia …

Jiayuguan Fort

The Gansu Corridor is a narrow piece of land between the Qilian Mountains and the Gobi Desert. Robbers used to attack people travelling on the Silk Road here. The Chinese emperor built the Jiayuguan Fort at the Western end of the Great Wall of China to protect the travellers.

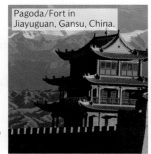
Pagoda/Fort in Jiayuguan, Gansu, China.

Historic Samarkand

From Samarkand, the silk sellers used to continue west to the Caspian Sea and then to the Middle East or Europe. Here, in Samarkand, we finally reach our journey's end and take a direct nine-hour flight back to London.

Ancient domes in Samarkand.

Camel Riders in the Taklimakan Desert

The Taklimakan Desert is one of the hottest places on the planet. The Silk Road travellers used to go around the north or south side of the desert to reach Kashgar. We will follow their route, including an excursion into the desert on camels.

A camel caravan in the Taklimakan Desert.

Dunhuang

After the Gansu Corridor, the silk sellers continued west until they reached the Eastern edge of the Taklimakan desert at Dunhuang. Here, we will see the cave homes built by Buddhist monks travelling on the Silk Road.

Woods and pagoda on edge of desert in Dunhuang.

The Pamirs

From Kashgar, the travellers used to cross the snowy Pamirs to continue in the direction of Samarkand. In the mountains, we will leave China and cross the border into Kyrgyzstan.

A snowy mountain range

2 The city walls of Xian, China

Xian used to be called Changan, and it was one of the biggest and most cosmopolitan cities in the world. In 750AD it was the capital of the Tang Empire, and the start of the Silk Road. From here, silk sellers used to travel west along the Gansu Corridor. We will have two days to explore the walls and monuments of this ancient city.

Pagodas on city walls of Xian/Changan.

A silk trader in Kashgar

At Kashgar, at the western end of the Taklimakan desert, people used to come from all directions to buy and sell their goods. It is still a very busy market town and we will have plenty of time to look around the bazaar.

silk salesman in Kashgar

How to describe a route

G *used to*   **V** prepositions of direction   **P** *used* /juːzd/ or /juːst/

A Vocabulary prepositions of direction

1 Look at the route plan. Complete the description with these words.

along   cross   end   follow   ~~leave~~
past   reach   takes   through   until

Geneva   Montreux   Brig   Milan
1hr   2hr 20min   *SWITZERLAND* | *ITALY*   4hr 20min

Lake Léman   *River Rhone*   *Simplon Tunnel* | *Lake Maggiore*

You ¹ *leave* Geneva and you go ² _____ the north side of Lake Léman. It ³ _____ about an hour to reach Montreux at the other ⁴ _____ of the lake. Then you ⁵ _____ the River Rhone. After that you continue along the Rhone Valley for about 80 minutes ⁶ _____ you reach Brig. Then you go ⁷ _____ the Simplon tunnel and ⁸ _____ the border into Italy. Finally, you go down a valley and ⁹ _____ Lake Maggiore until you ¹⁰ _____ Milan.

2 **10D.1▶** Listen and check your answers.

B Read and study the language

3 Look at **The Silk Road** opposite. Where would you find this text?
   a in a guide book   c in a holiday brochure
   b in a history book   d in an encyclopedia

4 Work with a partner. Put the text in order. Use the map to help you.

5 Underline the words that helped you to do exercise 4.
   Example   Paragraph 2 = the start of; west along the Gansu Corridor

6 Draw The Silk Road on the map opposite.

7 Work with a partner. Choose three of these words or phrases from **The Silk Road** and guess the meaning. Check in your dictionary.

trading   explore   ancient   robbers   fort
cave homes   edge   cross the border

C Grammar *used to*

8 Look at the text again and say true or false.
   1 The Silk Road used to be an important trade route.
   2 Robbers used to attack in the Gansu Corridor.
   3 Silk traders built the Jiayuguan Fort.
   4 The city of Xian used to have a different name.
   5 There used to be a market at Kashgar, but there isn't now.
   6 Samarkand is the last stop on the Silk Road.

9 Tick ✓ the uses of *used to*. Cross ✗ the things we can't use it for. Match the sentences in exercise 8 to the rules.
   We use *used to* for things that...
   a were true in the past and aren't true now ✓ *sentences 1, 4 and 5*
   b happened at one time in the past ✗ *sentence 3*
   c were true in the past, and are still true now
   d happened regularly in the past and don't happen now

10 Underline examples of *used to* in **The Silk Road**.

11 **10D.2▶** Pronunciation Listen to the difference. Then listen and say A or B.
   Example **A** use two /ˈjuːz ˈtuː/   **B** used to /ˈjuːstə/

12 **10D.3▶** Listen and repeat. Be careful to pronounce *used to* and *use* differently.
   They **used** to **use francs** in **France**
   To **buy** their **milk** and **bread**
   They **used** to **use francs** in **Bel**gium
   But **now** they **use eur**os in**stead**

13 How is travel different now? Make five sentences. Tell a partner. Do you agree?
   Example   Travelling by plane used to be very expensive. Now it's quite cheap.

More practice? **Grammar Bank ≫** p.145.

D Listen and draw a route plan

14 **10D.4▶** Listen. Which topic is Sara talking about?
   1 A route people used to take before air travel.
   2 A route she used to take to go on holiday as a child.
   3 The route of a long journey that she used to make.

15 Listen and tick the places you hear.
   ☑ Mallorca   ☐ Ibiza   ☐ Cyprus   ☐ London
   ☐ Paris   ☐ Rome   ☐ Barcelona   ☐ The Alps
   ☐ The Pyrenees   ☐ Palma

16 Listen again and draw a plan of the route.

   Start --- Finish

ABCD Put it all together

17 Think of a journey you used to make. Draw a route plan and make notes about how to get to the end of the journey.

18 Tell your partner about your route. Listen to your partner's route and draw a route plan.

I can describe a route.
Tick ✓ the line.   with a lot of help   with some help   on my own   very easily

Writing A letter to a holiday friend

A Read and guess the hidden information

1 Work with a partner. Look at the photos and describe what you see.

Dear Hakan,

Remember me? We met at that beach place near Marmaris. I've just printed my photos, and I'm sending this one of you as I promised. I'm also sending one of me at the harbour in Marmaris. Sorry it's taken me so long to send them. I've been very busy since I got back.

After Marmaris, I took a ferry across to Rhodes. I stayed there for a week and then I flew home. I've been back for three weeks now but it feels like months. It's been cold and wet here since I got home and I've lost my suntan already. It's great to look at the photos and remember the good times in Turkey.

How about you? Did you get back to Ankara with your old car in one piece? Have you fixed the broken mirror yet? And what about that Italian girl, Daniela – has she written to you yet?

If you ever come to Germany, give me a ring! You can sleep on the sofa bed.

Keep in touch.

All the best,

Alexis

2 Read the letter and discuss the questions with your partner.
1 Do you think Alexis knows Hakan well?
2 Why do you think he is sending Hakan a letter?
3 Where are Alexis and Hakan from?
4 How did they travel to Marmaris?
5 What do we know about Daniela?
6 Do you think Alexis wants Hakan to visit?
7 Does Hakan speak German?

3 Work in small groups. Discuss these questions.
1 Do you ever exchange addresses with people you meet when you are travelling?
2 Do they ever invite you to visit?
3 Did you visit them? Why? / Why not?

B Vocabulary letter-writing expressions

4 Find phrases with similar meanings in the letter.
Since I returned home   *Since I got back*
Did you arrive home?
Was your old car OK?
Phone me.
Don't lose contact.
Best wishes.

5 Write notes in the table.

letter structure	information in Alexis's letter
your name	*Dear Hakan*
why I'm writing	*sending photos as promised*
my news	
your news?	
what next?	
my name	*All the best, Alexis*

C Get ideas to write about

6 Work as a group. Follow these instructions.
Take a piece of paper. Think of a journey you have made or would like to make. Write some notes to complete this sentence:
1 *I was travelling in …* (write the name of a place in the world)
2 Fold the paper and give it to the next person.
3 Write some notes to complete this sentence: *I was …* (write an activity, e.g. camping; sitting on the train)
4 Fold the paper and give it to the next person.
5 Write some notes to complete this sentence: *I made friends with …* (write your own name)
6 Fold the paper and give it to the next person.
7 Write some notes to complete this sentence: *I promised to …* (write something you promised to your new friend)
8 Fold the paper and give it to the next person.
9 Write some notes to complete this sentence: *After that I …* (describe your journey home)
10 Give the paper to the next person.

7 Open the paper you have received and read out the notes.

ABC Put it all together

8 Write a letter to a holiday friend. Use the letter structure from exercise 5 and your page of notes from exercise 7 to help you. Add any other information you want.

9 Give the letter to the person.

10 Check the letter you receive. Does it have all the parts of the letter structure?

I can write a letter to a holiday friend.

Tick ✓ the line.   with a lot of help   with some help   on my own   very easily

Unit 10 Review

A Grammar

1 Present perfect with *just*, *already* and *yet* Add one of these words to the question or the response in each conversation.

already   yet   just

1 Why are your hands wet?
  I've washed them.   *I've just washed them.*
2 Have you had breakfast?
  No, I'll have it later.
3 Why don't you get this DVD?
  I've seen it.
4 Shall I check your homework?
  No, I haven't finished it.
5 Why is the TV warm?
  I've switched it off.
6 Let's go to Rome on holiday.
  No, I've been there.
7 Has your brother left school?
  Yes, he's at university now.
8 Can I borrow your newspaper?
  No, I haven't read it.

2 Present perfect with *for* and *since* Match the beginnings and ends of the sentences.

1 [c] Brasilia has been a capital city since
2 [ ] He's been asleep since
3 [ ] It's been dark for
4 [ ] I've had to wear glasses since
5 [ ] I've lived in London for
6 [ ] She's been off work with flu for
7 [ ] The USA has been independent for
8 [ ] They've been unemployed since

a five years.
b four days.
c ~~1960.~~
d over 230 years.
e they left school.
f I was a teenager.
g three hours.
h three o'clock.

3 *used to* Complete the sentences with *used to*. If *used to* is not possible, put the verb in the past simple tense.

1 New York _used to be_ (be) called New Amsterdam.
2 The emperor _____ (build) a great wall.
3 Marco Polo _____ (travel) to China.
4 The silk traders _____ (go) around the Taklimakan Desert.
5 Columbus _____ (want) to find a sea route to China.
6 The capital of Brazil _____ (be) Rio de Janeiro.
7 The traders _____ (sell) their silk in Europe.
8 Marco Polo _____ (be) in Venice.

B Vocabulary

4 Journey times Write two sentences for each sign.

1 🚶 **Metro** 5 minutes ❯
  The metro station is a five-minute walk from here   .
  The metro station is five minutes on foot from here   .
2 🚐 **Airport** 30 minutes ❯
  _____ .
3 🚂 **Scotland** 6 hours ❯
  _____ .
4 🐪 **Kashgar** 3 days ❯
  _____ .
5 🚗 **Coast** 4 hours ❯
  _____ .

5 Air travel Do the crossword. See clues on ❯❯ p.131.

6 Prepositions of direction Write the words in the gaps.

across (x2)   along   follow   ~~leave~~   past   reach   through

How to get to Ilha Grande

You ¹ _leave_ Rio de Janeiro and you go east
² _____ the coast. The road goes ³ _____
a short tunnel and ⁴ _____ Barra. After that,
you ⁵ _____ the beach for half an hour. Then
the road goes ⁶ _____ some hills to Campo
Grande. After about five hours you ⁷ _____
Angra. Then you take a ferry ⁸ _____ to
the island.

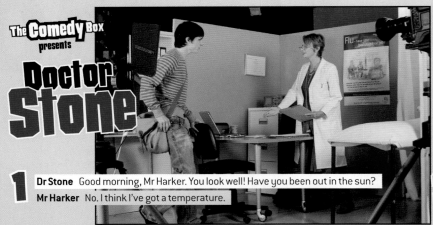

The Comedy Box presents Doctor Stone

1 **Dr Stone** Good morning, Mr Harker. You look well! Have you been out in the sun?
Mr Harker No. I think I've got a temperature.

2 **Dr S** Oh, very nice! So, how do you feel today?
Mr H I don't feel very well. I've got a sore throat and a head …

3 **Dr S** Say 'Aaah!'.
Mr H Aaah!

4 **Dr S** And are you still taking the pills?
Mr H No, I stopped. They made me feel sick and …

5 **Dr S** Good, good. And how's your backache? Is it getting any better?
Mr H It's worse. Now I'm aching all over and I've got a pain in the …

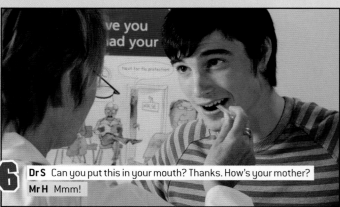

6 **Dr S** Can you put this in your mouth? Thanks. How's your mother?
Mr H Mmm!

7 **Dr S** Excellent!
Mr H Doctor Stone …

8 **Dr S** Yes, Mr Harker? What's the matter?
Mr H I don't think you're listening to me. You ask a question and then you don't …

9 **Dr S** Now, take these pills every four hours and come back and see me next week.
Mr H But …
Dr S Next!

FLUPAST®

fights flu fast

24 tablets • Available without prescription

USE FLUPAST® FOR FAST EFFECTIVE RELIEF OF PAIN. USE FOR:
• cold & flu • headache • toothache • backache
• sore throat • fever • a temperature

DO NOT USE FLUPAST®:
• for children under 7, except on medical advice
• for more than 7 days without medical advice
• if you're using other medicines that contain paracetamol
• during pregnancy
• if past the expiry date

HOW TO USE FLUPAST® TABLETS:

Age:	How often:
7–12	½–1 tablet every 4 hours with water maximum 4 in 24 hours
12–adults	1–2 tablets every 4 hours with water maximum 8 in 24 hours

If pain continues, or if you take more than the recommended dose, seek medical advice.

After opening keep below 30°C.
Each tablet contains 500mg Paracetamol.

Expiry date May 2012

How to describe symptoms

v symptoms of illness

A Vocabulary symptoms of illness

1 How often do you get a cold or flu? What symptoms do you have? What do you do? Tell a partner.

2 Work with a partner. Describe the symptoms in the pictures below with the phrases from this box.

I don't feel very well …			
I've got	a temperature.	I feel	sick.
	a sore throat.	I'm	aching all over.
	(a) backache. /ˈbækeɪk/		
	a cough. /kɒf/		
	a headache.		

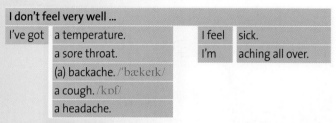

3 **11A.1▶** Listen, check, and repeat.

4 Read **Doctor Stone** opposite. What are Mr Harker's symptoms?

5 **11A.2▶** Listen to **Doctor Stone**. Why does the audience laugh?

6 What do you think Mr Harker wants to say? Work with a partner and finish his sentences.

B Read for specific information

7 Look at **Flupast** opposite. Read the instructions and answer the questions.
1 Do you need a prescription to buy *Flupast*?
2 How often should you take the tablets?
3 How many tablets should an adult take?
4 Who shouldn't take the tablets?
   a a child of nine
   b a pregnant woman
   c a child of six

8 <u>Underline</u> three words you don't know. Guess their meaning. Then check in a dictionary.

C Listen for useful phrases

9 **11A.3▶** Listen. Is this:
1 a radio advert for *Flupast*?
2 a doctor telling a patient about *Flupast*?
3 two friends talking about *Flupast*?

10 Listen again and answer the questions.
1 What are the man's symptoms?
2 What is the woman's advice?
3 What is the result?

11 Listen again and complete the woman's phrases.
What's the m_____?
Have you t_____ anything for it?
Get well s_____.
You look a lot b_____!
How do you f_____?

D Be a sympathetic listener

12 Which response is the most sympathetic?
1 I've got a terrible headache.
   a Me too!
   b You look OK to me.
   c Oh no! Would you like an aspirin?
2 I don't feel very well. I think I've got flu .
   a Have you taken anything for it?
   b Everybody's got flu these days.
   c Really? I feel fine.
3 My father's ill in bed at the moment.
   a Oh. Is there anything on TV tonight?
   b Oh dear. I hope he gets better soon.
   c Oh well. That's life.

13 Work with a partner. Take turns to be A and B.
A Ask your partner how he/she is.
B Tell your partner your symptoms.
A Be sympathetic.

14 Act a conversation with a partner, but with a more sympathetic doctor than Doctor Stone.
Example **A** I think I've got a temperature.
          B Oh dear! I'm sorry to hear that. When did it start?

ABCD Put it all together

15 Work in groups of three or four.
1 Think of one or more symptoms of illness.
2 Imagine the name of a medicine for these symptoms.
3 Read audio script 11A.3 on ≫ p.158. Write a similar advert for your medicine.

16 Act out your advert for the class.

I can describe symptoms.

Tick ✓ the line.   with a lot of help   with some help   on my own   very easily

Portrait of a young woman

The artist's model in this painting is a young woman called Suzon. You are standing in front of her. She's looking straight at you, and she doesn't seem happy. She's working in a bar in Paris. There are lots of people in the bar – you can see them in the mirror. But she seems lonely. She doesn't really want to be there. Perhaps she hates the job. Perhaps she has problems in her life. We can see Suzon's back in the mirror, and the face of a man in front of her. The man doesn't seem friendly. You are standing in front of her, so of course, <u>you</u> are the man in the mirror.

1 *Girl With a Pearl Earring*, Jan Vermeer (c1665)

2 *Mona Lisa*, Leonardo da Vinci (14th Century)

3 *A Bar at the Folies-Bergère*, Edouard Manet (1882)

4 *The Shrimp Girl*, William Hogarth (c1745)

How to say how people appear

G action or state verbs **P** unstressed words

A Listen for key words

1 Look at the paintings opposite. Which one do you like the most? Why? Tell a partner.

2 **11B.1▶** Listen and read **Portrait of a young woman** opposite. Which painting is the text about?

3 Which key words in the text helped you answer exercise 2? Underline them. Compare with a partner.

4 **11B.2▶** Listen to two more descriptions and note the key words. Match the descriptions with two of the other paintings.

B Grammar action or state verbs

5 Read audio scripts 11B.1 and 11B.2 on ≫ p.158. Underline all the verbs in the present continuous tense and circle all the verbs in the present simple tense. Write the verbs in the table.

verbs in the present continuous (action verbs)	verbs in the present simple (state verbs)
look	seem

Rule We do not normally use continuous tenses with state verbs.

Example ~~She's hating her job.~~
~~I'm not knowing him.~~

6 Do you think the verbs below are action or state verbs? Decide with a partner.

know walk listen hear like write
understand watch talk smile

7 In each pair of sentences, put one verb in the present simple and the other in the present continuous.

1 They're *speaking* a foreign language.
I *don't understand* them. speak / not understand

2 She _____ at me. I think she _____ me. smile / like

3 Do you _____ that man? He _____ at you. know / look

4 They _____ unhappy. I don't think they _____ the party. seem / enjoy

8 Put the verbs in brackets in the present simple or continuous tense.

¹She*'s standing* (stand) in front of you and ²she_____ (look) straight at you. ³She_____ (not work) or doing anything else. ⁴She_____ (smile). Behind her you can see countryside with a river. ⁵She _____ (be) very calm and relaxed. ⁶It _____ (seem) like ⁷she _____ (know) your thoughts. ⁸I _____ (like) this picture.

9 Which painting is the text in exercise 8 about? Do you agree with it? Tell your partner.
More practice? **Grammar Bank** ≫ p.146.

C Pronunciation unstressed words

10 **11B.3▶** Listen to the text in exercise 8. Which words are stressed?
a the black words
b the green words

11 Practise reading the text in pairs. Does your partner stress the correct words?

ABC Put it all together

12 Work with a partner. Look at these four portraits. Choose one and write notes to describe it. Look at audio scripts 11B.1, 11B.2, and 11B.3 on ≫ p.158 for ideas.

Example standing, wearing red, thinking, looking down, seems calm

13 Work in groups. Use your notes to describe one of the portraits. Remember – don't stress all the words. Guess which picture the other students in your group are describing.

I can say how people appear.
Tick ✓ the line. with a lot of help   with some help   on my own   very easily

Personality Test

Which do you follow – your **head** or your **heart**?

1. **Your friend is planning to marry someone you don't like.**

   a   You decide to tell your friend what you think.

   b   You try to say what you think, but in a nice way.

   c   You don't say what you really think. You prefer to tell a 'white lie'.

   d   You say nothing. You don't want to hurt your friend's feelings.

2. **Your friend hopes to become a singer but you don't think she can sing well.**

   a   You want to help her, so you tell her what you think.

   b   You try to suggest other careers you think will be better for her.

   c   You pretend to like her singing.

   d   You don't want to make her angry so you don't say what you think.

3. **You are planning to rent a flat. You have seen two places you like.**

   a   You try to think carefully about which flat will be better for your lifestyle.

   b   You decide to write a list of good and bad points for each flat and then compare them.

   c   You try to go with your feelings.

   d   You try to imagine what your family and friends will think of the two flats.

4. **Your friend is planning to cheat in an exam, and he wants you to help. You think it is wrong.**

   a   You refuse to help and you tell him why.

   b   You don't refuse to help completely, but you try to make your friend change his mind.

   c   You agree to help, but you say what you think.

   d   You agree to help. He's your friend and he knows what he's doing.

5. **You are going away for two weeks and your friend asks to stay in your flat. You don't want her to stay there.**

   a   You refuse to let her stay and you tell her why.

   b   You say you'd like to let her stay, but you think of a reason why she can't.

   c   You promise to think about it and hope she'll forget.

   d   You agree to let her stay, cross your fingers, and hope for the best.

6. **You are out with friends and they disagree about something. Everybody starts to get angry.**

   a   You try to talk about the problem calmly.

   b   You try to think of a solution.

   c   You decide to go home.

   d   You try to change the topic of conversation.

How to give your ideas

G verb + infinitive (with *to*)   **V** verbs for giving ideas   **P** stress in two-syllable verbs and nouns

A Vocabulary verbs for giving ideas

1 Look at the words in **Ideas** opposite.
1 Check new words in a dictionary.
2 Are any of the words similar in your language?

2 Complete the sentences with words from **Ideas**. More than one answer may be possible.
1 I *hope* to go to university next year.
2 I don't _____ to go out tonight.
3 She's only 15 but she _____ to be 18.
4 He _____ to go with me, so I went out alone.
5 Don't _____ to switch off your mobile on the plane.
6 I _____ to open the door but it was locked.

B Pronunciation stress in two-syllable verbs and nouns

3 **11C.1▶** Listen to this list of two-syllable verbs. Which one is pronounced differently? Underline it.

agree   become   compare   decide   forget
prefer   pretend   promise   refuse   suggest

4 **11C.2▶** Listen to this list of two-syllable nouns. Which one is different? Underline it.

exam   feelings   finger   lifestyle
problem   reason   singer   topic

5 Underline the correct words in these pronunciation rules.
1 All/Most two-syllable verbs have the stress on the first/second syllable.
2 All/Most two-syllable nouns have the stress on the first/second syllable.

6 Work with a partner. Practise saying the words in exercises 3 and 4. Check your partner's pronunciation.

C Read a personality test

7 Look at **Personality Test** opposite and answer the questions.
1 Where do you think the text comes from?
  a a Sunday magazine
  b a psychology text book
  c a newspaper
2 How old does the writer think the reader is? Why?
  a 10–17   b 18–24   c 25–40   d over 40

8 What do these phrases from the text mean?
1 tell a white lie   4 change his mind
2 go with your feelings   5 cross your fingers and
3 cheat in an exam   hope for the best

9 Do the **Personality Test** opposite. Choose a, b, c, or d.

10 Look at the **results** on ≫ p.131. Compare in small groups.

D Grammar verb + infinitive (with *to*)

11 Some verbs are followed by infinitives.

You don't | want | to hurt | your friend's feelings.

verb
infinitive (with *to*)

Underline examples of verb + infinitive in **Personality Test**. Make a list in your notebook.

verb + infinitive (with to)

– plan to   – decide to   – would like to

12 Write true sentences about you. Tell a partner.
1 I have always wanted to …
2 I'm planning to …
3 In the summer holiday, I hope to …
4 I have decided to …
5 At the moment, I'm trying to …

More practice? **Grammar Bank** ≫ p.146.

E Listen for general meaning

13 Read the **problem page** on ≫ p.131 and the dialogue below. Which problem are they discussing?
Mark You should refuse to get in the car.
Sonia Yeah, why don't you get a taxi?
Deb You could pretend you've lost the car keys and suggest a taxi.

14 **11C.3▶** Listen. Which problem are they discussing?

15 Listen again. Work with a partner and try to complete these sentences from the conversation.
1 You could promise to …
2 Why don't you ask him to …
3 I think you should refuse to …
4 What about your …
5 I don't want to …
6 You shouldn't agree to …

16 Listen again and check with the audio script on ≫ p.158.

ABCDE Put it all together

17 Work in small groups. Discuss the problems on ≫ p.131.

18 Read your best suggestions to another group. The other group must guess the problem.

I can give my ideas.

Tick ✓ the line.   with a lot of help   with some help   on my own   very easily

The face

cheek chin ear eyebrows
eyelashes forehead lips
neck nose skin

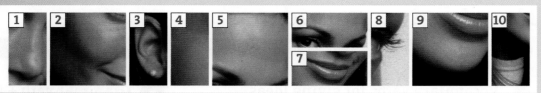

The Power of Make-up

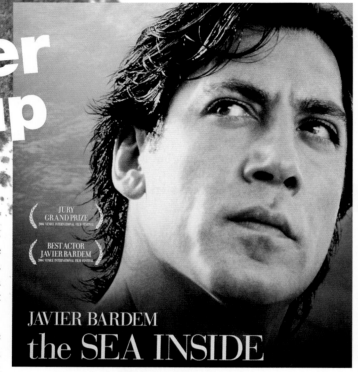

JAVIER BARDEM
the SEA INSIDE

Spanish actor Javier Bardem was 35 when he acted in *The Sea Inside*. In the film, he plays a man who is 20 years older. The man, Ramón Sampedro, was disabled after an accident at the age of 25. The film tells the true story of his life.

In the film, the make-up is so good that it's hard to believe it's Javier Bardem. He looks completely different, and you can't see the make-up at all. But it was very hard work and it took five hours each morning during the filming. First of all, Bardem's hair was shaved off the top of his head. His eyebrows were removed and his eyelashes were cut. Contact lenses were put in his eyes. A material called Dermaplast was used to change the shape of his face. The shape of his nose was changed, and bags were added under his eyes. Veins and spots were painted on his skin to make it look older.

The make-up had to be exactly the same each day, so photos were taken at every stage in the process. The make-up was finished at about 12.30 and then Bardem had to do about ten hours of filming. At the end of the day, the make-up was removed. Bardem's make-up was done by a British make-up artist called Jo Allen. Allen has also worked on other films such as *Gladiator* and *The Others*.

The Sea Inside was directed by Alejandro Amenábar and it won an Oscar for Best Foreign Language Film. The film was also given an Oscar for best make-up, and you can see why. In the film poster at the top, Bardem is playing Sampedro at the age of 25. In the picture at the bottom, he's playing Sampedro at the age of 55. The difference is amazing.

JAVIER BARDEM
MAR ADENTRO
"D'après l'histoire vraie de Ramón Sampedro"
un film de
ALEJANDRO AMENÁBAR

How to say how something was done

G past passive v the face

A Vocabulary the face

1 Make a list of words for parts of the face.
Example eye, ear ...

2 Look at **The face** opposite. Match the words with the numbers in the pictures. Do you know who this is?
Example 1 = nose

B Read and understand detail

3 Read **The Power of Make-up** opposite. What do you find out about these people? Tell a partner.

Javier Bardem   Ramón Sampedro
Jo Allen   Alejandro Amenábar

4 Read the text again and answer the questions. Compare with a partner.
1 How long did it take to do Bardem's make up?
2 What changes were made to Bardem's ...
    a hair?   c eyelashes?   e eyes?
    b eyebrows?   d nose?   f skin?
3 What time did Jo Allen finish doing his make-up?

5 Would you like to see this film? Why? / Why not?

C Grammar past simple passive

6 Read the sentences below from **The Power of Make-up**. Match questions 1–3 with answers a–c.
1 'Bardem's hair was shaved.' Who shaved it?
2 'Photos were taken at every stage.' Who did this?
3 'The film was also given an Oscar for best make-up.' Who gave the Oscar?

a Maybe a famous person. The article isn't about the Oscar ceremony.
b We don't know. It isn't important.
c Probably Jo Allen, but the article isn't about her, it's about the make-up.

7 Sentences 1–3 in exercise 6 are in the past simple passive. Answer the questions.
1 In a passive sentence, you can say what happened *without* saying who did it. This is sometimes useful. Why? (Clue – look at answers a, b, and c in exercise 6.)
2 When do you use *was* and when do you use *were*?
3 Which verb form follows *was* / *were*?
    a infinitive (*to do*)
    b past simple (*did*)
    c past participle (*done*)

8 Underline examples of the past passive in **The Power of Make-up**.

9 Imagine you're a star. Say how you were treated on a recent trip.
1 invite / New York
    I was invited to New York.
2 meet / airport
3 take / five-star hotel
4 give / best room
5 serve / breakfast in bed
6 show / on the evening news

10 Read the text and underline the correct option.
The Lord of the Rings [1] write / was written by JR Tolkien. It [2] made / was made into three films by Peter Jackson. The three films [3] made / were made at the same time. The project [4] took / was taken eight years to complete, and it cost $270 million. The film [5] won / was won seventeen prizes. It [6] filmed / was filmed in New Zealand. The scenery was very beautiful and many people [7] visited / were visited New Zealand because of the film.

More practice? **Grammar Bank** ≫ p.146.

D Listen for detail in a conversation

11 **11D.1▶** Ben worked as an extra in the film *Emma*. He's telling his friend Kath about it. Answer the questions.
1 Did Ben enjoy the work?
2 Is Kath interested in his story?

12 Listen again. What are Ben's answers to these questions?
1 Where did you go? *We were taken to a place in the middle of nowhere.*
2 Were you given a place to sleep?
3 What time were you woken up?
4 What were you given to wear?
5 How long were you given for lunch?
6 Were you given anything to eat?
7 What were you told to do?

ABCD Put it all together

13 Have you ever had any of these experiences? Choose one and make notes to answer these questions.

Where was it?   When was it?   What happened to you?
What was it like?   What were you told to do?
Were you given anything to eat?

1 a stay in hospital
2 your first day at school
3 a school or business trip
4 a part in a play
5 *your ideas*

14 Tell your partner about your experience. Does your partner's experience sound good? Why? / Why not?
Example A few years ago I had a job as an extra in a film. We were told to arrive at 8.00 a.m. and ...

I can say how something was done.

Tick ✓ the line.   with a lot of help   with some help   on my own   very easily

Writing A complaint

A Read a message of complaint

1 Do you complain in these situations? Tell a partner. Think of some other situations when you complain.

1 You took some medicine but it didn't work.
2 You don't like the food in a restaurant.
3 Your new shirt lost its colour in the washing machine.
4 Your doctor's appointment was two hours late.

2 Guess the order of Phillip Harker's actions when he was ill.

☐ I took the prescription to the pharmacy.
☐ I was given an appointment.
☐ 1 I phoned the health centre.
☐ I was seen by the doctor.
☐ I went to the health centre.
☐ The doctor gave me a prescription.

3 Now read Phillip's message of complaint about his visit to the health centre. Are the events in the same order you gave in exercise 2?

File Edit View Favourites Tools Help

Back · Next · Stop · Refresh · Home · Search · Favourites · ✉

Address http://www.healthservice/complaints

Health service: Online complaint form

Patient's Name:	Phillip Harker
Health Centre:	Park Green
Doctor:	Dr Stone
Date	24th April

Please write your message here:

I wish to make a complaint. Last week I didn't feel very well. I was aching all over and I had a sore throat. I phoned the health centre and I was given an appointment to see Dr Stone at 10.00 on Tuesday. However, when I arrived, I was told that my appointment was for Thursday, not Tuesday. I returned on Thursday at the correct time. However, I wasn't called in by Dr Stone until 12.00. Dr Stone asked a lot of questions but she didn't listen to my answers. Finally, she gave me a prescription. I thought it was for a flu drug. However, when I took it to the pharmacy I found that it was a prescription for a pregnancy test! Clearly, this is not good enough. I would like to be registered with a different doctor. I hope to hear from you soon.

SUBMIT

4 Phillip makes four complaints. What are they?

B Use sentence adverbs

5 You can use sentence adverbs to show how a sentence connects to the rest of the text. Underline these sentence adverbs in the message in exercise 3. Then match them with their meanings below.

However, ... Clearly, ... Finally, ...

1 _____ It is easy to see that this is true.
2 _____ What happened is the opposite of what I wanted or expected to happen.
3 _____ This is the last part of my story.

6 Complete the sentences with adverbs from exercise 5.

1 I told the doctor about my problem. _____, she didn't listen.
2 I phoned five times and nobody answered. _____, I went to speak to them in person.
3 Phillip Harker is a man. _____, he can't be pregnant!

C Practise making complaints

7 Work with a partner. Have three-line conversations. Use the first lines below and the example to help you.

Example **A** (angrily) I was seen by the doctor at 12.30!
B What's wrong with that?
A My appointment was for 10.00!

1 I was seen by the doctor on Thursday!
2 The doctor said there's nothing wrong with me!
3 I was given a prescription for a stomach ache!
4 The doctor asked me lots of questions!
5 The doctor said it's normal for old people to get hand pains.
6 The doctor thought I could be pregnant.

8 Write three sentences using your ideas from exercise 7. Try to use the sentence adverbs.

Example My appointment was for 10.00. However, I wasn't seen by the doctor until 12.30!

ABC Put it all together

9 Think of your situation from exercise 1, or another situation when you have complained. Explain the situation to a different partner.

10 With your partner, write a message of complaint. Use sentence adverbs and phrases from Phillip's message.

11 Read another pair's message. Could they explain the problem more clearly? How?

I can write a complaint.

Tick ✓ the line. with a lot of help with some help on my own very easily

Unit 11 Review

A Grammar

1 Action or state verbs Put the verbs in present simple or present continuous.

In this picture, we can see a man.
He [1] *'s looking* look to the left.
He [2] _____ wear a red hat.
He [3] _____ not seem very
friendly. He [4] _____ not smile.
Perhaps he [5] _____ listen to somebody.
Perhaps somebody [6] _____ say something and
he [7] _____ not like it. He [8] _____ seem angry.

2 Verb + infinitive Complete the sentences.
1 We're going to have a baby. We've decided.
   We've decided *to have a baby* _____.
2 Jack asked Anita to marry him. She agreed.
   Anita agreed _____.
3 I didn't take my pills this morning. I forgot.
   I forgot _____.
4 Marcus will help me. He promised.
   Marcus promised _____.
5 I couldn't call you. Your phone wasn't working.
   I tried _____.
6 I asked my parents to lend me the car. They refused.
   My parents refused _____.

3 Past passive Correct the sentences.
1 ~~My dog killed a lorry.~~
   My dog was killed by a lorry _____.
2 The money took a robber.
   _____.
3 The robbers caught the police.
   _____.
4 The car drove a young woman.
   _____.
5 The robbery didn't see the neighbours.
   _____.
6 The patients checked a doctor.
   _____.
7 The photographs didn't take a professional.
   _____.
8 This message didn't write an adult.
   _____.

4 Past passive Write sentences using the following verbs and phrases.
1 invite / New York   *I was invited to New York.*
2 meet / airport
3 put / five-star hotel
4 give / best room
5 serve / breakfast in bed
6 drive / everywhere in a fantastic car
7 take / to the airport

B Vocabulary

5 Parts of the body and symptoms Find eighteen more symptoms and parts of the body. Some letters are used twice.

F	O	R	E	H	E	A	D	C	C
S	H	O	U	L	D	E	R	O	H
A	W	M	U	S	C	L	E	U	I
F	E	E	L	S	I	C	K	G	N
R	T	B	A	C	K	A	C	H	E
S	O	R	E	T	H	R	O	A	T
K	U	L	O	A	F	E	L	I	D
I	N	E	C	K	R	L	E	I	O
N	E	B	L	O	O	D	U	K	P

6 Discussing illness Put these words in the conversation

aching   better   feel   hope   how
matter   pills   taken   ~~well~~

A You don't look [1] *well* _____. What's the [2] _____?
B I don't [3] _____ very well. I'm [4] _____ all over.
A Have you [5] _____ anything for it?
B I've taken some [6] _____. Now I'm going to bed.
A Good night. I [7] _____ you feel better in the morning.
A [8] _____ do you feel today?
B I feel much [9] _____ thank you.
A Good. You can help me with the shopping!

7 Action and state verbs Underline the best word.
1 I hope / pretend / imagine to go to university next year.
2 We're wanting / suggesting / planning to go to Spain this summer.
3 They've tried / decided / forgotten to move to a bigger flat next year.
4 She pretended / imagined / refused to be angry, but really she was happy.
5 I asked for a day off and my boss hoped / promised / preferred to think about it.

8 Sentence adverbs Complete the sentences with these words.

However, ...   Clearly, ...   Finally, ...

1 Mr Harker asked me the same question three times.
   _____ he wasn't listening to me.
2 I went to the doctor's on Monday afternoon.
   _____ my appointment was for Monday morning.
3 I arrived at the health centre at 6.00 and waited for a long time. _____ the doctor arrived and started seeing people.

Mixed Messages

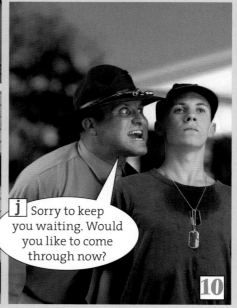

How to ask people to do things

G gerund or infinitive   V polite requests

A Read and match

1 Look at the photos in **Mixed Messages** opposite. Do you know the names of the people's jobs?

2 Look at **Mixed Messages**. Work with a partner. Match photos 1–10 with the things the people say a–j.
Example   1 = c

3 **12A.1▶ Pronunciation** Listen, check, and repeat. Try to sound like the speakers.

4 Match these responses with four of the requests.
1 I'd like to help, but I'm afraid I'm in a hurry. Good luck with your research!
2 Yes, go straight ahead. It's opposite the bank.
3 Yes, of course. OK, first of all, click on this icon …
4 Yes sure. Where do you want to take them?

B Vocabulary polite requests

5 Decide if the requests in **Mixed Messages** are polite or not polite. Why are some of the speakers not being very polite?

6 What do you notice about the more polite requests? Say *true* or *false*.
1 They are questions.   *True*
2 They aren't questions.
3 They are shorter sentences.
4 They are longer sentences.
5 They often begin with an apology.

7 Put the words in order to make requests.
1 opening mind window the you would ?
Would you mind opening the window?
2 wait moment a here could for you ?
3 seat like would take to a you ?
4 me switching mobile phone off you excuse would your mind ?

8 Work with a partner. Look at the situations on ≫ p.135. Make polite requests and replies.

C Grammar gerund or infinitive

9 Match 1–4 with a–d.
1 I'd like   a helping you for a few minutes.
2 Would you mind   b to help, but I'm in a hurry.
3 Would you like   c to come through now?
4 I don't mind   d giving me a hand?

10 Which of the sentences in exercise 9 are requests, and which are responses?

11 Some verbs are followed by gerunds (-*ing* form) and some by infinitives. Look at this list for a minute. Then cover the box and complete the text.

verbs followed by gerund	verbs followed by infinitive
enjoy go hate* like* love* mind	agree decide need plan promise refuse want would like

* You sometimes see infinitive after *like, love*, and *hate*, especially in American English.

I enjoy ¹_____ (cook) so I decided ²_____ (invite) four friends for dinner. One of them needed ³_____ (study) for an exam and refused ⁴_____ (come). The other three agreed ⁵_____ (come) and promised ⁶_____ (arrive) at eight. I planned ⁷_____ (serve) the meal at nine, because I wanted ⁸_____ (have) a drink first. However, my friends arrived at ten! I don't mind ⁹_____ (wait) for a short time, but I hate ¹⁰_____ (eat) burnt food!

More practice? **Grammar Bank** ≫ p.147.

D Predict before you listen

12 Work with a partner. What requests do people make when they're travelling on a train? Write a list.
Example   Would you mind moving your bag?

13 **12A.2▶** Listen to a comedy sketch about two people on a train. What requests does the man make?

14 Listen again and answer the questions.
1 Why does the audience laugh? Tick two reasons.
a The man makes too many requests.
b The man does not use polite words.
c The man's requests are making the woman angry.
2 What would you do in the woman's situation?

15 Look at the audio script on ≫ p.159. Act the conversation with a partner. Remember to sound polite when you make requests.

ABCD Put it all together

16 Choose one of these situations (or think of another). Imagine that one of the people makes a lot of requests to the other. Work with a partner and make a list of possible requests. Practise having a conversation.
two colleagues at work   two neighbours two customers in a queue   two passengers on a bus
Example two colleagues at work – open the window, lend a pen, answer the phone …

17 Act out your conversation in small groups. Can you guess the situation?

I can ask people to do things.
Tick ✓ the line.   with a lot of help   with some help   on my own   very easily

PARTY PLANET

WHAT'S YOUR IDEA OF FUN? HAVE A LOOK AT SOME OF THE STRANGEST FESTIVALS FROM AROUND THE WORLD AND FIND THE PARTY FOR YOU!

HOW ABOUT ELEPHANT FOOTBALL?

THE SURIN ELEPHANT FESTIVAL NOVEMBER, THAILAND

1 First of all, everybody gets together to watch the elephant feeding ceremony. There are five tons each of pineapples, bananas, watermelons, cucumbers, potatoes, and sugar cane. Everything is put carefully on tables. Then the elephants arrive for the feast. After that there are four days of elephant dancing, elephant racing, elephant football, and elephant everything.

WHAT AN ICE PARTY!

SAPPORO SNOW FESTIVAL FEBRUARY, JAPAN

2 People come from everywhere to see this festival of snow and ice statues. There are hundreds of them and some are enormous. There is a statue competition and teams come from everywhere, even tropical places such as Hawaii and Singapore. There's something for everybody – playgrounds for the children, nightlife, bars, and karaoke for the adults. And everything's made of ice.

LOOKING FOR LOVE?

IMILCHIL WEDDING FESTIVAL AUGUST, MOROCCO

3 Anybody looking for a wife or husband will want to be here. This is where the young Berber people from all over the Atlas Mountains come to find a partner. But anybody who is married or happily single will find plenty to do as well. There are ceremonies, folk musicians, and traditional dances. There's also a lively market where you can buy anything, from a camel to a coffee pot.

FANCY A NICE LONG MUD BATH FOLLOWED BY A BIT OF BODY PAINTING?

THE GOROKA SHOW SEPTEMBER, PAPUA NEW GUINEA

4 People from everywhere in the Eastern Highlands meet in Goroka for this popular festival. There are people from 80 different tribes. It's a colourful celebration, with everybody wearing their traditional costume and body paint. The drums start and the action begins. Nobody stops dancing for two days. If you're looking for something strange and exotic, this is the party for you!

IF YOU'RE A FOG FAN, THIS IS THE PARTY FOR YOU!

NEWFOUNDLAND FOG FESTIVAL OCTOBER, CANADA

5 In October, everybody gets together for a day of fun in the fog. There are boat races, fishing competitions, and everyone wears funny hats. Then, at midday, there's a procession to the beach. Everybody takes their clothes off and jumps into the water. But you can't see anything, of course, because it's too foggy.

How to describe a festival

G indefinite pronouns / adverbs   V festivals and celebrations   P stress in words ending -ion

A Read and identify

1 Which of these things can you find in the photos opposite? Use a dictionary.

a ceremony   a colourful celebration   traditional costumes
a carnival procession   a fight   elephants   camels
a tropical country   a competition   a tribe

2 Read **Party Planet** opposite. Match the festivals with the photos. Which festival is false? Which six photos are not mentioned in the texts?

3 Which festival would you like to go to? Why? Tell a partner.

B Pronunciation   stress in words ending -ion

4 Write the words in the box.

congratulations   procession   action   competition

●●	●●●	●●●●	●●●●●
station	tradition	information	pronunciation

5 **12B.1▶** Listen, check, and repeat.

6 Are the rules *true* or *false*?

In all the words ...
1 The last syllable is /ʃn/ (the letter is pronounced like *sh*).
2 The stress is on the last syllable.

C Grammar   indefinite pronouns / adverbs

7 Complete the grammar box.

people				
	someone	anyone		no one
things			everything	nothing
places	somewhere			

You can use *-body* instead of *-one*, for example *somebody, anybody* etc.

8 Read **Party Planet** again. Underline examples of indefinite pronouns in the text.

9 Are indefinite pronouns singular or plural? (Clue: look at the verbs that go with them.)

10 Match 1–6 with a–f.

1 There isn't	*f*	a	nothing to do.
2 There's		b	everybody leaving.
3 I saw		c	everybody do?
4 Did you see		d	anything?
5 What did		e	no one answered.
6 I called but		f	anywhere to sit.

11 Underline the correct word.
1 I heard someone / anyone playing a guitar.
2 Anybody / Nobody wanted to leave the party.
3 It was foggy and I couldn't see anything / nothing.
4 Everything / Anything is covered in mud.
5 Everything's free – you don't have to pay for nothing / something / anything.
6 There's something / everything / nothing / anything in his hand – I think it's a photo.
7 There isn't somewhere / everywhere / nowhere / anywhere interesting to go.

More practice? **Grammar Bank** ≫ p.147.

D Predict before you listen

12 Look at the pictures of the six festivals <u>not</u> in the texts. You will hear people talking about three of these festivals. What words do you expect to hear? Write a list. Compare with a partner.

13 **12B.2▶** Listen and match the conversations with three of the photographs. Which words on your list did you hear?

14 Listen again. What do they say about these things? Compare with a partner.

Conversation 1 balloons
Conversation 2 the crowd
Conversation 3 an animal

15 Choose a festival from the four descriptions in **Party Planet** opposite. Make notes about what happens and what people do. Work with a partner. Ask and answer questions using your notes.

ABCD Put it all together

16 Work with a partner. Think of a festival you know, or invent one. Write notes under these headings.

Where and when?
How long does it last?
What does everyone do?
How does it begin?
How does it finish?

17 Work in small groups. Tell the other students about your festival.

I can describe a festival.

Tick ✓ the line.   with a lot of help   with some help   on my own   very easily

A Date with Des

Oh no –
I think he wants to
ask me out!

1 **Des** Are you doing anything tonight?
Lucy Oh, well I'm a bit busy actually …

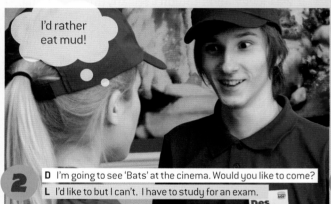

I'd rather
eat mud!

2 **D** I'm going to see 'Bats' at the cinema. Would you like to come?
L I'd like to but I can't. I have to study for an exam.

If you come
near my house,
I'll call the police!

3 **D** Oh come on! You'll enjoy it, I promise!
I'll collect you from your house at 7.30.
L That's very kind of you, but really …

Thanks, but
I'd prefer to sit in
a box of fish!

4 **D** OK, I'll wait and we can go tomorrow.
L I'm sorry, but I'm meeting
some friends tomorrow.

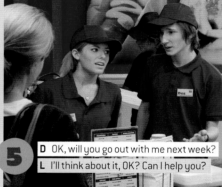

5 **D** OK, will you go out with me next week?
L I'll think about it, OK? Can I help you?

Oh great –
he wants to
ask me out!

6 **D** Are you doing anything tonight?
Cath Oh, nothing much. Why?

I'd love to!

7 **D** I'm going to see 'Bats' at the cinema. Would you like to come?
C Oh, I don't know …

8 **D** Oh, come on! It'll be fun!
C OK, I'll come!

How to accept and refuse invitations

G future forms V going out phrases P *yes* or *yes, but* intonation

A Read a comedy sketch

1 Look at the pictures in **A Date with Des** opposite. Answer the questions with a partner.
   1 What kind of place is it?
   2 What can you say about the people's age / appearance?

2 Read the story and answer the questions with a partner.
   1 Which girl would like to go out with Des?
   2 Do the girls say what they really think?
   3 Somebody you don't like asks you out. What do you say and what do you think? Think of some funny endings for these sentences!
   I'd like to, but …   I'd rather …   I'd prefer to …
   Example   I'd rather stay at home and do a Sudoku.

3 **12C.1▶** Look at **A Date with Des** with a partner. Guess where the audience will laugh. Write *L* in the text. Then listen and check.

B Grammar future forms

4 Look at the grammar box. Find the example sentences in **A Date with Des** and fill the gaps.

will (deciding, offering, promising)	OK, I'll _____ and we can go tomorrow. I'll _____ about it …
going to (talking about plans)	I'm going to _____ 'Bats'.
present continuous (talking about arrangements)	I'm meeting some _____ tomorrow. Are you doing anything _____?

5 Underline the correct words.
   1 I'll / I'm going to help you if you like.
   2 I'm looking / I'm going to look for a job next year.
   3 I think I'm having / I'll have a coffee, please.
   4 I'll never / I'm never going to leave you, I promise!
   5 We'll go / We're going to the cinema tonight.
   6 My holiday plans? I'm going to relax / I'm relaxing by the pool!

6 Ask and answer with a partner. Then decide if you're talking about plans, arrangements, or decisions.
   Example   What are you doing tonight?
   I'm going to watch TV. = plan
   I'm meeting my girlfriend at 7.00. = arrangement
   I don't know. I think I'll rent a DVD. = decision
   1 What are you doing tonight?
   2 Have you got any plans for the weekend?
   3 What are you doing for your next holiday?
   4 Have you got any career plans for the future?

More practice? **Grammar Bank** ≫ p.147.

C Listen and follow a conversation

7 How many different conversations can you find from *Start* to *Finish*? (You can move → or ↓)
   Example   Start – 1 – 2 – 3 – 7 – 11 – Finish

START	**1** Are you doing anything on Friday evening?	**2** Well, I'm a bit busy actually … Why?	**3** Do you fancy going for a drink?
4 What are you doing at the weekend?	**5** Oh, nothing much. Why?	**6** I'm having a party. Do you want to come?	**7** I'd rather not. I have to get up early in the morning …
8 Well, I'm going out on Saturday but I'm free on Friday.	**9** How about going out for dinner?	**10** Well, I'd prefer not to. I'm on a diet.	**11** Ok then. Maybe some other time …
12 Would you like to come round and see my photos?	**13** I'd love to. What time?	**14** Let's meet around 8 o'clock.	FINISH

8 **12C.2▶** Listen to two conversations and follow them in the maze in exercise 7.

9 Work with a partner. Act out two or three conversations from the maze in exercise 7.

D Pronunciation *'yes'* or *'yes, but'* intonation

10 **12C.3▶** Listen to the difference and repeat.
   Yes   I'd **love** to!
   Yes, but ☹ I'd **like** to … (but I can't)

11 **12C.4▶** Listen to the first part of each sentence. Which ending do you expect to hear, a or b?
   1 I'd like to come …
      a ☺ What time shall we meet?
      b ☹ but I can't, I'm afraid.
   2 That's very kind of you,
      a ☺ thanks. I'll come.
      b ☹ but really, I can't.
   3 That would be lovely …
      a ☺ Where shall we meet?
      b ☹ but I've got to study for an exam.
   4 Oh, I'd love to come …
      a ☺ What time does it start?
      b ☹ but I've arranged to go out with a friend.

12 **12C.5▶** Listen and check.

ABCD Put it all together

13 Work with a partner. Try to find a time when you can meet.
   Student A Look at the **diary** on ≫ p.131.
   Student B Look at the **diary** on ≫ p.135.

I can accept and refuse invitations.

Tick ✓ the line.   with a lot of help   with some help   on my own   very easily

Ideal World

In an ideal world
People would be kind
You could just be yourself
And nobody would mind
We'd all make friends
We wouldn't fall out
We wouldn't have to cry
And we wouldn't have to shout

People in an ideal world
Living in an ideal world

In an ideal world
People wouldn't fight
In an ideal world
Snakes wouldn't bite
We'd all live together
We'd all live in peace
We wouldn't need lawyers
And we wouldn't need police

People in an ideal world
Living in an ideal world

In an ideal world
We'd live and let live
In an ideal world
We'd learn to forgive
And we'd all get along
With the neighbours next door
And people would be friends
With their mothers-in-law

People in an ideal world
Living in an ideal world

Gallery of Dreams

'If we lived in an ideal world, there would be peace in Africa. It's terrible there now, because there are so many wars there and the people haven't got enough to eat. I think those countries are poor because of wars. If there was peace, they would become richer.'

'If I could be a famous person for one day, I'd be someone like Shakira, the pop singer from Colombia, because I'd really love to go on stage in front of thousands of people, you know. I think it would be really exciting, with everybody dancing and the lights and the music and everything.

Clare Russell

How to talk about imagined situations

G 2nd conditional

A Read and listen to a song

1 What do you think are the most important problems in the world today? Make a list with a partner.
Example war, not enough food, oil …

2 **12D.1▶** Listen and read **Ideal World** opposite. Does the song talk about any of your ideas from exercise 1?

3 Find words and expressions in the song with these meanings.
1 nice and friendly k*ind*____
2 stop being friends f_____ _____
3 speak very loudly s_____
4 opposite of war p_____
5 a law expert l_____
6 stop feeling angry f_____
7 have a good relationship g_____ _____
8 your husband or wife's mother m_____-____-_____

4 According to the song, what happens in the *real* world?
Example People aren't kind.

5 Think about five things to describe *your* ideal world and compare your ideas in groups. Are any of your ideas the same?

B Grammar 2nd conditional

6 **12D.2▶** Look at the pictures in **Gallery of Dreams** opposite. Read and listen to Clare's ideas. Match her imagined situations with two of the pictures.

7 Read this sentence and answer the questions.
If we lived in an ideal world, there would be peace in Africa.
1 Do we live in an ideal world?
2 Is there peace in Africa?

8 Match imagined situations 1–4 with imagined results a–d. Then complete the rule below.

imagined situation	imagined result
1 If there was peace,	a everybody would want to be my friend.
2 If I could travel anywhere,	b what would you do?
3 If I had a million dollars,	c poor countries would get richer.
4 If you didn't have to work,	d I'd visit India.

Use the _____ _____ tense in the imagined situation.
Use _____ + verb in the imagined result.

9 Complete the sentences.
1 If I _had___ more time, I _would learn_ Chinese. have / learn
2 If I _____ rich, I _____ my job. be / leave
3 If I _____ near the coast, I _____ to the beach every weekend. live / go
4 If we all _____ to work, the air _____ cleaner. walk / be
5 If I could _____ any job, I _____ a vet. choose / be

10 Answer these questions. Tell a partner.
1 If we lived in an ideal world, what would be different?
2 If you could be a famous person for one day, who would you be?
3 If you were an animal, what would you be?
4 If you could live anywhere in the world, where would you go?
5 If you had a time machine, where would you go in history?
6 If you had a chance to meet a celebrity, who would you choose?

More practice? **Grammar Bank** >> p.147.

C Listen for detail

11 Work with a partner. Describe the pictures in **Gallery of Dreams**.

12 You will hear Clare answering questions 3–6 in exercise 10. Look at the pictures in her **Gallery of Dreams** and guess what she will say.

13 **12D.3▶** Listen and check your guesses.

14 Listen again. What reasons does she give to explain her answers?

15 What pictures would be in your *gallery of dreams*? Tell a partner.

ABC Put it all together

16 Read the **questions** on >> p.132. Choose five questions and ask three students in the class about imagined situations and results.

17 Who gave the most interesting answers to exercise 16? Tell a partner.

I can talk about imagined situations.

Tick ✓ the line. with a lot of help | with some help | on my own | very easily

Writing An email conversation

A Read and follow an email conversation

1 Read and put the email conversation in order. One of the emails is not part of the conversation.

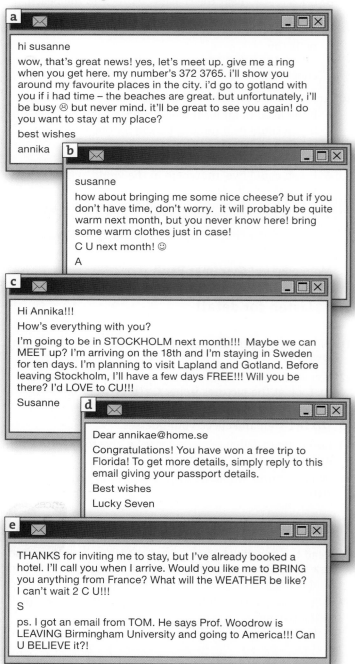

a

hi susanne

wow, that's great news! yes, let's meet up. give me a ring when you get here. my number's 372 3765. i'll show you around my favourite places in the city. i'd go to gotland with you if i had time – the beaches are great. but unfortunately, i'll be busy ☹ but never mind. it'll be great to see you again! do you want to stay at my place?

best wishes

annika

b

susanne

how about bringing me some nice cheese? but if you don't have time, don't worry. it will probably be quite warm next month, but you never know here! bring some warm clothes just in case!

C U next month! ☺

A

c

Hi Annika!!!

How's everything with you?

I'm going to be in STOCKHOLM next month!!! Maybe we can MEET up? I'm arriving on the 18th and I'm staying in Sweden for ten days. I'm planning to visit Lapland and Gotland. Before leaving Stockholm, I'll have a few days FREE!!! Will you be there? I'd LOVE to CU!!!

Susanne

d

Dear annikae@home.se
Congratulations! You have won a free trip to Florida! To get more details, simply reply to this email giving your passport details.

Best wishes

Lucky Seven

e

THANKS for inviting me to stay, but I've already booked a hotel. I'll call you when I arrive. Would you like me to BRING you anything from France? What will the WEATHER be like? I can't wait 2 C U!!!

S

ps. I got an email from TOM. He says Prof. Woodrow is LEAVING Birmingham University and going to America!!! Can U BELIEVE it?!

2 Choose subject lines for the emails from the ones below.
1 coming to Stockholm!   4 what to bring
2 you're the winner!   5 my phone number
3 weather?

3 Answer the questions.
1 Where does Annika live?
2 Where does Susanne live?
3 What is Susanne going to do?
4 What is Annika going to do?
5 Can you guess where Annika and Susanne met?
6 Can you guess what time of year it is?

B Think about style

4 People use many different styles in their emails. Who are these sentences about? Say *Annika* or *Susanne*.
1 She uses little pictures, for example, good news ☺, bad news ☹.
2 She doesn't use capital letters.
3 She uses a lot of exclamation marks (!).
4 She uses netspeak for example, *you* – U, *see* – C, *be* – B.
5 She writes important words in capital letters.

5 Here are some formal phrases. Find informal phrases with a similar meaning in the emails in exercise 1.
1 You can't predict the weather here.
   You never know, here.
2 Thank you very much for your invitation.
3 I look forward to seeing you.
4 Would you mind bringing …
5 Telephone me.
6 Would you like to meet?
7 If you don't mind me asking, will you be there?

6 Write an email to your partner with this subject line.
cinema Saturday?

7 Reply to your partner's email with this subject line.
how about Sunday?

AB Put it all together

8 Rewrite this email in informal language. Add a subject line at the top.

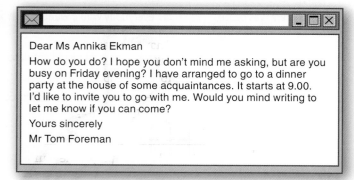

Dear Ms Annika Ekman

How do you do? I hope you don't mind me asking, but are you busy on Friday evening? I have arranged to go to a dinner party at the house of some acquaintances. It starts at 9.00. I'd like to invite you to go with me. Would you mind writing to let me know if you can come?

Yours sincerely

Mr Tom Foreman

I can make an email arrangement.

Tick ✓ the line.   with a lot of help   with some help   on my own   very easily

Unit 12 Review

A Grammar

1 Gerund or infinitive Match the beginnings and ends of the sentences.

1 [g] I hate
2 [ ] Ann and Joe have decided
3 [ ] Would you mind
4 [ ] I really enjoy
5 [ ] To pass the exam, he needs
6 [ ] She promised
7 [ ] I think
8 [ ] What are you planning

a to study more.
b listening is important.
c cooking Indian food.
d opening the window?
e to pay me back.
f to do in the holidays?
g ~~waiting for buses.~~
h to get married.

2 Indefinite pronouns Complete the text with these words.

anything   someone   everywhere
~~somewhere~~   nobody   everyone

I'm at a carnival in a small town [1] _somewhere_ in North East Brazil. There are drums and guitars and [2]_____ is playing a trumpet. [3]_____ is dancing. There are street decorations [4]_____. There are lots of food stalls and you can get [5]_____ from mangoes to meat balls. It's late at night but [6]_____ is going to sleep tonight!

3 Future forms Underline the correct verb form.

1 Would you like tea or coffee?
  I think I'm having / I'll have tea, please.
2 What have you arranged to do with Simon?
  We're meeting / will meet for a drink at 8 o'clock.
3 Sasha will have / 's going to have a baby in March.
  Oh. I didn't know she was pregnant.
4 Have you got any plans for next year?
  Yes, I'm learning / going to learn Chinese.

4 2nd conditional Make sentences from the words.

1 If we walk to work have cleaner air
  If walked to work, we'd have cleaner air .

2 If we have nothing to do people be bored
  _____ .

3 If the world be one country we speak the same language
  _____ .

4 If I have more time learn to play the trumpet
  _____ .

5 If you have a time machine where go?
  _____ .

B Vocabulary

5 Polite requests Find seven polite requests.

[1] Would	[2] Do	you	mind	if
you	[3] Could	you	[4] Would	I
mind	opening	help	you	sit
[5] Do	the	me?	mind	here?
you	window	[6] Could	waiting	here?
mind	please?	you	write	it
if	[7] Can	I	help	for
I	leave	now?	you?	me?

6 Festivals and celebrations Do the crossword. See the clues on >> p.132.

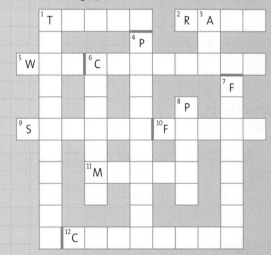

7 Going out Put the words in order to make sentences.

1 What doing are weekend you the at ?
  What are you doing at the weekend?
2 Saturday on I'm free
3 to not I'd prefer
4 to I'd love
5 dinner How out going about for?
6 much nothing Oh
7 bit actually a busy I'm

Pairwork

1D Put it all together
Student A Definitions!

1 What does *fan* mean?
  a It's an adjective. It means the same as cold. For example, It was a long, fan winter. ·
  b It's a noun. You use it to stay cool in hot weather. For example, I'm hot. Can you switch on the fan, please?
  © A fan is a follower, of a football team for example. For example, My brother's a Manchester United fan.

2 What does *jam* mean?
  a It's a kind of food with fruit and sugar. For example, He always has toast and jam for breakfast.
  b _____.
  c It's when there are too many cars and the traffic stops. For example, Sorry I'm late. I was in a traffic jam.

3 What does *green* mean?
  a _____.
  b It's a colour. For example, _____.
  c It's a place on a golf course. For example, the eighteenth green.

2A Exercise 13
Student A Places to visit

	how high	how long	how much
Eiffel Tower			
London Eye	140 m	30 mins	£12.50

2B Exercise 9
Student A Holiday picture

3D Put it all together
Student A Film Studio

Predict what these people are going to do and find the differences between your pictures.

  Dracula   Frankenstein   James Bond
  Kate and Leonardo   Laurel and Hardy

Example **A** In my picture, Dracula is going to eat an apple.
        B Oh. In my picture, he's going to fall.

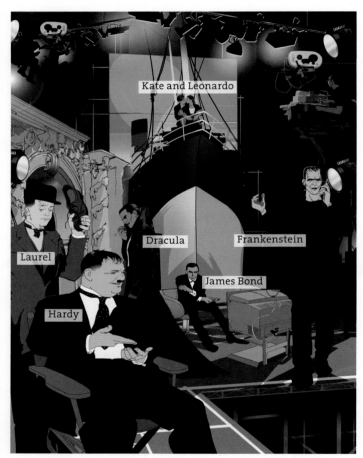

4B Put it all together
Student A The Kitchen

Describe what has happened and find the differences.

Example
A In my picture, the cups have fallen off the shelf.
B In my picture, the plates have fallen off the shelf.

4C Exercise 8
Lisa's house

4D Put it all together
Liar!

Play this game in small groups.

1 Write six *Have you ever … ?* questions.
   Example Have you ever lived abroad?

2 Take turns to ask your questions to one of the other players.

3 When somebody asks you a question, you can choose to tell the truth or to lie.

4 Listen to the other players' answers. Ask for more details and decide if they are lying.
   Example **A** Have you ever met a famous film star?
   B Yes, I have.
   A Who was it?
   B Samuel Jackson.
   A Oh yes? Where did you meet him? …

5A Put it all together
Student A What are they wearing?

Work with a partner. Ask your partner questions to find Maria, Charles, Elsa, and Tommy.

Example **A** What's Maria wearing?
   B She's wearing a blue cardigan.

5B Put it all together
Shopping Maze

START	B phones A. Arrange to meet.	A hasn't got enough money for shoes. B offers to lend it.
A meets B in street. Go for coffee.	Have coffee. A hasn't got any money. B pays.	A gets money from cash machine and offers to pay B back.
B needs to phone but has no mobile. A offers one.	B has lots of things to carry. A offers help.	It's raining. Go home. A's got a car.
A wants to try on shirt. B offers to hold bag.	It's raining. A offers umbrella to B.	FINISH

5D Put it all together
Rules

Student A B is visiting the place you made a list for in exercise 13. Tell B what the place is and explain the rules to him/her.

Student B You are visiting the place A made a list for in exercise 13. Ask questions about the rules.

Example **A** OK, we're in a youth hostel. These are the rules. First, you must be in bed by 11 o'clock.
   B 11 o'clock? Why?
   A Well, we turn off the lights at 11.00.

Pairwork

6A Put it all together

Caller cards

Choose any of these cards and 'phone' your partner.

> You phone Central College (726 8915). You want to speak to Ms Breen, Mrs Wilson, or Mr Nailer.

> You phone Central College (726 8915). You want to speak to Ms Green, Mrs Nilson, or Mr Mailer.

> You phone Kwikfix Garage (726 8515). You want to speak to Don or Tim.

> You phone Kwikfix Garage (726 8515). You want to speak to Dan or Tom.

Answerer cards *garage*

Choose any of these cards and answer the call from your partner.

> You are a secretary at Central College (726 8915). Here are some of the people in your department:
> **Ms Green** She's in class at the moment. Her class finishes at 17.15.
> **Mr Nailer** He's talking on the phone at the moment.
> **Mrs Wilson** She's free. You can put the caller through.

> You are a secretary at Central College (726 8915). Here are some of the people in your department:
> **Mr Mailer** He's on holiday at the moment. He's back on the 13th.
> **Ms Breen** She's talking on the phone at the moment.
> **Mrs Nilson** She's in class at the moment. Her class finishes at 9.50.

> You work at Kwikfix Garage (726 8515). You work with two other people:
> **Don** He's busy at the moment.
> **Tom** He's in the office. You can put the caller through.

> You work at Kwikfix Garage (726 8515). You work with two other people:
> **Tim** He's busy at the moment.
> **Dan** He's gone home. He starts work at 9.15 in the morning.

6B Put it all together
Different forms of transport

Choose two forms of transport. Make notes about the obligations connected with them. Use some of the ideas below.

wear a helmet   wear a seat-belt   go through security
wait for a long time   smoke   eat   drive   buy petrol
get a licence   buy a ticket   book a seat   *your ideas*

Example Cycling   have to   wear helmet
                      don't have to get licence
                      mustn't   ride on pavement

Use your notes to say which form of transport you prefer.

Example **A** I prefer driving to travelling by bus. You can smoke if you want, and you don't have to wait for a long time.
B Yes, but you have to buy petrol ...

6C Put it all together
Student A Picture story

6D Exercise 12
Student A What were they doing?

Ask and answer questions about the pictures with your partner. Ask about Benny, Jerry, Gareth, and Ernest and Frances.

Example **A** What was Benny doing when the police arrived?
B He was talking on the phone.

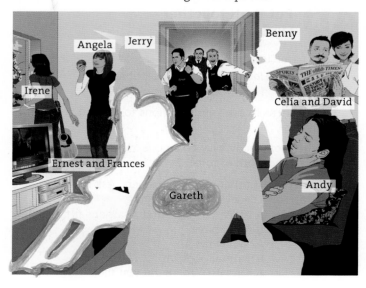

7B Exercise 12
Team A Jobs Quiz

What do you call...

a doctor who does operations? (surgeon)
the room where hospital patients sleep? (ward)
a person who makes and mends shoes? (cobbler)
a person who makes things with wood? (carpenter)
a thing which you use to cut wood? (saw)
a building where a farmer keeps animal food? (barn)

You can ask for clues:

What's the first letter?
And the second letter?
How many letters are there in the word?
Is the word similar in our language?
Is the word _____ in our language?

7B Put it all together
Describing a job

Answer these questions about your job (or a job that you'd like to have).

1 What's your occupation?
2 Who do you work with or for?
3 What place or places do you spend time in at work?
4 What are the things that you use in your job?

Write definitions to explain your answers to the questions.
Example I'm a motorcycle courier. That's a person who delivers packages on a motorcycle. I work with ...

7C Exercise 11
Student A Office

8B Put it all together
Describing objects

8D Put it all together
Options

1 New computer ...

desktop? | laptop?

2 Language lessons ...

Latin? | Chinese?

3 Holiday ...

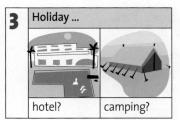

hotel? | camping?

4 New home ...

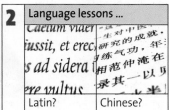

house? | flat?

5 Journey ...

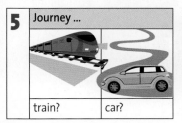

train? | car?

6 Birthday dinner ...

restaurant? | home?

7 Music lessons ...

piano? | guitar?

8 New pet ...

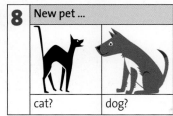

cat? | dog?

Pairwork

9C Put it all together
Lifestyle Pyramids

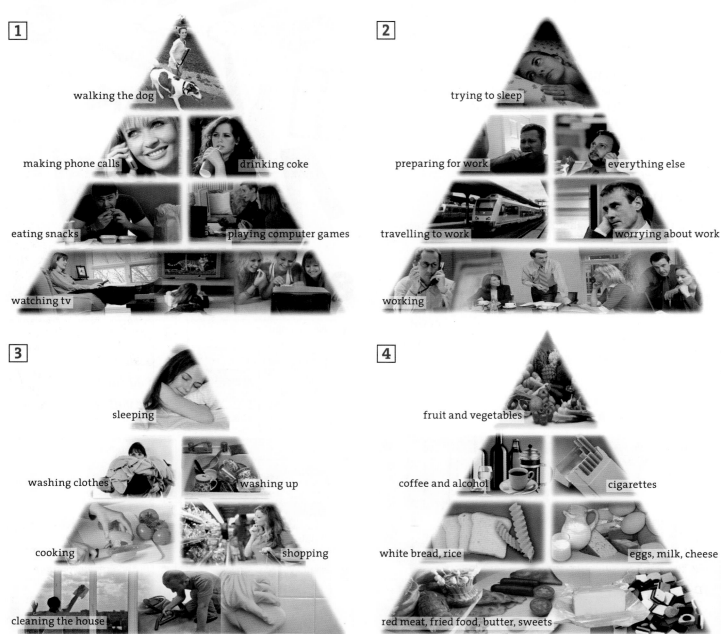

1

walking the dog

making phone calls

drinking coke

eating snacks

playing computer games

watching tv

2

trying to sleep

preparing for work

everything else

travelling to work

worrying about work

working

3

sleeping

washing clothes

washing up

cooking

shopping

cleaning the house

4

fruit and vegetables

coffee and alcohol

cigarettes

white bread, rice

eggs, milk, cheese

red meat, fried food, butter, sweets

10C Put it all together
Flight to Athens

Role card 1 Erik / Erika

You're travelling for work. You're a tour guide and you work for a company called *Sun Tours*. You've worked for them since 2007. Before that, you worked for *Golden Holidays*. You've been a tour guide for seven years. You're from Denmark, but you've lived in Brussels, Belgium, since 2001. You enjoy painting and reading detective novels. Your boyfriend / girlfriend is from Manchester, in England.

Role card 2 Manuel / Manuela

You're Mexican and you're on holiday in Europe. You've been in Europe since April. You've visited Britain and Belgium. You're going to tour Greece with a company called *Golden Holidays*. You've lived in Houston, Texas, in the USA, since 2002. You've been a full-time writer for five years. You write detective novels. You're married and your wife / husband works for a company called *Techno-Sonic*.

Role card 3 Josef / Josefina

You're travelling for work. You're a translator and you're travelling with a group of tourists from Prague in the Czech Republic. The group is going to tour Greece with a company called *Golden Holidays*. You've been a translator since you left university in 2004. You've lived in Prague since 1999. You speak Czech, Greek, English, and Italian. Sometimes you work at the European Union in Brussels.

Role card 3 Justin / Justine

You're on holiday with a tour company called *Sun Tours*. You're from Manchester but you've lived in London for six years. You work for a company called *Techno-Sonic*. The company makes intercom systems. You've worked there since 2003. You often travel for work – last year you went to Brussels, Copenhagen, and Houston. You're married. Your husband / wife is from Prague, in the Czech Republic.

10R Exercise 5
Crossword clues

Across

3 What time does the plane _____ in Beijing?
5 Please _____ your seat-belts.
6 Don't open your seat-_____ until the plane has stopped.
7 The captain has switched on the seat-belt _____.
8 Have you been _____ customs yet?
10 You wait for your plane in _____.
12 You have to sit down for _____ and landing.

Down

1 Which _____ does the plane leave from?
2 Have you been through _____ control yet?
4 I bought your present in the _____-free shop.
6 Please _____ the plane through gate 53.
9 Can I have a _____ near the front of the plane, please?
11 Customs officers sometimes _____ you to open your bags.

11C Exercise 10
Personality test

Results key

More **a** and **b** answers = you think from the **head**
More **c** and **d** answers = you think from the **heart**

11C Exercises 13 to 18
Problem page

Choose three problems from below and ask for advice. Whose advice is best?

Example **A** I've got too much work. I'm stressed and I've got a headache.
B Why don't you try to relax? Ask your boss to give you some time off ...

1 You've got too much work. You're stressed and you've got a headache.	2 You live with your parents. You haven't got enough money to get a flat.	3 Your wife / husband smokes and you want her/him to stop.
4 Your girl / boyfriend has had a few beers. Now she / he wants to drive home.	5 You've studied English for 5 years but you still can't speak it.	6 You're planning to travel in Africa but you're worried about your health.
7 You've decided to go out more because you haven't got many friends. But where?	8 Your girl / boyfriend wants to get married. You are not sure that you love her/him.	9 Every day, your son asks for money. You don't know what he wants it for.
10 Your friend wants to be a guitarist but he can't play the guitar very well.	11 Every time you decide to do something, your wife / husband disagrees.	12 Your daughter is pretending to study, but really she's playing computer games.

12C Put it all together
Student A Diary

	lunchtime	early evening	night
Monday	Free		Cinema with friends
Tuesday	Meet Jackie		Prepare for exam
Wednesday	Free	Free	Concert
Thursday	Free		Free
Friday	Free	Pack bags	Going away
Saturday	Away for the weekend		
Sunday			

Invite your partner out. Try to find a time when you are both free.

Example **A** Are you doing anything on Monday lunch time?
B Yes, I've arranged to have lunch with Peter. How about Monday early evening?

Pairwork

12D Put it all together
'Imagined situations' questions

If you could give a message to the whole world, what would you say?

If your house was on fire, what would you take?

If you had three wishes, what would they be?

If you were a world leader, what would you do?

If you could change one thing about yourself, what would it be?

If someone gave you 50 million pounds, what would you do?

If you could do any job, what would you like to do?

If you could go on holiday anywhere in the world, where would you go?

If you could start your life again, what would you do differently?

If you had 24 hours to live, what would you do?

If you found 1,000 euros on the floor, what would you do?

12R Exercise 6
Crossword clues

Across
1 A group of people in New Guinea, for example.
2 A competition to find the fastest.
5 A fight between countries.
6 A formal celebration – a wedding for example.
9 A large model of a person or a thing.
10 A party with a lot of food.
11 Folk musicians play folk _____ .
12 A very big street party.

Down
1 At the Goroka Show, everybody wears their _____ costumes.
3 Most traditions started many years _____ .
4 People walking and dancing along the street behind decorated lorries.
6 A set of clothes.
7 A traditional celebration.
8 Opposite of 5 across.

green fields

1D Put it all together
Student B Definitions!

1 What does *light* mean?
   a It's an adjective. It's the opposite of dark. For example, It isn't light enough to read.
   b It's a noun. You use it to see at night. For example, It's dark. Can you switch on the light, please?
   c It's a verb. It means the same as run. For example, She was late so she lighted all the way to school.

2 What does *fly* mean?
   a _____
      _____ .
   b It's a small insect. For example, The kitchen was dirty and there were flies everywhere.
   c It's a verb. It means to travel by air. For example, I never go by plane because I hate flying.

3 What does *room* mean?
   a It's a part of a house. For example, _____
      _____ .
   b _____
      _____ .
   c It means the same as space. For example, There isn't enough room for two cars in their garage.

2A Exercise 13
Student B Places to visit

	how high	how long	how much
Eiffel Tower	320 m	about 1 hour	€10.70
London Eye			

2B Exercise 9
Student B Holiday picture

Spain
Santiago
Madrid

3D Put it all together
Student B Film Studio

Predict what these people are going to do and find the differences between your pictures.

Dracula   Frankenstein   James Bond
Kate and Leonardo   Laurel and Hardy

Example   **A** In my picture, Dracula is going to eat an apple.
           B Oh. In my picture, he's going to fall.

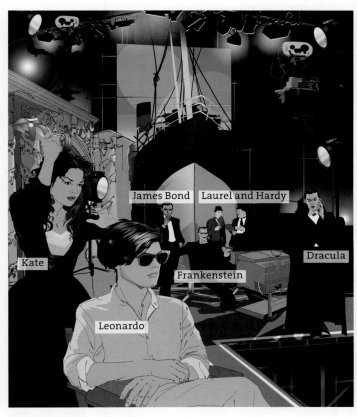

4A Put it all together
In a hotel

Do a hotel role play. Take turns to be A and B. Have a conversation at the reception desk, and then two or three phone conversations.

You are a hotel guest. Look at the ideas below to help you. Decide what you would like.

guest – ask for / about
– a single room for two nights
– a sandwich and a cup of tea
– an alarm call at 6 a.m.
– someone to fix the TV

4B Put it all together
Student B The Kitchen

Describe your picture and find the differences.

   Example
   A In my picture, the cups have fallen off the shelf.
   B In my picture, the plates have fallen off the shelf.

5A Put it all together
Student B What are they wearing?

Work with a partner. Ask your partner questions about Anna, Jamie, Kate and Claire, and Holly.

   Example   **A** What's Maria wearing?
            B She's wearing a blue cardigan.

Pairwork

6C Put it all together
Student B Picture story

6D Exercise 12
Student B What were they doing?

Ask and answer questions about the pictures with your partner.
Ask about Irene, Angela, Andy, and Celia and David.

Example **A** What was Benny doing when the police arrived?
B He was talking on the phone.

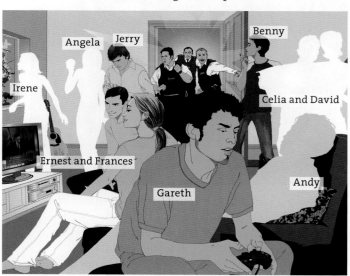

7B Exercise 12
Team B Jobs Quiz

What do you call...

a small machine which you use to fix papers together? (stapler)
a person who moves things on and off ships? (docker)
a person who makes jackets and suits? (tailor)
a shop where you buy fish? (fishmonger's)
a machine which lifts heavy things? (crane)
the room where the captain works on a ship? (bridge)

You can ask for clues:

What's the first letter?
And the second letter?
How many letters are there in the word?
Is the word similar in our language?
Is the word _____ in our language?

7C Exercise 11
Student B Office

134

9A Exercise 9
Healthy, tasty, or *easy* questionnaire

Now count your score. Do you have more *healthy, tasty* or *easy* answers?

Question	Healthy	Tasty	Easy
1	a	b	c
2	c	a	b
3	b	c	a
4	b	a	c
5	a	c	b
6	a	b	c
7	c	b	a
8	b	a	c
9	a	b	c
10	a	b	c
Your total			

12A Exercise 8
Situations

1 You're in a bank and you haven't got a pen. Ask the person next to you.
2 You've lost your money. Ask a stranger for your bus fare home.
3 You're on the train and it's too hot. Ask another passenger to open the window.
4 You're on holiday. You want somebody to take a photo of you with your camera.
5 You're waiting in line at the airport check-in. You're late. Ask the person at the front of the queue to let you in first.

12C Put it all together
Student B Diary

	lunchtime	early evening	night
Monday	Lunch with Peter	Free	Free
Tuesday	Free		Free
Wednesday		Play football	Free
Thursday	Free		Play cards
Friday	Meet Sophie	Free	Free
Saturday	Free	Free	Cinema with Jackie
Sunday	Free		

Invite your partner out. Try to find a time when you are both free.

Example **A** Are you doing anything on Monday lunch time?

B Yes, I've arranged to have lunch with Peter. How about Monday early evening?

Grammar Bank

1A possessive 's

Use the possessive 's to say who something belongs to.

after a singular noun	apostrophe + s	Anna's surname is Conde. My dog's name is Rover.
after a plural noun that doesn't end with s	apostrophe + s	Our children's names are Sue and Rod.
after a plural noun that ends with s	apostrophe	My brothers' names are Ruy and Edson.

>> Now go to **exercise 1.1** to practise.

1B present simple -s / -es endings

Use s/es to make the third person singular.

most verbs	+ s	I / You / We / They start He / She / It starts
verbs ending with o / s / sh / ch / x	+ es	I / You / We / They finish He / She / It finishes
verbs ending with y	y + ies	I / You / We / They study He / She / It studies

>> Now go to **exercise 1.2** to practise.

1C *be* and *do* in questions

	be	*do*
present	Are you the new boss? How is Holly?	Do you like your job? Where does Anna work?
past	Were you late for work? Where was Justin?	Did they go to work? Which watch did he buy?

>> Now go to **exercise 1.3** to practise.

present simple and present continuous

Use the present simple to talk about things that happen sometimes or all the time, and things that are generally true.

+	–	?
I / You / We / They go to work.	I / You / We / They don't go to work.	Do I / you / we / they go to work?
He / She / It goes to work.	He / She / It doesn't go to work.	Does he / she / it go to work?

Use the present continuous to talk about what's happening now.

+	–	?
I'm driving to work.	I'm not driving to work.	Am I driving to work?
You / We / They're driving to work.	You / We / They aren't driving to work.	Are you / we / they driving to work?
He / She / It's driving to work.	He / She / It isn't driving to work.	Is he / she / it driving to work?

>> Now go to **exercise 1.4** to practise.

subject pronouns and possessive adjectives

Use subject pronouns with verbs.
Use possessive adjectives with nouns.

subject pronouns	I	you	he	she	it	we	they
possessive adjectives	my	your	his	her	its	our	their

>> Now go to **exercise 1.5** to practise.

1.1 Right or wrong? Tick (✓) or correct the sentences.
Example My friends name is Jane. *My friend's name is Jane.*

1 Her parents' names are Luis and Eva.
2 Mr Jones is my brothers teacher. They don't like him.
3 Our teacher's name is Marcus.
4 Guy Ritchie is Madonnas husband.
5 Their names are Mike and Joe.
6 That's Mrs Smiths childrens school.

1.2 Complete the text with the verbs in the correct form.
Duane _'s_ be an English teacher. He ¹_____ teach in a university in Libya. He ²_____ work from 10 a.m. to 4 p.m. every day. When he ³_____ finish work, he ⁴_____ walk home and ⁵_____ have dinner. In the evenings, he ⁶_____ watch football on TV or he ⁷_____ study Arabic. At the weekend, he ⁸_____ go to an Internet café and ⁹_____ read his emails.

1.3 Complete the questions. Use the correct form of *be* or *do*.
Example What _is_ his mobile phone number?

1 _____ these your children?
2 Who _____ your teacher last year?
3 _____ Peter work in an office?
4 What _____ she doing now?
5 _____ you like your job?
6 _____ you send Tom an email last week?
7 Where _____ they yesterday?
8 Which _____ your desk?

1.4 Complete the sentences. Put the verb in the present continuous or the present simple.
Example Who is Anna _speaking_ to now? speak

1 Justin's lazy. He _____ much work. not / do
2 _____ you _____ an email now? write
3 I _____ on Saturdays. not / work
4 Justin _____ the computers every day. check
5 Shh! I _____ to the teacher. listen
6 Where _____ they _____ from? come
7 We _____ now. not / study
8 She _____ to work by bus. go

1.5 Right or wrong? Tick (✓) or correct the sentences.
Example This is Hans. His my secretary.
         This is Hans. He's my secretary.

1 Are these your books?
2 Its is a very good dictionary.
3 Mr Crawley is we English teacher.
4 My birthday is in June.
5 Him watches football a lot.
6 What's they address?
7 How old is she?
8 What does him do?

2A *How* questions

Use *How* + adjective ... ? to ask for information about price, age, distances, etc.

How questions	answers
How long is the journey to Snowdon?	It's an hour.
How old is the Colosseum in Rome?	It's 2,000 years old.
How far is the London Eye from Big Ben?	It's 500 metres.
How high is the Eiffel Tower?	It's 320 metres tall.
How much is an Adult ticket?	It's £21.00.

>> Now go to **exercise 2.1** to practise.

2B adjective order

Use adjectives to describe people and things.

Put an adjective before a noun.	A pretty village. A white village.
Put adjectives of *opinion* before adjectives of *fact*.	A pretty white village.

>> Now go to **exercise 2.2** to practise.

2C comparative and superlative adjectives

Use comparative + *than* to compare two things.

one-syllable adjectives	+ *er* or *r*	old > older large > larger
one-syllable adjectives that end vowel + consonant	double the consonant + *er*	big > bigger hot > hotter
adjectives that end *y*	*y* + *ier*	heavy > heavier pretty > prettier
adjectives with more than one syllable	*more* + adjective	famous > more famous interesting > more interesting
irregular adjectives		good > better bad > worse

Use *the* + superlative to compare more than two things.

one-syllable adjectives	*the* + *est* or *st*	old > the oldest large > the largest
one-syllable adjectives that end vowel + consonant	*the* + double the consonant + *est*	big > the biggest hot > the hottest
adjectives that end *y*	*the y* + *iest*	dry > the driest pretty > the prettiest
adjectives with more than one syllable	*the most* + adjective	famous > the most famous interesting > the most interesting
irregular adjectives		good > the best bad > the worst

>> Now go to **exercise 2.3** to practise.

2D past simple

Use the past simple to talk about actions that are finished.

+	–	?
I / You / He / She / It / We / They visited Spain.	I / You / He / She / It / We / They didn't visit Spain.	Did you / we / they visit Spain? Where did he / she / it visit?

short answers	
Yes, I / you / he / she / it / we / they did.	No, I / you / he / she / it / we / they didn't.

• For a list of irregular verbs, see >> p.148.

Spelling note: *-ed* endings

most verbs	+ *ed*	visit > visited
verbs that end *e*	+ *d*	live > lived
verbs that end consonant + *y*	*y* + *ied*	study > studied
one-syllable verbs that end one vowel + one consonant	double the consonant + *ed*	stop > stopped

>> Now go to **exercises 2.4 and 2.5** to practise.

2.1 Complete the *how* questions.

Example **A** How _far_ is New York from Moscow?
　　　　　B It's 7,557 kilometres.

1 **A** How _____ is the Great Wall of China?
   B Over 2,000 years.
2 **A** How _____ is the journey to Rome?
   B It's two hours.
3 **A** How _____ is a return ticket to Brighton?
   B It's £24.
4 **A** How _____ is the London Eye?
   B It's 135 metres.

2.2 Put the green words in the correct order to complete the sentences.

Example They're visiting a _lovely little village_ . (village little lovely)

1 This is an _____. (interesting castle old)
2 Portugal has some _____. (beaches long beautiful)
3 We live in a _____. (village English pretty)
4 It's a _____. (sunny beautiful day)
5 It was a _____. (town dirty horrible)
6 There are some _____ in Greece. (ruins old amazing)

2.3 Complete the sentences. Use a comparative or superlative form. Add other words you need.

Examples Is France _the biggest_ country in Europe? big
　　　　　　The USA is _bigger than_ Britain. big

1 July was _____ month this year. wet
2 Tokyo is _____ Sydney. expensive
3 Do you think hot weather is _____ cold weather? bad
4 What are _____ places to visit? good
5 Yesterday was _____ today. warm
6 What's _____ place in the world? dry
7 I think the car is _____ way to travel. comfortable
8 Spring is _____ winter. nice

2.4 Write the sentences in the past.

Example Bernie lives in Prague. Bernie _lived_ in Prague.

1 I have coffee for breakfast.
2 Jaime gives me a t-shirt for my birthday.
3 We buy souvenirs on holiday.
4 Clara doesn't like her present.
5 We go to Cuba in the summer.
6 Does it snow in winter?
7 Petra doesn't want a carpet.
8 Do they get up at seven o'clock?
9 The journey takes an hour.
10 Jen buys the train tickets on the Internet.

2.5 Put the words in order to make questions.

Example he holiday did his enjoy ? *Did he enjoy his holiday?*

1 poster that get did where you ?
2 Chile did what do they in ?
3 buy you souvenir a did ?
4 castle did the visit they ?
5 to she did when Sydney go ?

3A *like doing, would like to do*

Use *like* + verb + *-ing* to talk about things you like / dislike now.

+	–	?
I / You / We / They like swimming. He / She / It likes swimming.	I / You / We / They don't like swimming. He / She / It doesn't like swimming.	Do I / you / we / they like swimming? Does he / she / it like swimming?

short answers	
Yes, I / you / we / they do. Yes, he / she / it does.	No, I / you / we / they don't. No, he / she / it doesn't.

Use *would like* + infinitive to talk about things you want / don't want to do in the future.

+	–	?
I / You / He / She / It / We / They 'd like to play tennis.	I / You / He / She / It / We / They wouldn't like to play tennis.	Would I / you / he / she / it / we / they like to play tennis?

short answers	
Yes, I / you / we / they would. Yes, he / she / it would.	No, I / you / we / they wouldn't. No, he / she / it wouldn't.

>> Now go to **exercises 3.1 and 3.2** to practise.

3B *can, could* (ability)

Use *can* for ability in the present. Use *could* for ability in the past.

+	–	?
I / We / He can swim. I / We / He could swim.	I / We / He can't swim. I / We / He could swim.	Can I / we / he swim? Could I / we / he swim?

short answers	
Yes, I / we / he can. Yes, I / we / he could.	No, I / we / he can't. No, I / we / he couldn't.

- Use an infinitive without *to* after *can / could*.
- We use *be able to* to talk about ability, e.g. *I was able to swim when I was four.* However, this is less common than *can / could*.

>> Now go to **exercise 3.3** to practise.

3C *could* (possibility)

Use *could* to talk about past ability and present possibility.

ability in the past	I could read when I was three. He could run fast when he was a young boy.
possibility in the present	We could go to the cinema tonight. We could play tennis.

>> Now go to **exercise 3.4** to practise.

3D *going to* (prediction)

Use *going to* to predict the future, based on things happening now.

+	–	?
I'm going to cry.	I'm not going to cry.	Am I going to cry?
You / We / They're going to start work.	You / We / They aren't going to start work.	You / We / They going to start work?
He / She / It's going to fall.	He / She / It isn't going to fall.	Is he / she / it going to fall?

short answers	
Yes, I am.	No, I'm not.
Yes, you / we / they are.	No, you / we / they aren't.
Yes, he / she / it is.	No, he / she / it isn't.

>> Now go to **exercise 3.5** to practise.

3.1 Put the words in order to make sentences and questions.
Example dancing my like doesn't father
My father doesn't like dancing.

1 like I to Antarctica visit 'd
2 walking Jim in forest like the does ?
3 try like we to canoeing wouldn't
4 like swimming they the sea don't in
5 to language a like she learn would foreign ?
6 would drive Helen like a to sports car
7 mountain they go 'd to like climbing
8 like on you watching do sport TV ?

3.2 Right or wrong? Tick (✓) or correct the sentences.
Example They'd like to swimming in the sea.
They'd like to swim in the sea.

1 Ivan likes go scuba-diving at weekends. C
2 I'd like to buy a sports car. C
3 Do you like playing tennis? —
4 They'd like to going surfing. —
5 We like meet new people. C
6 Would Jana like to come climbing? C
7 She wouldn't like to trying snowboarding. —
8 Alicia doesn't like learn new sports. C

3.3 Complete the sentences with *can, can't, could,* or *couldn't*.
Example *Could* you speak French when you were three?

1 My sister can't swim. She's frightened of the water.
2 Steve could play the piano quite well when he was six.
3 He can speak English but he can't speak German.
4 Look! You can see the sea from here.
5 He couldn't dive when he was a child, but he can now.
6 The homework was difficult. We couldn't do it.
7 Can your children ski?
8 Millie could dance well when she was young.
9 My brother could play chess as a child, but I couldn't

3.4 Match 1–5 with a–e. Are the pairs of sentences about ability or possibility?

1 [c] Can you run fast? *ability*
2 [e] Could you swim well when you were younger? A
3 [b] There's nothing on TV. P
4 [d] What would you like for dinner? P
5 [a] Could you speak Greek before you started school? A

a Yes, I was born in Athens.
b You could watch a DVD.
c No, I'm very slow.
d We could have pizza.
e No, I couldn't. I didn't like going in the water.

3.5 Complete the sentences with the correct form of *going to*. Some answers are negative.
Example This is a great film. You *'re going to* enjoy it.

1 They're still packing their bags. _____ they _____ miss their train?
2 They're in love. I think they _____ get married.
3 It's a lovely day. I _____ need an umbrella.
4 Katrin looks terrible. _____ she _____ be alright?
5 It's very cold. I think it _____ snow.
6 Bruno's running very slowly. He _____ win the race.
7 Hurry up. You _____ be late for school.

4A *can / could* (requests)

for things	Can / Could I have **a cup of tea**, please?
for permission to do something	Can / Could I **open** the door, please?
for someone to do something	Can / Could you **help** me, please?

- *Could I / Could you … ?* is more polite and formal than *Can I / Can you … ?*

>> Now go to **exercise 4.1** to practise.

4B present perfect with a present result

Use the present perfect to talk about something which happened in the past, but has important results now.

past action	present result
I / You / We / They've washed the cups.	The cups are clean now.
He / She / It's broken the computer.	The computer doesn't work now.

- To form the present perfect, use *have / has* + a past participle.
- For a list of irregular past participles, see >> p.148.

>> Now go to **exercises 4.2 and 4.3** to practise.

4C present perfect ⊞⊟⍰

+ ('ve = have, 's = has)	– (haven't = have not, hasn't = has not)	?
I / You / We / They've fed the dog.	I / You / We / They haven't fed the dog.	Have I / you / we / they fed the dog?
He / She / It's washed the towels.	He / She / It hasn't washed the towels.	Has he / she / it washed the towels?

short answers	
Yes, I / you / we / they have. Yes, he / she / it has.	No, I / you / we / they haven't. No, he / she / it hasn't.

>> Now go to **exercises 4.4** to practise.

4D present perfect with *ever / never*

Use *ever* and *never* with the present perfect for emphasis.

ever + present perfect question	= at any time before now	Have you ever travelled abroad?
never + present perfect positive form	= at no time before now	We've never been to Canada.

>> Now go to **exercise 4.5** to practise.

4D present perfect and past simple

Use the present perfect to talk about an event which happened at some time before now. It isn't important exactly when it happened.

Use the past simple to talk about an event which happened in the past and is not connected to now.

present perfect	past simple
I've been to London this year. He's never played chess. We've visited Dublin twice.	I went to London last week. He didn't play chess yesterday. We went to Dublin twice last year.

Use expressions of unfinished time with the present perfect, and expressions of finished time with the past simple.

expressions of unfinished time	expressions of finished time
before now, today, this week, in my life	last summer, yesterday, last week, in 2001, when I was five

>> Now go to **exercise 4.6** to practise.

4.1 Order the words to make requests.
  Example you make can our please beds
  Can you make our beds, please?
  1 we double have please could a room
  2 you can me tomorrow please phone
  3 towels please you change can my
  4 a have sandwich cheese I could please
  5 drink have a please I can
  6 another please of bottle I can have shampoo

4.2 Write the past participles of the verbs in the correct box.
~~work~~ swim put stop break live listen think do like fall study burn decide

regular	irregular
worked	

4.3 Match 1–7 with a–g.
  1 ⟦c⟧ Someone has opened the window.
  2 ☐ I've lost my keys.
  3 ☐ We've washed the cups.
  4 ☐ He's broken his finger.
  5 ☐ I've switched on the radio.
  6 ☐ You've burnt the toast.
  7 ☐ She's dropped the eggs.

  a You can hear music.
  b They're on the floor.
  c ~~It's cold in here.~~
  d I can't open the door.
  e They're clean.
  f It smells terrible.
  g He can't write.

4.4 Complete the sentences. Use these verbs in the present perfect.
~~buy~~ not do cook not pay drink not send invite put take
  Example Lisa's parents *have bought* a new car.
  1 You _____ your homework!
  2 _____ you _____ all your friends to the party?
  3 They _____ dinner. It's on the table.
  4 _____ she _____ the cheese in the fridge?
  5 She _____ the gas bill.
  6 He _____ all the fruit juice.
  7 I _____ an email to my friend.
  8 Lisa _____ the dog for a walk.

4.5 Add *ever* or *never* to the sentences in the correct places.
                    never
  Examples I've ⸝ had flu.
                           ever
             Have you ⸝ been skiing?
  1 Have you broken your arm?
  2 We've stayed in a hotel.
  3 She's eaten Japanese food.
  4 Has Jamie worked in an office?
  5 I've used a computer.
  6 Have they lived abroad?

4.6 Right or wrong? Tick (✓) or correct the sentences.
  Example We have been to Corfu last year on holiday.
            We went to Corfu last year on holiday.
  1 We have seen a great film last night.
  2 Did she do the homework yesterday?
  3 **A** Did you lose your passport?
    B Yes. Can you help me look for it?
  4 They haven't bought their house in 1997.
  5 He didn't study French when he was at school.
  6 My team won two matches this year.
  7 I have been to the sports centre twice on Tuesday.
  8 Has he worked in Spain before?

5A adverbs of degree

Use adverbs of degree to say how much an adjective is true.

	+/−	+++/−−−
neutral 😐 + positive adjectives	These jeans are quite comfortable.	Lara's dress is very pretty. This shirt is really nice.
negative 😞 + negative adjectives	Pete's a bit lazy. Those clothes are a little boring.	These trousers are too expensive.

- The opposite of *too* is *enough*.
- Use an adverb of degree before an adjective, but use *enough* after an adjective.

>> Now go to **exercises 5.1 and 5.2** to practise.

5B *will / shall* (offers and promises)

Use *will / shall* to make offers and promises.

promises	*will / won't* + verb	I won't forget to post your letters. We'll send you a postcard. You won't find a cheaper computer.
offers	*will / shall* + verb	I'll open the door for you. Shall I lend you some money?

- Use *will / won't* + infinitive without *to*.
- Use *will / won't* in a statement and *shall* in a question.

>> Now go to **exercise 5.3** to practise.

5C phrasal verbs with *on* and *off*

Many phrasal verbs have two parts, a *verb* and an *adverb*. For example: *try on*; *try* is the verb and *on* is the adverb.

phrasal verb + noun	verb + noun + adverb verb + adverb + noun	Can I try this dress on? Can I try on this dress?
phrasal verb + pronoun	verb + pronoun + adverb not verb + adverb + pronoun	Can I try it on? Can I try on it?

>> Now go to **exercise 5.4** to practise.

5D *must / mustn't*

Use *must / mustn't* to talk about rules. *Must* means it is important to do something.

Mustn't means it is important **not** to do something.

must + verb	You *must pay* for things before you leave the shop.
mustn't + verb	He *mustn't eat* in the shop.

- Use *must / mustn't* + infinitive without *to*.

>> Now go to **exercise 5.5** to practise.

object pronouns

Use a subject pronoun to say who / what does an action.
Use an object pronoun to say who / what receives the action.

subject pronouns	object pronouns	
I	me	He doesn't like me.
you	you	I'll meet you.
he	him	Can you hear him?
she	her	Listen to her.
it	it	I sent it yesterday.
we	us	Can you help us?
they	them	Don't drop them.

- Use an object pronoun in the place of a noun and after a verb. *Can you hear John?* > *Can you hear him?*

>> Now go to **exercise 5.6** to practise.

5.1 Order the words to make sentences.
Example jeans tight are these too
These jeans are too tight.

1 cheap are jackets the quite
2 trainers enough big aren't these
3 bit are bright a colours the
4 little is shop this expensive a
5 dress really that nice is
6 very coat is old my

5.2 Match 1–5 with a–e

1 [c] Are those sandals comfortable?
2 ☐ Do you like the jeans in the shop window?
3 ☐ Does this skirt look good on me?
4 ☐ Is this sweater big enough for John?
5 ☐ This suit is quite cheap.

a Yes, it really suits you.
b Yes, but it isn't a very good fit.
c ~~Not really. They're a little big for my feet.~~
d No, it's too small. He needs a bigger size.
e They're really nice, but they're very expensive.

5.3 Complete the dialogues with *will*, *shall*, or *won't* and the green words.
Example **A** Oh dear! I haven't got enough money.
B Don't worry. *I'll pay* with my credit card.   I/pay

1 **A** Have you talked to your friends?
B Don't worry! _____ anybody your secret.   I/not tell
2 **A** I'm really hungry.
B _____ you a sandwich?   I/make
3 **A** Remember to phone me when you arrive in New York.
B _____. we/not forget
4 **A** Mum! I can't do this homework.
B _____ you, if you like.   I/help
5 **A** _____ those books for you?   I/carry
B Yes, please.

5.4 Put the green words into the sentence in the correct place.
Example Did you turn the TV?   on
Did you turn on the TV? OR Did you turn the TV on?

1 Did you try them?   on
2 Shall I the heating on?   turn
3 She put on.   it
4 I took my sunglasses.   off
5 He turned off.   it
6 Why don't you off the light?   turn

5.5 Complete the office rules with *must* or *mustn't*.
Example You *must* keep your desk clean.

1 We start work at 9 o'clock, so you mustn't be late.
2 If you want to smoke, you must go outside.
3 You mustn't leave bags on the floor. It's dangerous.
4 When you leave the office you must turn off the lights.
5 You mustn't use the office phone to call your friends.
6 It's important to look smart so you must wear a suit.

5.6 Underline the correct words.
Example **A** I like that dress.
B Why don't you buy it / them?

1 **A** Jane's trousers are nice.
B Oh, I don't like it / them.
2 **A** Are you going out now?
B Yes, I'll see you / me later.
3 **A** Has Peter arrived?
B I haven't seen him / he.
4 **A** How are we going to get to the airport?
B My brother will take we / us.

6B have to / don't have to

Use *have to* / *don't have to* to talk about obligation.
Use *don't have to* to show it's not necessary to do something.

+	–	?
I / You / We / They have to start work now.	You / We / They don't have to start work now.	Do I / you / we / they have to start work now?
He / She / It has to start work now.	He / She / It doesn't have to start work now.	Does he / she / it have to start work now?

>> Now go to **exercise 6.1** to practise.

6C past simple: irregular verbs

regular verbs	end with -*ed* (see **2D**)	change > changed	open > opened
		close > closed	print > printed
irregular verbs		be > was / were	lose > lost
		drive > drove	run > ran

• For a list of irregular verbs, see >> p.148.

>> Now go to **exercises 6.2** to practise.

6D past continuous

Use the past continuous to talk about actions in the past which were in progress at a particular time.

+	–	?
I / He / She / It was sitting in the garden.	I / He / She / It wasn't sitting in the garden.	Was I / he / she / it sitting in the garden?
You / We / They were playing tennis.	You / We / They weren't playing tennis.	Were you / we / they playing tennis?

short answers	
Yes, I / he / she / it was.	No, I / he / she / it wasn't.
Yes, you / we / they were.	No, you / we / they weren't.

>> Now go to **exercise 6.3** to practise.

6D past continuous and past simple

Use the past continuous and the past simple together to describe two things that happen at the same time in the past.
Use the past continuous to describe a longer action which started first, and was in progress.

past continuous	past simple
I was driving in the rain	and I crashed.
Were they having dinner	when you arrived?

>> Now go to **exercise 6.4** to practise.

6E clause linking with *when*

Use *when* to join actions in the past continuous and past simple.

I was waiting for the train. It started to rain.	I was waiting for the train when it started to rain. When it started to rain, I was waiting for the train.

>> Now go to **exercise 6.5** to practise.

past time expressions

Use a past time expression with a past tense to say when something happened.

last night / month / Friday / weekend	I saw a car accident last month.
yesterday, yesterday morning	They caught the criminal yesterday.
the day before yesterday the week before last	Somebody knocked down Miss Setter the day before yesterday.
two days / a week / a month / a year ago	We bought this car two years ago.

>> Now go to **exercise 6.6** to practise.

6.1 Complete the sentences. Use *have to*, *don't have to*, or *mustn't*.
Example You _have to_ arrive at the station early.

1 You can't buy a ticket on the train, so you _have to_ buy it before you travel.
2 You _don't have_ book a seat, but it's a good idea.
3 You _mustn't_ smoke on the train.
4 You _mustn't_ talk to the train driver.
5 You can buy food before you travel, so you _don't have_ buy it on the train.
6 There is a place for large bags, so you _don't have to_ carry them with you all the time.
7 When the trains are busy you sometimes _have to_ stand.
8 You _mustn't_ put your feet on the seats.

6.2 Write the infinitive form of these verbs.
Example broke _break_

1 brought _bring_
2 drove _drive_
3 heard _hear_
4 made _make_
5 put _put_
6 ran _run_
7 rang _ring_
8 sat _sit_
9 took _take_
10 think _think_

6.3 Complete the sentences. Use the verbs in the past continuous.
Example We _were waiting_ for the bank manager. wait

1 What _were_ you _doing_ do
2 She _wasn't talking_ to her friend. not / talk
3 They _____ for a train. wait
4 _Was_ he _driving_ his new car? driving
5 We _weren't playing_ computer games. not / play
6 I _was cycling_ along Bridge Road. cycle
7 You _weren't working_ not / work
8 _Was_ the dog _running_ in the park? run

6.4 Underline the correct tense, past continuous or past simple.
I had a terrible day yesterday. First of all, I was dropping / (dropped) my coffee when I (was making) / made breakfast. Then, when I [2](was walking) / walked to work, it [3]was starting / (started) to rain. I was late for work and I was wet. Then my computer [4]was breaking / (broke) when I [5](was using) / used it. At lunchtime I [6](was eating) / ate my sandwich in the park, when a cyclist [7]was crashing / (crashed) into me!

6.5 Join the sentences with *when*.
Example I had an accident. I was driving to the hospital.
I had an accident when I was driving to the hospital. OR
When I was driving to the hospital, I had an accident.

1 We got lost. We were going to London.
2 It started to snow. I was cycling home.
3 The phone rang. They were leaving the house.
4 She was working in a bank. She met her future husband.
5 You were running along the High Street. I saw you.

6.6 Which event happened first? Look at the past time expressions, and order the events.

a ☐ There was an accident last night.
b ☐ We got married two months ago.
c ☐ The day before yesterday someone stole my purse.
d ☐ Yesterday morning she lost her keys.
e ☐ The week before last they were on holiday.
f ☐ 1 He passed his driving test last year.
g ☐ She started her new job at the bank three days ago.

7B defining relative clauses

Use defining relative clauses to say which person, thing, or place you are talking about.

for people	who / that	Fred's the man who cleans the school. A dentist is someone that takes care of people's teeth.
for things	which / that	A watch is a thing which shows the time. A dictionary is a book that tells you the meanings of words.
for places	where	This is the office where I work.

- When you use a relative pronoun (who / which / that / where) you don't need to use a subject or object pronoun (he / they / it / her / them, etc.).

≫ Now go to **exercises 7.1 and 7.2** to practise.

7C can / can't (permission)

Use *can* to give permission (to say it's OK to do something).

Use *can't* (= cannot) to refuse permission (to say it isn't OK to do something).

+	–	?
I / You / We / They can borrow the bike.	I / You / We / They can't smoke here.	Can I / you / we / they go out?
He / She / It can use my mobile phone.	He / She / It can't park here.	Can he / she / it use your car?

Short answers	
Yes, I / you / we / they can.	No, I / you / we / they can't.
Yes, he / she / it can.	No, he / she / it can't.

- Use an infinitive without *to* after *can*.

≫ Now go to **exercises 7.3 and 7.4** to practise.

7D because, so

| Use *because* to explain why something happens. | I was late for work because I missed the bus. |
| Use *so* to explain what the result is. | I missed the bus so I was late for work. |

≫ Now go to **exercises 7.5** to practise.

prepositions of place: in / on / at

in	for an enclosed space (e.g. rooms, towns, continents)	My brother works in a big hotel. The children are in the playground.
	for private cars and taxis	He went to work in his car.
on	for surfaces (e.g. rivers, mountains) and lines (e.g. paths, coasts, roads)	We've got a villa on the Mediterranean coast. We had a lovely holiday on the River Thames.
	for public transport (e.g. planes, trains, buses, boats)	She got a job on a ship. I don't like travelling on buses.
at	for a particular point, or building	We met at the station. Wait at the reception desk.
	with *home* and *work*	They're at work. He's working at home.
	to say where people study	He's a pupil at Park School. My daughter is at university.

≫ Now go to **exercise 7.6** to practise.

7.1 Match 1–8 with a–h.

1 [e] A chemist is a person
2 ☐ A canteen is a place
3 ☐ A mechanic is someone
4 ☐ A bus is a vehicle
5 ☐ A postman is someone
6 ☐ A camera phone is a phone
7 ☐ An airport is a place
8 ☐ A classroom is a place

a that mends cars.
b where planes arrive and leave.
c which carries people around town.
d that takes pictures.
e who sells medicines.
f where you have lessons.
g who brings letters to your house.
h where you eat in a school.

7.2 Underline the correct word.
Example He's the man that / he mended our car.

1 This is the house where / which we had a party.
2 He's the man who / he teaches my children.
3 Our college has a machine that / who makes hot drinks.
4 A nurse is someone that / where works in a hospital.
5 What do you call a shop where / which you buy newspapers?
6 French is one of the subjects that / it we study at school.

7.3 Order the words to make sentences and questions.
Example photocopy can a make I ?
     Can I make a photocopy?

1 have a can today we lunch break long ?
2 can't you in office smoke the
3 jeans you at wear work can ?
4 the use can't you computer boss'
5 classroom in we eat our can't

7.4 Complete the library rules with *can / can't* and a verb from the box.

✓ read make do	✗ play eat bring write

Example You *can't write* in the library books.

1 You _____ photocopies on the library photocopier.
2 You _____ food in the library.
3 You _____ newspapers in the library.
4 You _____ computer games at the library.
5 You _____ your homework here.
6 You _____ animals into the library.

7.5 Complete the sentences using *because* or *so*.
Example I was ill *so* I stayed at home.

1 Your boss was angry because you were late this morning.
2 The roads aren't very good, so Rajendra uses a bicycle to deliver the mail.
3 I joined a travel agency because I can get cheap holidays.
4 Sua doesn't sign her name, because she can't write.
5 It's the weekend, so we don't have to work today.
6 He's learning English because he wants to work in the USA.

7.6 Right or wrong? Tick (✓) or correct the sentences.
Example Don't run on the corridor.
     Don't run in the corridor.

1 I don't like travelling at busy trains.
2 My sister's studying Maths at university.
3 Their house is in the south coast.
4 Meet me in the coffee machine.
5 Holly and Anna work in an office.
6 They got on the taxi and sat down.

8A possessive pronouns

Use possessive pronouns to talk about possessions.

subject pronouns	possessive adjectives	possessive pronouns
I	my bag	Her bag is black, so she's borrowing mine.
you	your drink	That's not my drink, it's yours.
he	his umbrella	My umbrella is broken, so Jake lent me his.
she	her coat	I want a coat that's similar to hers.
we	our car	Mike and Stella's car is larger than ours.
they	their flat	Our flat is too small for a party, so we're using theirs.

≫ Now go to **exercises 8.1 and 8.2** to practise.

8B present passive

Use the present passive when you don't know who does an action, or when the action is more important than the person who does it.

	subject	verb		object
active	I/We/You/They	see		me/him/her/it/you/us/them.
	He/She/It	sees		me/him/her/it/you/us/them.
passive	I	'm	seen	
	He/She/It	's	seen	
	We/You/They	're	seen	

• To form the present passive, use *am/is/are* + a past participle.

≫ Now go to **exercises 8.3** to practise.

8C will (prediction)

Use *will/won't* to make predictions about the future.

+	–	?
I/You/He/She/It/ We/They'll win the race.		Will

short answers	
Yes, you/we/they will.	No, you/we/they won't.
Yes, he/she/it will.	No, he/she/it won't.

• Use an infinitive without *to* after *will* or *won't*.

≫ Now go to **exercise 8.4** to practise.

8D first conditional

Use first conditionals to talk about possible future actions and their results.

If you give me your email address,	I'll write to you.
If he doesn't know how to use a computer,	he won't get a good job.
You'll save money	if you don't go out tonight.
The camera won't work	if you drop it in the water.

• Use *if* + present simple for a possible future action, and *will/won't* for its result.
• When a conditional sentence begins with an *if* clause, use a comma to separate the two clauses.

≫ Now go to **exercises 8.5 and 8.6** to practise.

8.1 Replace the underlined words with a possessive pronoun.
Example Are these your books? *Are these yours?*

1 This camera is good but their camera is better. *But theirs is better*
2 Are these History books your books? *Are those History books is yours?*
3 Which computer is her computer, the desktop or the laptop?
4 He left his phone at home so I lent him my phone. *so I lent him mine phone*
5 Our car is red, their car is blue.
6 This isn't Mike's coat, that's his coat on the chair.

8.2 Underline the correct words.
Example It isn't your bag, it's my /mine.

1 Their/Theirs house is bigger than our /ours.
2 Our/Ours children go to that school.
3 My/Mine pen doesn't work. Can I borrow your /yours?
4 Her/Hers computer is broken but his/her isn't.
5 Are they your /yours?
6 What's his/hers phone number?

8.3 Complete the sentences. Use the present passive of the verbs.
Example Coffee _is grown_ in Africa and South America. grow

1 The coffee beans _____ from the coffee plant. take
2 The beans _____ to factories. drive
3 They _____ to make coffee. use
4 The coffee _____ into boxes. put
5 The boxes _____ to other countries. send
6 Cups of coffee _____ in shops and cafés. sell
7 Coffee _____ all over the world. drink

8.4 Make sentences and questions with *will/won't*.
Example they/pass/the/exam ? *Will they pass the exam?*

1 everyone/have/a computer.
2 houses/be/more expensive.
3 there/be/more cars/on the roads?
4 there/not/be/diseases or hospitals.
5 we/not/have/TVs.
6 everything/be/very expensive?
7 we/have/school/on/the Internet.
8 he/go/to university?
9 I/not/get married.
10 more people/work/at home?

8.5 Match 1–7 with a–g to make first conditional sentences.

1 [e] I won't delete this file
2 ☐ This window will close
3 ☐ If you don't go to the interview,
4 ☐ We'll call a computer technician
5 ☐ If you download that song,
6 ☐ I'll send you a message
7 ☐ If you lend me your laptop,

a if you tell me your email address.
b you won't get the job.
c I'll listen to it.
d if we get a virus.
e ~~if you need it for work.~~
f I won't break it.
g if you click on that button.

8.6 Correct the sentences.
Example I'll call the police if someone will steal my money.
I'll call the police if someone steals my money.

1 If you'll buy your ticket on the Internet, you'll save money.
2 He'll be sick if he ate all the biscuits.
3 If she not go to the meeting, her boss will be angry.
4 I have time, I'll phone you.
5 If we don't have any money, we won't to go out.
6 If their car has problems again, they are calling a mechanic.
7 He doesn't pass his exam if he doesn't study.
8 You'll be tired if you won't go to bed.

9A countable and uncountable

Countable nouns are nouns that you can count. They can be singular or plural.

Uncountable noun are nouns that you can't count. They can't be singular or plural.

	countable nouns	uncountable nouns
+	I want a mango. I want some sausages. I want three apples.	I want some coffee.
–	I don't want a mango. I don't want any sausages.	I don't want any milk.
?	Do you want a mango? Do you want any sausages?	Do you want any sugar?

• Some nouns can be countable or uncountable but the meaning is different. *A potato, some potatoes, some (mashed) potato.*

>> Now go to **exercise 9.1** to practise.

9B quantifiers

Use quantifiers to say how much or how many of something there is.

	+	–	?
plural countable nouns	There are a lot of sausages. There are a few sausages. There are none.	There aren't many sausages.	How many sausages are there?
uncountable nouns	There's a lot of sugar. There's a little sugar. There's none.	There isn't much sugar.	How much sugar is there?

• Use *a lot of* with plural countable and uncountable nouns. Only use *of* before a noun.

>> Now go to **exercise 9.2** to practise.

9B sequencers

Use sequencers to show the order of a series of actions.

first	First, we had the soup.
then next after that	Then, we had a salad. Next, we had chicken and vegetables. After that, we had a dessert.
finally	Finally, we had coffee.

• *then, next,* and *after that* have similar meanings.

>> Now go to **exercise 9.3** to practise.

9C *should* (advice)

Use *should/shouldn't* to give and ask for advice.

+	– (shouldn't = should not)	?
I/You/He/She/It/ We/They should sleep eight hours a night.	I/You/He/She/It/ We/They shouldn't go out every night.	Should I/you/he/ she/it/we/they do more exercise?

short answers	
Yes, you/we/they should.	No, you/we/they shouldn't.
Yes, he/she/it should.	No, he/she/it shouldn't.

>> Now go to **exercise 9.4** to practise.

9D *should/must*

Use *should/shouldn't* and *must/mustn't* to give advice.

You should wash the fruit before you eat it.	You shouldn't eat your food quickly.
You must wash you hands before you eat.	You mustn't put food on the floor.

• Use *must/mustn't* to give very strong advice.

>> Now go to **exercise 9.5** to practise.

9.1 Underline the correct words.
Example Can I have some /<u>a</u> baked potato for dinner?

1 She usually has a / an boiled egg for breakfast.
2 Tom's making some toast / toasts.
3 Can I have some / a cup of coffee?
4 We're going to buy some / two fruit.
5 You need a / an onion for this recipe.
6 Have you got any / some milk?
7 I'm having a sandwich / sandwiches for lunch.
8 There's one / some sausage in the fridge.

9.2 Complete the sentences. Use these words.
~~much~~   many   a few   a little   none   a lot (x2)

Example **A** How _much_ oil is there?
       B About a litre.

1 **A** How _____ tomatoes have you got?
  B Two or three.
2 **A** She bought _____ of strawberries.
  B Yes, She's going to make strawberry jam.
3 **A** Have we finished all the soup?
  B Yes, we have. There's _____ left.
4 **A** How much sugar does he have in his coffee?
  B Just _____. He's on a diet.
5 **A** Are there any biscuits in the cupboard?
  B There are _____. We need to get some more.
  A Can I have one, please?
6 **A** We've got four kilos of potatoes.
  B That's _____! We won't eat them all.

9.3 Put the sentences in the correct order 1–5.
a ☐ Finally, you put the egg in an egg cup and eat it.
b ☐ Then you cook the egg for three minutes.
c ☐ After that, you take the egg out of the water.
d ☐ Next you put the egg into the boiling water.
e ☐1☐ To make a boiled egg, first you boil some water in a pan.

9.4 Match 1–8 with a–h.
1 ☐f☐ He hasn't got much money.
2 ☐ I want to lose weight.
3 ☐ Should I make some coffee?
4 ☐ She's not a good student.
5 ☐ The children are very tired.
6 ☐ Should I buy this shirt?
7 ☐ There aren't any clean cups.
8 ☐ He doesn't feel very well.

a You shouldn't eat chocolate.
b No, you've had four cups today.
c No, it's too expensive.
d He shouldn't go to work.
e She should work harder at school.
f ~~He should get a job.~~
g You should do the washing up.
h They shouldn't go to bed late.

9.5 Rewrite the sentences. Use *You + should/shouldn't* or *must/mustn't*.
Example It's very bad manners to throw food.
       You mustn't throw food.

1 It's very bad manners to start eating before everyone is ready.
2 It isn't polite to smoke during meals.
3 It's polite to offer to help with the washing up.
4 It's very bad manners to touch someone else's food.
5 It isn't very polite to eat with your mouth open.
6 In some countries, it's very bad manners to eat with your hands.

10B present perfect with *yet*, *just*, and *already*

Use *yet* to say that something hasn't happened up to now, or to ask about something that you expect to happen.

Use *just* to say something has happened, when the action is very recent.

Use *already* to say something has happened before now, or to say it happened earlier than you thought.

yet	+ question OR + negative	**A** Have you had breakfast yet? **B** No, not yet. I haven't had a shower yet.
just	+ positive sentence	I've just made some coffee. They've just got up.
already	+ positive sentence	She's already been for a run. They've already gone to work.

- Use *yet* at the end of a sentence or question.
- Use *just* and *already* before the main verb.

≫ Now go to **exercises 10.1 and 10.2** to practise.

10C present perfect with *for* or *since*

Use the present perfect + *for/since* to talk about the duration of actions and states that began in the past and continue in the present.

for	**A** How long have you worked here? **B** I've worked here for six years.
since	**A** How long have you lived in this house? **B** We've lived in this house since 1995.

- Use *for* + a period of time (*two hours, four weeks, six years, a long time*, etc.) that continues until now.
- Use *since* + a point in the past (*1995, four o'clock, last year, four years ago*) to say this is when the action started.

≫ Now go to **exercises 10.3** to practise.

10D used to

Use *used to* to talk about things that happened many times in the past, but which don't happen now.

Use *used to* to talk about states which were true in the past, but which aren't true now.

used to + verb	I used to work in a hotel.
	You used to be a flight attendant.
	He / She / It used to travel a lot.
	We used to live in Mexico.
	They used to have a red car.

- Don't use *used to* to talk about single events in the past. *People used to travel by horse.* BUT *Nicolas-Joseph Cugnot invented the first car in 1769.*

≫ Now go to **exercise 10.4** to practise.

10D prepositions of direction

Use prepositions of direction, e.g. *along, across,* and *between,* to describe movement. *They travelled along the coast. They sailed across the Mediterranean. The Alps are between Italy and Switzerland.*

≫ Now go to **exercise 10.5** to practise.

10.1 Order the words to make sentences and questions.
Example they their haven't yet bags packed
They haven't packed their bags yet.

1 been the we travel agent's to 've just
2 plane tickets they the have yet bought ?
3 a I already 've taxi booked
4 found his 's he just passport
5 've you already twice been Spain to
6 her changed she yet has money ?

10.2 Complete the conversation with *yet, just,* or *already*.
A Hi Mum, we've *just* arrived in the centre of Paris.
B Have you seen the Eiffel Tower [1]_____?
A Yes, we've [2]_____ seen it. We drove past it in the taxi.
B What's your hotel like?
A Oh, we haven't found a hotel [3]_____.
B Where are you going to stay?
A Justin's [4]_____ gone to the tourist office to book a hotel.
B What are you doing while he's gone?
A I'm in a café and I've [5]_____ finished lunch.
B Well have a good time and send me a postcard.
A Oh, I've [6]_____ sent one. I posted it before lunch.
B But you haven't seen anything interesting [7]_____!

10.3 Right or wrong? Tick (✓) or correct the sentences.
Example We've studied English for January.
We've studied English since January.

1 They've been in Paris for two days.
2 I haven't heard from Jamie for a week ago.
3 This building has been here since many years.
4 The photocopier has been broken since two or three days.
5 They've been married since 1999.
6 He's been at the airport for 3 o'clock.
7 I haven't seen Marco since we left university.
8 Sandra hasn't played the piano since a long time.

10.4 Complete the sentences. Use *used to* and these verbs.
travel ~~be~~ take buy have like cost
Example There *used to be* two airports in London, but now there are four.

1 They _____ to New York every month, but they don't now.
2 It _____ 10 hours to get to Berlin, but the trains are faster now.
3 We _____ a villa in the South of France but then we sold it.
4 Plane tickets _____ a lot of money, but now they're cheaper.
5 She _____ flying, but she prefers to travel by train now.
6 I _____ tickets at a travel agent's, but now I use the Internet.

10.5 Underline the correct words.
Example The ferry sails between / across Greece and Egypt.

1 We walked across / into the bridge to the other side.
2 They walked all the way around / along the island.
3 She cycled from North Africa up / down to South Africa.
4 The dog ran across the road and into / in the park.
5 We walked along / into the river to reach the village.
6 I have to drive along / through the city to get home.
7 He was walking in / out the direction of the beach.
8 They visited the museum, then went around / back to their hotel.

11B action or state verbs

action verbs can be used with continuous tenses	Miriam's talking to Sonia. Wafa and Nawal are taking photos.
state verbs are not usually used with continuous tenses	David likes art and music. Phil and Julie have three children.

Some common state verbs are:

verbs connected with thinking and opinions	believe, feel, hate, know, like, love, prefer, think, understand, want
verbs connected with the senses	appear, feel, look, seem, smell, sound, taste

>> Now go to **exercise 11.1** to practise.

11C verb + infinitive (with *to*)

I sometimes forget to switch off my computer.
You're planning to buy a house.
She didn't want to go to the party.
They decided to have a meal out.

• Use an infinitive with *to* after some verbs.

>> Now go to **exercise 11.2** to practise.

11D past passive

Use the past passive when you don't know who did an action, or when the action was more important than the person who did it.

active	passive
I took …	I was taken by taxi.
You / We / They woke up …	You / We / They were woken up by a noise.
He / She / It visited …	He / She / It was visited by friends.

• To make the past passive, use *was/were* + a past participle.
• Use *by* with the passive to say who or what did an action.

>> Now go to **exercises 11.3** to practise.

11E sentence adverbs

Use sentence adverbs to show how a sentence connects to the rest of a text.
Use *clearly* to say that something is true.
Use *however* to add a contrast.
Use *finally* to add your last point.

clearly	Global warming is a big problem. Clearly, we have to find a solution.
however	The hotel was expensive. However, it wasn't very good.
finally	I was ill for two weeks. Finally, I decided to go and see the doctor.

>> Now go to **exercise 11.4** to practise.

imperatives

Use imperatives to tell a person or people what to do or what not to do.

+	–
Take one pill every four hours. Go and see the doctor.	Don't drive. Don't give the pills to children.

• To make the imperative, use (*don't* +) the infinitive of the verb without *to*.

>> Now go to **exercise 11.5** to practise.

11.1 Right or wrong? Tick (✓) or correct the sentences.
Example He isn't understanding the teacher.
　　　　　He doesn't understand the teacher.

1　They're smiling at their mother.
2　Are you liking this painting?
3　Are you knowing my cousin Sam?
4　This dinner is tasting great.
5　They're standing outside John's house.
6　He's seeming very tired.
7　He's wearing a suit.
8　I'm thinking this is a nice song.

11.2 Complete the sentences with *to* and a verb.
　　help　take　learn　call　work　turn　visit　~~marry~~　get
Example She promised _to marry_ him.

1　We decided _____ a taxi to the airport.
2　There was a lot of work, but he refused _____ me.
3　I wanted _____ you but I lost your mobile number.
4　He's hoping _____ his friends in Berlin.
5　This computer is useless. I want _____ a new one.
6　I'd really like _____ Arabic.
7　They agreed _____ together.
8　Did you forget _____ off the heating?

11.3 Complete the text. Put the verbs into the past passive.
Two paintings _were stolen_ (steal) from a museum. They
[1]_____ (take) by a museum employee. The theft
[2]_____ (not/plan) very well. It [3]_____ (film)
on a security camera and the manager of the museum
recognized his employee. The police [4]_____ (call) and
the thief [5]_____ (catch). The paintings [6]_____
(return) to the museum, and the thief [7]_____ (send)
to prison.

11.4 Complete the sentences. Use *however*, *clearly*, and *finally*.
Example They don't listen. They don't do their homework.
　　　　　Clearly they won't pass the exam.

1　First I wrote to them, then I called them. _____, I decided to go to their office.
2　More than 50,000 people live in this town but we only have one dentist. _____ this is a big problem.
3　I've written to them several times. _____, no one has replied to me yet.
4　When I phoned, they told me that I had to go down to the office in person. _____, when I went there the office was closed!
5　You're not listening. _____, you're not interested.

11.5 Match 1–8 with a–h.
1　[d] Follow this advice
2　[ ] Don't go
3　[ ] Drink plenty
4　[ ] Stay in bed
5　[ ] Turn the
6　[ ] Have some
7　[ ] Phone the doctor if
8　[ ] Take some

a　heating on and stay warm.
b　to work if you're ill.
c　chicken soup.
d　~~if you catch flu.~~
e　you start to feel worse.
f　and sleep until you feel better.
g　medicine.
h　of water.

12A verb + gerund (-ing) and verb + infinitive

verb + infinitive (+ to)	agree, decide, hope, need, learn, offer, plan, promise, refuse, want, would like	They agreed to help. She promised to come.
verb + (-ing)	enjoy, finish, go, hate, mind, like, love, practise	I go skiing in winter. I've finished cooking.

>> Now go to **exercises 12.1 and 12.2** to practise.

12B indefinite pronouns

Use indefinite pronouns when you don't know exactly who, what, or where.

	one	one	all	none
people	someone	anyone	everyone	no one
	somebody	anybody	everybody	nobody
things	something	anything	everything	nothing
places	somewhere	anywhere	everywhere	nowhere

- Use *someone*, *somebody*, *something*, and *somewhere* in positive sentences.
- Use *anyone*, *anybody*, *anything*, and *anywhere* in questions and negative sentences.
- Use *no one*, *nobody*, *nothing*, and *nowhere* in short negative answers, or in sentences with a positive verb.

>> Now go to **exercise 12.3** to practise.

12C future forms

Use *will* for deciding, promising, and offering.
Use *going to* to talk about plans.
Use *going to* to predict the future, based on what you can see.
Use the present continuous to talk about arrangements.

will	going to	present continuous
We'll do the washing up.	She's going to look for a job.	They're leaving next week.
I won't be late.	It isn't going to rain today.	We aren't going to the party.
Shall I help you?	Are they going to fly to Rome?	Are you staying in tonight?

- Use *shall* instead of *will* in questions with *I* and *we*. *Shall we meet at the station? Shall I bring my coat?*

>> Now go to **exercise 12.4** to practise.

12D second conditional

Use *if* + past simple for an imagined situation, and *would* + a verb for its imagined result.

If we moved to a new country,	we'd* go to New Zealand. * 'd = would
If he was rich,	he would buy a boat and sail to Africa.
They'd buy that house	if it was cheaper.

- The *if* clause can go before or after the *would* clause.
- When a conditional sentence begins with an *if* clause, use a comma to separate the two clauses.

>> Now go to **exercise 12.5** to practise.

prepositions of time: *in, on, at*

at	at 7.30, at the weekend, at night, at breakfast, at Christmas
on	on Saturday morning / evening, on 12th August
in	in the afternoon, in January, in (the) spring, in 2001
no preposition	tonight, tomorrow, last week, this morning, every day

>> Now go to **exercise 12.6** to practise.

12.1 Complete the sentences with the correct form of the verbs.
lend ~~see~~ go pass invite speak live
Example I'd like _to see_ that film.
1 They didn't want _____ Ramsay to the party.
2 Would you mind _____ me your pen?
3 I practise _____ English with my friend.
4 Does she enjoy _____ in Australia?
5 He needs _____ his driving test before he buys a car.
6 Where did they decide _____ for their holiday?

12.2 Order the words to make sentences.
Example the getting up hates morning he early in
    He hates getting up early in the morning.
1 buy planning they a to 're house
2 the you to go to meeting agree did ?
3 to learning she drive is ?
4 the love I in running park
5 refusing Toby come is us to with

12.3 Replace the underlined words with an indefinite pronoun.
Example <u>All of the people</u> enjoyed the festival.
    Everyone enjoyed the festival.
    OR *Everybody enjoyed the festival.*
1 I've looked <u>in all the places</u>.
2 There was <u>no place</u> to stay.
3 There was <u>no food</u> in the fridge. It was empty.
4 <u>None of the people</u> likes that teacher.
5 Is there <u>a place</u> we can have a coffee?
6 The children ate <u>all the food</u>.
7 We didn't see <u>a person</u>.

12.4 Underline the correct words.
Example A <u>Shall</u> / Will I make a cup of coffee?
    B That's a good idea.
1 A Have they made any plans for the holiday?
    B Yes, they're going to / 'll sail to Ireland.
2 A What are you doing / will you do tonight?
    B Nothing.
3 A Do you think it's going to snow / snowing today?
    B No, the sky's blue, and it's too warm.
4 A Did you arrange to see Emily?
    B Yes, we're meeting / we'll meet tomorrow.
5 A Have you decided what to do?
    B No, I'm deciding / I'll decide tomorrow.
6 A Why are you cleaning the house?
    B My parents are coming / will come tonight.

12.5 Complete the sentences with the correct form of the verbs.
Example If I _get_ to work earlier, I _'ll do_ more work.
    get / do
1 If I _____ more work, my boss _____ me more money.
    do / give
2 If he _____ me more money, I _____ you to marry me.
    give / ask
3 If I _____ you to marry me, you _____ 'yes'. ask / say
4 If you _____ 'yes', we _____ married. say / get
5 If we _____ married, we _____ children. get / have

12.6 Right or wrong? Tick (✓) or correct the sentences.
Example They went on holiday on Easter.
    They went on holiday at Easter.
1 I called him 6 p.m. but he was out.
2 We had a big party on Christmas Day.
3 Shall we meet on the afternoon?
4 There's an exam next week.
5 I'm going to finish my homework at the morning.
6 Romania joined the European Union in 2007.

Irregular verbs

verb	past simple	past participle
be	was	been
	were	
break	broke	broken
buy	bought /bɔːt/	bought /bɔːt/
can	could /kʊd/	been able to
come	came	come
cut	cut	cut
do	did	done
draw	drew	drawn
drink	drank	drunk
drive	drove	driven /'drɪvn/
eat	ate	eaten
find	found	found
forget	forgot	forgotten
get	got	got
give	gave	given
go	went	gone
		been
have	had	had
hear	heard /hɜːd/	heard /hɜːd/
know	knew /njuː/	known
learn	learnt	learnt
	learned	learned
leave	left	left
lose	lost	lost

verb	past simple	past participle
make	made	made
meet	met	met
put	put /pʊt/	put /pʊt/
read	read /red/	read /red/
ring	rang	rung
run	ran	run
say	said /sed/	said /sed/
see	saw /sɔː/	seen
sell	sold	sold
send	sent	sent
sing	sang	sung
sit	sat	sat
sleep	slept	slept
speak	spoke	spoken
spend	spent	spent
stand	stood /stʊd/	stood /stʊd/
swim	swam	swum
take	took /tʊk/	taken
tell	told	told
think	thought /θɔːt/	thought /θɔːt/
understand	understood	understood
wake up	woke up	woken up
wear	wore	worn
write	wrote	written /'rɪtn/

« Look at the verb column. Cover the past simple and past participle columns and test yourself.

Pronunciation

Vowel sounds

/æ/ apple /æpl/	/e/ egg /eg/	/ɪ/ fish /fɪʃ/	/ɒ/ office /'ɒfɪs/	/ʌ/ uncle /'ʌnkl/	/ʊ/ book /bʊk/
/ɑː/ car /kɑː(r)/	/ɜː/ girl /gɜː(r)l/	/iː/ eat /iːt/	/ɔː/ four /fɔː(r)/	/uː/ two /tuː/	
/eə/ hair /heə(r)/	/ɪə/ ear /ɪə(r)/	/ʊə/ newer /njʊə(r)/	/əʊ/ phone /fəʊn/	/aʊ/ mouth /maʊθ/	
/aɪ/ ice /aɪs/	/eɪ/ eight /eɪt/	/ɔɪ/ boy /bɔɪ/	/ə/ cinema /'sɪnəmə/		

Consonant sounds

/p/ pen /pen/	/b/ bed /bed/	/t/ table /teɪbl/	/d/ door /dɔː(r)/	/tʃ/ chair /tʃeə(r)/	/dʒ/ jeans /dʒiːnz/
/f/ food /fuːd/	/v/ visit /'vɪzɪt/	/θ/ thing /θɪŋ/	/ð/ father /'fɑːðə(r)/	/k/ cup /kʌp/	/g/ garden /'gɑːdən/
/s/ sister /'sɪstə(r)/	/z/ zoo /zuː/	/ʃ/ shoe /ʃuː/	/ʒ/ television /'telɪvɪʒn/	/h/ house /haʊs/	/l/ lunch /lʌntʃ/
/m/ man /mæn/	/n/ nine /naɪn/	/ŋ/ sing /sɪŋ/	/r/ red /red/	/w/ water /'wɔːtə(r)/	/j/ young /jʌŋ/

The alphabet

A /eɪ/	B /biː/	C /siː/	D /diː/	E /iː/	F /ef/	G /dʒiː/	H /eɪtʃ/	I /aɪ/	J /dʒeɪ/	K /keɪ/	L /el/	M /em/	N /en/
O /əʊ/	P /piː/	Q /kjuː/	R /ɑː(r)/	S /es/	T /tiː/	U /juː/	V /viː/	W /'dʌbljuː/	X /eks/	Y /waɪ/	Z /zed/, *American* /ziː/		

Stressed and unstressed words

Stress 'vocabulary' words ...	
nouns	*book, girl, time ...*
main verbs	*walk, speak, play ...*
adjectives	*big, green, old ...*
adverbs	*easily, fast, slow ...*
question words	*Who, What, How, ...*
negatives	*not, aren't, can't ...*

Don't stress 'grammar' words ...	
articles	*a, an, the ...*
prepositions	*in, on, of ...*
conjunctions	*and, but ...*
auxiliary verbs	*is, was, do ...*
pronouns	*you, we, them ...*
possessives	*me, your, their ...*
demonstratives	*this, that ...*

Example stress patterns

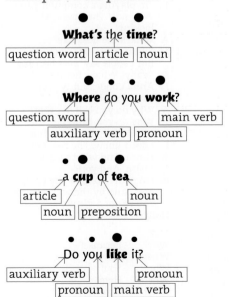

149

Audio scripts

1

1A.1
1 H-O-N-D-A
2 L-A-C-O-S-T-E
3 H-I-L-F-I-G-E-R
4 S-C-H-W-E- double P-E-S
5 M-small C- capital D-O-N-A-L-D apostrophe S.

1A.2
1 This is the surname of a French woman. Her first name was Gabrielle. She also had a nickname – Coco. Her surname begins with a *C*.
2 This is the surname of a Swedish man. His first name is Lars and his middle name's Magnus. His surname means 'Eric's son'.
3 This man's first name was Michio. His surname means 'bell tree'. It's a very common surname in Japan. It begins with the letter *S*.
4 This is the surname of four brothers – Harry, Albert, Sam and Jack. They started a famous film studio. The name of the studio includes the name B-R-O-S. This means 'brothers'.
5 This is the surname of an Italian man. His first name was Enzo. He started a car company. This surname has the same meaning as 'Smith' in English. It begins with the letter *F*.

1A.3
A What's your name?
B Chico.
A Is that your first name?
B Yes. It's short for Francisco.
A Oh. And what's your surname?
B My surnames are Oliveira Cardoso.
A Oliveira Cardoso?
B Yes. Oliveira's my mother's surname and Cardoso's my father's surname.
A Oh I see. So it's Francisco Oliveira Cardoso?
B That's right, but just call me *Chico*!

1B.1
Um, My name's Caroline, um Caroline Watt, and I'm from Louth, that's L-O-U-T-H, Louth – it's in Lincolnshire, in England. I wasn't uh … I wasn't born in Louth, I was born in Lincoln in 1981, so I'm British. I'm married and uh … my husband's name is Paul. OK, my job – well, I'm a nurse and I work in a hospital … A typical day? Well, I, uh, get up at half past six in the morning, half past six yeah, and uh, well I have a shower and breakfast … oh, and I give some breakfast to the cats, 'cause we've got two cats, they're called Felix and Oscar. I start work at eight and I finish at five. Oh, I go to work on my bike. It's great, but it's awful in the rain! So yeah, and in the evening, well, sometimes I play tennis, and oh, I like cooking … I like Thai food, so um, I make a lot of that … so … yes, well, that's it really. Oh, and I go to bed at about eleven o'clock.

1B.2
1 I sit and read.
   She sits and reads.
2 You sing and dance.
   She sings and dances.
3 We watch football.
   He watches football.
4 They open and close.
   It opens and closes.
5 I go swimming.
   She goes swimming.
6 You start and finish.
   It starts and finishes.

1C.1
Justin Hi. Are you new?
Anna Yes.
J When did you start?
A On Monday.
J Where do you work?
A Just along the corridor. What do you do?
J I'm a computer technician. I check the system for viruses.
A How often do you check it?
J Not very often. They don't pay me enough!
A So what are you doing now?
J I'm playing a computer game. Why not? The boss isn't looking!
A What's the boss like?
J I don't know her. She's new. But people say she's horrible.
A Really? What's her name?
J Anna Conde. But we call her Anaconda.
A Why do you call her that?
J Why do you think?!
A Where does she come from?
J I don't know. The zoo, probably!
A Hmm. And what's your name?
J Justin. And you?
A I'm Anna Conde – the new boss. And by the way, I think you've got a virus.
Holly Ouch!

1C.2
Why?	Because!
When?	Now!
Who?	You!
Where?	Here!
How?	Carefully!
Which?	That one!
What?	Nothing!

1C.3
Who was he **with**?
Where were your **keys**?
When does she **start**?
What do they **do**?
Why are you **here**?
Which is her **desk**?
How did it **end**?

1D.1
debt	quay
receipt	rough

1D.2
Definitions! Which one is wrong?
1 What does *book* mean?
   a It means to get tickets, a room in a hotel or a table in a restaurant.
   b A book is something that you read.
   c It means the same as *fast*.
   … and the wrong definition is … c!
2 What does *park* mean?
   a It's an adjective. It's the opposite of *long*.
   b It's a place in a town with trees and grass.
   c It's a verb. It means leave the car somewhere.
   … and the wrong definition is … a!
3 What does *left* mean?
   a It means the same as *difficult*.
   b It's the opposite of *right*.
   c It's the past of *leave*.
   … and the wrong definition is … a!
4 What does *match* mean?
   a It means the same as *game*. For example, a football match.
   b It's a kind of drink. It's similar to tea.
   c It's a small piece of wood to light a cigarette or fire.
   … and the wrong definition is … b!
5 What does *fit* mean?
   a It's a verb. We say clothes or shoes fit if they are not too big and not too small.
   b It's an adjective. It means the same as *healthy*.
   c It's a noun. It's a kind of chair in a church.
   … and the wrong definition is … c!
6 What does *ring* mean?
   a It's a noun. You wear a ring on your finger.
   b It means the opposite of *large*.
   c It means to call someone on the phone.
   … and the wrong definition is … b!

1E.1
I'm learning English because um, I want to go um … to visit Canada um … I've got an uncle in Canada, and so, and I want to go there maybe, I dunno, for a year and work … Well, I have two English lessons a week and so I have English lessons, and homework, I do homework, and I practise speaking, yes. And there's an Irish pub in my town, and I've got a lot of friends there, and they speak English, and there's English television too.

2

2A.1
Natural
beach desert forest island lake mountain river

Man-made
castle church lighthouse railway ruins village

2A.2
How high is it?
How old is it?
How far is it?
How much are they?
How long is it?

2A.3
Ticket Seller Can I help you?
Sara Hello, yes, um, are there any good day trips from here?
T Well, you can go up Snowdon.
S Oh I don't know - I haven't got good shoes for mountains …
T But you can go up on the mountain railway. Snowdon's the highest mountain in Wales.
S Oh. How high is it?
T About 3,500 feet. That's about 1,000 metres.
S How far is it from here to the station?
T It's 4½ miles. There's a bus from here to the station.
S Oh – so it's not far. How long's the journey?
T The round trip's 2½ hours, but of course you can stay longer at the top.
S Is it cold?
T Yes, it's often quite windy, but there's a restaurant.
S Oh really? How much is the train fare?
T The return fare's £21.
S Oh, right. It's a bit expensive.
T OK. Another trip you can take is Anglesey …

2B.1
Barb I'm just going out for a coffee, Jen. If any customers come in, remember we want to sell holidays in Scandinavia this week.

Jen OK, Barbara.

M Excuse me!

J Oh! Hello …

M We want to book a safari.

J Are you sure? How about a nice holiday in Scandinavia?

M No thanks. We want to see the animals, you know – elephants …

W … lions

M … zebras …

J Insects.

W … giraffes … Sorry, what did you say? Insects?

J Yes. There are lots of horrible little insects in Africa. Some horrible big insects too! But there aren't any insects in Scandinavia …

M We don't want to go to Scandinavia!

J Why not? Picture it – beautiful white beaches, lovely blue water, palm trees …

M Palm trees? In Scandinavia?

J Well, maybe not, but there's a lot to see. Pretty white villages. Fine old castles. Aztec ruins …

M Listen, we came in here to book a safari. If that's not possible, we're leaving.

J Right, so you want a nice long safari with elephants and things. No problem. In fact, we've got a special offer at Oslo zoo this week … Hey wait! Where are you going?

2B.2

1 beautiful old railway
2 pretty white villages
3 beautiful white beaches
4 horrible little insects
5 lovely blue water
6 nice long safari
7 pretty little island

2B.3

nice blue lakes
lovely quiet beaches
interesting African animals

2B.4

beautiful colourful villages
fine old trees
pretty little islands

2B.5

Well, there are lots of beaches, um … nice quiet beaches, and it's very green, um, it's not like the south of Spain, it's not hot and dry I mean, there are lots of lovely big forests and green fields, and there's a lot of rain here in the North, so um it's quite wet, and um … there are some beautiful old towns and um … colourful villages … Santiago or er … Lugo. And um … the mountains – there are some very high mountains, really nice … Most tourists go to the South of Spain, but the North is beautiful too.

2C.1

1 It's raining.
2 There's a storm coming.
3 There are a lot of clouds.
4 It's dry.

5 The temperature is very high.
6 There isn't any wind.

2C.2

colder weather
cold weather
windier city
windiest city
heavier snow
heavy snow
hottest summer
hotter summer

2C.3

People say it rains a lot in London, but the rain's much heavier in Sydney.

London's cloudier, but the rain's lighter. In Sydney, when it rains, it *really* rains. But then it's sunny. It's much sunnier than London. Sunnier and hotter. The temperature in summer is often higher than 40 degrees. The most uncomfortable months are January and February. But for me, hot's better than cold. When I left Australia it was summer, and I arrived here on the coldest day of winter. It was minus two. I wanted to get back on the plane!

2D.1

Picture 1 those are fans.
Picture 2 those are rugs.
Picture 3 those are mugs.
Picture 4 those are key rings.
Picture 5 those are cups.
Picture 6 that's a knife.
Picture 7 those are plates.
Picture 8 those are posters.
Picture 9 those are caps.
Picture 10 those are T-shirts.
Picture 11 those are bags.
Picture 12 those are postcards.

2D.2

A OK, well these caps. I think they're from New York.

B Uh huh, yeah. Looks like an American city.

A 'Cause you can read on the front *NYC. NYC.* That's New York City.

B Oh, right. Yeah. So that's the USA then.

2D.3

A That's nice. I love the blue colour.

B Mmm, yes.

A Where did you get it?

B My boyfriend gave it to me. Because of the two fish. I'm a Pisces.

A Oh. Where did he get it?

B He bought it on a beach in Mexico.

A Mexico? Did you go with him?

B No, I didn't go. I just got the plate!

A Oh well. Better than nothing.

2D.4

A These posters are great. Where did you get them?

B They were a present from my aunt. She went on a boat trip in the Baltic and she visited St Petersburg.

A Wow.

B And she bought me these posters in a street market.

A Does she travel a lot?

B Yeah. Last year she went to Tunisia. She sent me this camel postcard from there.

A Did she give you that camel rug too?

B No. I bought that in Egypt.

A Oh. When did you go to Egypt?

B Last summer.

A Did you like it?

B Yeah, it was great.

A Did you buy anything else there?

B No, just the rug.

3

3A.1

A Paul skis.
B Paula's keys.
A The ski school.
B The skier's cool.
A She skates.
B She's a skater.
A Snowboard.
A A snowboarder.
A Spanish sport.
B A Spanish supporter.

3A.2

Paula's keys.
The ski school.
She's a skater.
Snowboard.
A Spanish supporter.

3A.3

Conversation 1

A Do you like swimming?

B Yes, I do.

A Me too. And I'd like to try scuba-diving.

B Oh, not me. It's too dangerous!

Conversation 2

A Would you like to try skydiving?

B Yes, I'd love to. I like exciting sports.

A What sports do you do?

B Oh, rock climbing, ice climbing …

3B.1

When I was five
I was able to dive
I could swim really well
But I couldn't drive

Now, I can cook
And I'm able to drive
I can swim quite well
But now I can't dive

3B.2

Ben What are you doing at the weekend, Sarah?

Sarah I'm going windsurfing in Cornwall.

B Windsurfing? I didn't know you were a windsurfer.

S Yeah. I could windsurf when I was six. My uncle taught me.

B Really? Can you surf too? Normal surfing, I mean …

S No, I can't. I tried it once, but I couldn't stand up. What about

you? Do you do any water sports?

B Not really. I mean, I can swim and everything, but I prefer mountain sports.

S What, like climbing?

B Yeah, climbing. And mountain walking. And I can ski.

S Oh yeah? I never go to the mountains. I think I'd get lost. I can't read maps.

B You can't read maps?

S No, I've never been good at that. Don't know why.

3C.1

The carpet's green
The sofa's blue
The TV's boring
And you are too

I could go to town
And meet some friends
But no one goes out
Except at weekends

We could switch it off
And go to the park
But there's nothing to do
In the park in the dark

This programme's so boring
Oh, what shall we do?
Let's change the channel
And find something new

Nowhere to go
Nothing to do
Watching TV
On the sofa with you

3C.2

1

Man Is there anything good on TV this evening?

Woman Well, I want to watch the *Money Programme* on TVC 2.

M Hey look – there's a film on TVC 1 *Anaconda*. Shall we watch that?

W No, look, it finishes at quarter to eleven and the *Money Programme* starts at ten.

M Oh come on, let's watch the film.

W We could video it.

M Yeah, OK, we can video it. Anything else?

W Half past ten – *Change your Husband*. That could be interesting!

M Ha ha!

2

Boy What shall we watch?

Girl What time is it?

B Nearly eight o'clock.

G Let's see – we could watch the National Lottery …

B Oh no, boring! We haven't even got tickets. What's on the other channels?

G There's *Mad House* on TVC1.

B Oh yeah, cool, let's watch that. And what's on after it?

G A film called *Anaconda*.

B Nah, saw that last year.

G All right then, we could watch *Big Brother* on channel 3.

B *Big Brother*? I'm your big brother!

G Yeah, right! So OK, let's watch *Big Brother*.

3C.3

1 What shall we watch?
2 Shall we watch the news?
3 How about playing a game?
4 Let's switch off the TV.
5 We could go out.

3C.4

A What shall we do?
B Shall we just stay at home and watch TV?
A OK. What's on?
B Let's see … We could watch *Sports Week*.
A No, let's watch the *National Geographic* programme.
B OK. Good idea!

3D.1

actor star story crime director thriller

character horror Harrison Ford Laurel and Hardy

Harry Potter Star Wars

3E.1

Hi Zofia
I've got two tickets to see the *Phantom of the Opera* on Thursday evening. Would you like to come? It's at the *Palladium* at 7.00. We could meet at 6.30 at *Esperanto's*. What do you think?
Marek

4

4A.1

The bed's too hard
The blanket's old
The pillow's small
The sheets are cold

The towel's wet
The floor is too
The taps don't work
There's no shampoo

The lamps don't work
The room's too hot
The ashtray's full
And the mini-bar's not

No glass, no soap
No toilet roll
And someone stole
The remote control!

4A.2

A Can I help you?
B Yes, I'd like a room please.
A Just for one night?
B Yes. How much is it?
A It's €80 a night, breakfast included.
B OK.
A Could I see your passport, please?
B Yes, here you are.
A Thanks. Here's your key. It's room 224 on the second floor.
B Thanks. What time's breakfast, please?
A Breakfast's from 7.30 to 10 a.m.
B 7.30 to ten. Thanks.

4A.3

Can I have an alarm call at 7.30 a.m., please?

Could I have a cup of coffee, please?

The TV doesn't work. Could you send someone to look at it, please?

Can you give me an outside line, please?

4B.1

M Oh no!
W What's happened? What have you done?
M I've burnt the toast!
W Yeah, I can smell it!

4B.2

M Oh no!
W What's happened? What have you done?
M I've burnt the toast!
W Yeah, I can smell it!

M Oh no! Look!
W What's happened? What have you done?
M I've broken my glasses.
W Oh no!

W Oh no!
W What's happened? Are you OK?
W The plates have fallen out of the cupboard.
M Ooops! What a mess!

W Ouch!
M What's happened?
W I've burnt my finger!
M Are you alright?
W Yeah, it's not too bad.

M Oh no!
W What's happened?
M I've dropped an egg on the floor!
W Has it broken?
M What do YOU think?!

M Yuck!
W What?
M I've put salt in my coffee!
W You idiot!
M It's disgusting!

M Oh no!
W What've you done?
M I've dropped my breakfast and it's gone all over the floor.
W Oh dear …

M Oh no!
W What have you done now?
M I've dropped the sugar and it's gone all over the floor.
W Oh no! What a mess!

W Ouch!
M What's happened?
W I've cut my finger!
M Let's see … oh, that looks bad …

M Oh no, help!
W What's happened?
M The bottles have fallen on the floor!
W Ooops.

W What's that smell?
M Oops, um.. I've had a little accident.
W What?
M I've burnt a shirt.
W Oh no!

W Oh no!
M What's happened?
W I've broken a cup!
M Are you all right?
W Yeah, but the cup isn't!

4B.3

I've cut my hand.
You've burnt the toast.
She's dropped an egg.
He's broken a glass.

4C.1

Home Alone
Lisa Hello?
Mum Hi Lisa, it's Mum here. Is everything OK? How's the house?
L It's fine.
M Have you fed Toby?
L Yes.
M And have you taken him for a walk?
L Yes.
M Have you cleaned the bathroom?
L Yes.
M And have you watered the plants?
L Yes.
M And the cactus?
L Yes. I mean no! I haven't watered the cactus.
M Good girl. And have you kept the kitchen clean?
L Yes. I've washed up and put everything away, and I've cleaned the floor.
M What's that noise? You haven't invited all your friends for a party, I hope!
L No, don't worry. It's just a TV programme. Just a moment … ssshhh! … There. I've turned it off.
M Have you done the shopping?
L Yes.
M Have you turned on the heating?
L Yes. Anyway, Mum, how's the holiday?
M We've decided to come home early. We'll be there in ten minutes.
L What?!

4C.2

What have you **done** this **morn**ing?
What have you **done** today?
Have you **cleaned** the **floors**?
Have you **cleaned** the **doors**?
What have you **done** today?

I **haven't washed** the **sheets**
I **haven't made** the **bed**
I've **cleaned** the **floors**
I've **cleaned** the **doors**
But I **haven't bought** the **bread**

4C.3

I'm really tired 'cause um, I've got Mum and Dad coming to stay for the weekend. So you know, I'm trying to clean the house, and I've washed the sheets and made the bed for them and everything, and towels, I've washed all the towels and um, I've cleaned the bathroom. But there's still lots to do, I mean, I haven't started in the kitchen yet. It's really dirty and I haven't cleaned the cooker or the fridge and um, or the floors, and I haven't got time, you know, so … . Yeah, and I'm really busy at work too.

4D.1

A OK Callum so first I need to know how old you are. Are you under 18, between 18 and 22 or over 22?
B I'm 24.
A All right, so *over 22* then. OK, first question. Have you ever lived alone?
B No, I haven't.
A And have you ever lived in another town or country?
B No, I haven't.
A No, OK, and … um … have you ever paid for the shopping?
B Yes, uh huh.
A What about the electricity, gas or telephone bill?
B No, I haven't paid that.
A And rent. Have you ever paid rent?
B No.
A OK, and have you ever bought any of these things – a towel, knives, forks and spoons or a fridge?
B Well, I've bought a towel, but not the other things.
A A towel, OK. Have you ever had your own room?
B Yes.
A And your own house keys?
B Yeah, uh huh.
A And your own home?
B My own home? No, I haven't.
A Have you ever turned on the cooker?
B Yes, sure.
A And what about the heating and electricity?
B Yes, I've turned those on.
A Have you ever cooked a meal for yourself?
B Yes, I have.
A And for your family?
B Yes.
A And for guests?
B Um … let's see … No, I don't think so.
A Right. Have you ever put a battery in the TV remote control?
B Yes, sure.
A And have you ever put soap in the washing machine?
B Yeah, uh huh.
A And last question, have you ever put a shelf on the wall?
B Um … no, I haven't done that, no.
A OK, thanks Callum.

4D.2

James Have you ever broken your arm?
Alice No, I haven't. Have you?
J Yes, once, my left arm.
A When was that?
J It was, er, in 2001.
A What happened?
J I fell downstairs.
A Ouch!

4E.1

Hi Phillipa
I've had a great time!
I've fed the cat.
I've left the keys with your neighbour.

Sorry, I dropped your box of eggs on the floor. I've cleaned the floor and bought some more eggs. My towel was wet so I've left it in the washing machine.
Thanks for everything!
Ana

5

5A.1

Gavin Nice suit Jeff! Everybody's looking at it, have you noticed?
Jeff Well, that's because it's half price in the sales.
G No, but it's really nice. Very smart. And the jacket's a really good fit.
J Thanks. Don't you think the trousers are too short?
G They're quite short, yes, but long enough. And I love the colour. It really suits you.
J Thanks. What do you think of the shirt?
G Well, the colour's a bit bright, perhaps …
J Oh, I quite like it … Hey, quiet somebody's coming.
G You see! *She* looked at you.
J What, the woman in the red top? I thought she looked at *you*.
G Me? Oh no! *I* haven't got anything on!

5A.2

G It's **really nice**.
G It **really suits** you.
J They're **quite short** …
J The **colour**'s a bit **bright**, perhaps …

5B.1

Sadie Hi Vic! Where are you?
Vic I'm in Bridge Street Market. I'm going for a coffee and cake in *Maxine's*. Do you want to come?
S Yeah, sure. I'll be there in fifteen minutes.
V OK. I'll see you there.
S How much is the bill?
V Let's see, um … it's six pounds fifty.
S Oh no – I'm sorry, I haven't got enough. Could I borrow some from you and I'll go to the cash machine and pay you back.
V Oh, don't worry about it. I'll pay for it. You can pay next time!
S Well, OK then. Thanks.
S There's a sale at *Style Factory*. Let's go and see.
V Yeah, OK.
S Shall I carry one of your bags for you?
V Oh, yes please.
S Wow, that's heavy. What's in here?
V A set of plates. They were cheap in the market, so …
S Ha ha. And what's in the other?
V Cups.
V I like this scarf, but I haven't got enough money for it …

S Why? How much is it?
V £19.99. I've only got £15.
S I'll lend you five pounds. I've just got fifty from the cash machine.
V Will you? Oh great, thanks. I'll pay you back tomorrow.
S OK. Go and pay. I'll hold your bag for you.
V Thanks.
Woman That's £19.99, please. And there's a penny change. Shall I wrap it for you?
V No, thanks. I can just wear it.
M OK, then. Bye now.
V Bye.

5B.2

We'll **call** you **later**.
I **won't** for**get**.
Shall **I** car**ry** it?

5B.3

We'll **call** you **later**.
I'll **hold** your um**brel**la.
I'll **lend** you my **jack**et.
I'll **pay** you **back**.
I **won't** for**get**.
You **won't** be **sorry**.
Shall **I** car**ry** it?
Shall **I pay** for **you**?

5C.1

Dean's Jeans
Clean jeans, neat jeans
Sitting on your seat jeans
Dear jeans, cheap jeans
Wear them on the beach jeans
Wear them with a sweater
Great in any weather
Dirty jeans, clean jeans
The trousers of your dreams
Dean's Jeans!

5C.2

S Can I help you?
A Yes, I'm looking for a pair of jeans.
S Do you like these ones?
A Yes. How much are they?
S £54.99.
A Can I try a pair on?
S Yes, of course. What size are you?
A I'm not sure.
S OK, try this pair on. The changing room's over there.
S How are they?
A They're a bit small.
S OK, try the next size. Here you are.
A Thanks.
S What do you think?
A Yes, they're fine. I'll take them.
S How would you like to pay?
A I'll pay in cash.

5C.3

Do you like these ones?
Do you like this one?

How much are they?
How much is it?

Try this pair on.
Try this one on.

They're fine.
It's fine.

I'll take them.
I'll take it.

How are they?
How is it?

They're a bit small.
It's a bit small.

I'm looking for a pair of jeans.
I'm looking for a sweater.

Can I try a pair on?
Can I try one on?

5D.1

1 You mustn't cycle here.
2 You must walk on the path.
3 You mustn't enter in your swimming costume.
4 You must take off your cap or hood before you enter.

5D.2

Simon OK, now it's a good idea to put your membership card with your gym stuff. Don't forget it, 'cause you must show it at the door – I sometimes forget, and can't come in.
Judy What a pain!
S Yeah, I know. OK, so these are the machines.
J Wow! This place is big, isn't it?
S You must have a towel with you on the machines, to put over the seat.
J Right, OK.
S And you mustn't wear your street shoes in here.
J Oh, there's a pool.
S Yeah. Have you got your swimming stuff with you?
J Sorry?
S Your swimming costume and stuff. Have you got them with you?
J Oh, um … no. I'll bring them next time.
S Yeah – and remember, you must have a swimming cap to go in there.
J Swimming cap, OK. There are lots of rules. Are there any more?
S Um … let's see … Oh yeah, you mustn't eat when you're on the machines, but it's OK to drink water. And if you want to join the aerobics class, it's free. But remember, you must put your name on the list. It fills up very quickly.
J OK, is that all?
S I think so.
J Great. So we can smoke, then!
S Ha ha!

6

6A.1

Recep Hello, Central College?
Paola Yes, can I speak to Mr Hardy, please?
R Yes, who's calling?
P Paola Nes.. . *(phone cuts off)*
Mechanic Hello, Kwikfix Motors.
P Kwikfix Motors? Oops, sorry, wrong number!
R Hello, Central College?
P Yes, can I speak to Mr Hardy, please?

R Did you say Mr Ardy?
P No, Mr *Hardy* – with an H.
R Ah, Mr Hardy, OK. Who's calling?
P Paola Nesta. I called a moment ago but I got cut off.
R Oh, yes. Just a moment … I'm sorry, he's busy at the moment. Would you like to leave a message?
P No, thanks. I'll call back later. Thanks.
R Hello, Central College?
A Yes, can I speak to Mr Hardy, please? This is Paola Nesta. I called earlier.
R Oh, yes. Hold the line, Ms Nesta. Don't hang up. I'll put you through.
Mr Hardy Hello?
P Oh hi … Is that Mike Hardy? This is Paola Nesta speaking.
H Hi Paola! I can't speak now. Can I call you back later?
P Aaaaarrrgggghhhhhh!

6A.2

Can I speak to …
Sorry, wrong number!
I called a moment ago.
I got cut off.
I'll call back later.
Is that … ?
This is … speaking.
Who's calling?
Just a moment.
He's busy at the moment.
Would you like to leave a message?
Hold the line.
Don't hang up.
I'll put you through.

6A.3

Automated Message
Thank you for calling, hold the line
Please press one and we'll waste your time
Press two and we'll put you through
Don't hang up, you're in a queue
Hello, my name's Caroline
Please press three
And hold the line
Hold the line
If you want some music, just press four
Then press five and hear some more

Press six to speak to an operator
Sorry, she's busy, call back later
Press seven for an answerphone
And leave a message after the tone
Press eight and wait and then press nine
If no one answers
Just hold the line
Just hold the line
If you're calling from abroad, press ten
Get cut off and dial again

6A.4

1
A Hello?
B Hello, Frank?
A I'm sorry, I think you have the wrong number.
B Is this 726 8915?
A No, 726 8515.
B Oh, I'm sorry. Goodbye.

2
A Hello. Central College?
B Hello. Can I speak to Ms Perry?
A Did you say Ms Berry?
B No, Ms Perry, P-E-R-R-Y.
A Oh, sorry, Ms Perry. Yes, of course. Hold the line, I'll put you through.

3
A Hello?
B Hello. Can I speak to Mr Mills, please?
A I'm sorry, I'm afraid he's busy. Would you like to leave a message?
B No, thanks. I'll call back later.
A OK. Call after five thirty. He's in a meeting until then.
B Four thirty. OK.
A No, five thirty.
B Oh, OK, sorry – half past five.

6A.5

No, **five** one five.
No, five one **five**.

No, **Mr** Ardwick.
No, Mr **Ardwick**.

No, seven **fifteen**.
No, **seven** fifteen.

6B.1

They have two clean windows.
They have to clean windows.

6B.2

You have to wear a seat-belt.
You mustn't drive through a red light.
You don't have to wear a helmet.
You mustn't park on the motorway.
You have to drive on the right in most countries.
You don't have to wear training shoes.
You mustn't drive on the pavement.
You don't have to listen to the radio.

6B.3

I Hello, and welcome to *Meet the People*, and on today's show, we've got PC Robert Ellis in the studio to talk about his work as a traffic police officer, and if you want to ask Robert a question, just phone the number 0207 543 9584. So, good morning Robert.
R Good morning.
I So tell us something about your work. What's it like being a traffic policeman?
R Well the worst thing about the job is the hours. I often have to start work at four in the morning. But I like the work. I think it's a very important job. I mean, we sometimes save lives, and I feel good about that.

I Uh huh. Ok, now we'll take the first question from the listeners. This is Brenda Jackson from Horsham. Brenda?
B Yes, hello. Hello Mr Ellis. My question is this: What qualities do you need to be a traffic cop?
R Hello Brenda. Well, you have to be a good driver. You have to get an advanced driving licence, and um ... You have to be good with people, I think, you mustn't get angry, and um ... you have to think quickly in an emergency you always have to stay calm, you know, you mustn't panic. And you have to be fit. I mean, you don't have to be an athlete, but you have to be fit and healthy.
I Ok, and another question from the listeners at home. Mike Windsor from Croydon. Mike?
M Yes, thank you. Hello Mr Ellis. I'd like to know this. Do you have to follow the rules of the road as a traffic police officer? Do you have to wear a seat-belt, for example?
R Hi Mike. Well, we don't always have to wear a seat-belt, but I usually do, you know, for safety. And we don't have to keep to the speed limit, because obviously, we have to get to an emergency fast.
I Uh huh. Ok, we'll have a quick pause here, but we'll be right back after the break ...

6C.1

I bought a stamp.
I changed a traveller's cheque.
I'd like to open an account.
I sent him a letter.
I took out £100 in cash.
I wrote a cheque.
I wrote to the company.
Someone stole my credit card.
The cashier asked me for some ID.

6C.2 & 6C.3

My neighbour's daughter Pat
Thought she bought a hat
She brought it back
And it caught a rat
So I guess she bought a cat

6D.1

Terror on Dock Street
Mr Basset
I was driving along Dock Street and he ran in front of me. I put my foot on the brake, and the car behind crashed into me. I called the police immediately.

Miss Setter
I was standing in front of the post office. I was waiting for the number 94 bus.

Then *he* ran past and knocked me down. He didn't help or say sorry.

Mrs Samoyed
I was standing in a queue in the butcher's and he came in. He didn't say anything. He just went to the front of the queue and he took something from the counter. I think it was a leg of lamb. Then he ran out without paying!

Mr Collie
I was at the National Bank cash machine on Dock Street. I was taking some money out of the machine and I heard a noise. I looked round and I saw him. He was running towards me, and I saw blood on his face. He had something in his mouth. I think it was red meat. He was like a ... a wild animal!

Judge
Quiet please!

Mrs Beagle
It was a nice, sunny day, and I was sitting in my garden, and the children were playing. They were making a castle out of old boxes, Then *he* came into the garden and he knocked it down. The children started crying, and he just ran away.

PC Shepherd
When we were putting him into the police car, he bit me!

Judge
Do you have anything to say?
Woof!

6D.2

The bus is coming.
The bus was coming.
The boss is watching.
The boss was watching.
The boys are playing.
The boys were playing.
The birds are singing.
The birds were singing.

6D.3

The bus was coming ... past
The bus is coming ... present
The boss was watching ... past
The boss was watching ... past
The boys are playing ... present
The boys are playing ... present
The birds were singing ... past
The birds are singing ... present

6D.4

Nick
I was sitting on a bus and um, it was going past a TV shop, and there were lots of people looking in the window, so I thought, what's happening, you know, and I looked and I could see these pictures on the TV, and that was the first I knew about it.

Sarah
Um, I remember I wasn't feeling well, so I didn't go to work that day, and I was lying in bed, and um, reading a book I think, and anyway the phone rang and it was my sister, and she said have you heard? And I said, heard what? And she said switch on the TV now, so I got out of bed and switched on the TV and well, that's when I first saw it.

Tom
I was in class, I think it was History, yeah, History, and the teacher was talking about the Romans and I was thinking about lunch, and then I got a text message, and I thought *oops!*, 'cause we aren't allowed to use mobile phones in class. But anyway I looked at the message and it was from a friend, and that's when I heard the news.

6E.1

Um, well, I was driving home, and er ... I was, I was on Wellington Road, um ... It was half past eleven at night. Anyway, I was passing the sports centre when a young man ran in front of me, and well, I, I turned to the left and I crashed into a traffic light. I told the police immediately. Um.. I was wearing a seat-belt, but I hurt my neck, so um, I had to go to hospital.

7

7A.1

Andy What do you do?
Belén I'm a Spanish teacher.
A Oh yeah? Where do you work?
B In a school called *Lingo City*.
A Do you like it?
B Yes, it's fun. What do YOU do?
A I'm a limousine driver.
B Oh. Interesting!

7A.2

Andy What do you do?
Belén What do you do?

7A.3

What do you **do**? ... S
What do **you** do? ... R

Where do **you** live? ... R
Where do **you** live? ... R

Where are **you** from? ... R
Where are you **from**? ... S

Where do **you** work? ... S
Where do **you** work? ... S

7A.4

A What do you do?
B I'm a nurse.
A Oh really? Where do you work? In a hospital?
B No, I go out to people's houses, um, old people, you know. If they have a problem at home, I go there to help ...
A Oh right. So you travel?
B Yeah, I have to travel a lot, yeah ...
A Do you like it?
B I like the work, but it's not very well paid, and the hours are quite long.
A Oh.
B What about you? What do YOU do?
A I'm an actor.
B Wow. What, do you work in the theatre or on TV?
A No no, I work on cruise ships.
B Really? That's great! Do you like it?
A Yeah, I enjoy it. I work for two weeks on the ship and then I get two weeks off.
B Lucky you. And is it fun on the ship?

A Yeah, I like working in a team, and I do, you know, I work with musicians and comedians, yeah, and we have a good time.

B And is it well paid?

A Yeah, the money's not bad, and you don't spend it, you know, 'cause you're on the ship and all expenses are paid, so …

B Sounds great! Do they want any nurses?

A Well, actually, they do …

7B.1

This is me, Kevin Taylor. I'm an English literature teacher. And this is the school where I work.

This is me with my form class.

This is Chris Walton, head of Maths. He teaches in the next classroom.

This is the room where we sit in the breaks. The woman who's sitting on the right is Linda. She's the school secretary. She often joins us for coffee.

This is one of the computers which we use to prepare lessons. These are two of my colleagues Josh and Maria Carmen. Josh teaches Geography. He's new here. Maria Carmen's our Spanish teacher, all the way from Madrid.

This is Lenny. He's the man who takes care of the building. If you want any keys, Lenny's your man.

This is the place where the kids have lunch, and that's Moira, one of the women who serves there. I sometimes go to the canteen, but usually I have sandwiches in the staff room.

This is the lab where the kids have Chemistry lessons, and Jack Peterson, head of Science. Jack's the oldest teacher in the school and he's going to retire next year.

This is the room where the kids have IT lessons, and Andy, the school technician. They're looking at the camera that students use for projects. I guess Andy's showing them how it works. Andy's really helpful and all the kids love him.

So that's it. That's my workplace. Not a bad place to work. I'm happy with it, anyway.

7C.1

Holly Boss alarm!

Anna Justin, this is Joan. She's new. Can you show her around and tell her the office rules?

Justin OK, let's start with coffee. The rules say you can't have more than four cups a day. So I've started drinking tea.

J This is the smoking room. Nobody can go in there because smoking isn't allowed.

Jo So why is there a smoking room?

J Don't ask. Now, this is the office supplies cupboard. You can take anything you want, if you can find the key.

Jo Are there any dress rules?

J Yes, but they're quite flexible. You aren't allowed to wear jeans, but you can wear any colour socks you want.

Jo Hmm. Can you send personal emails?

J Yes, but not before six.

Jo But the office closes at six!

J True. Now, we also have our own office rules. You can't arrive early, you can't leave late and you can't work in the lunch hour.

J And finally, this is the boss alarm. If you see her coming, you have to ring this bell. That gives us time to start working.

Jo Ahem …

7C.2

This is John.
This is Joan.

They want work.
They won't work.

They're not books.
They're notebooks.

7C.3

boss
closes
coffee
don't
go
not
office
own
show
smoking
socks

7C.4

Let's see, um … well, we can't run in the corridor, we're allowed to run outside in the playground, but not in the corridor. And um … we can't be late for class … Um … we have two free lessons a week and we can do anything we want, and um, that's great … Um … we can't eat in the classroom, you know, 'cause it isn't allowed. We don't have a uniform, but we can't wear jeans, we have to wear trousers or a skirt … and um … That's all … Oh yes, and we can't talk in the library.

Um, in my school, there aren't any rules. I mean like, you can't hit people, and you can't call the teachers bad names, you know. But you can miss lessons if you want. Um, you can choose the lessons you want to go to. Um, the older kids can go out at lunch time. We can go to the café in the village for lunch if we want, it's great … I mean, in most schools there are lots or rules and things, but we're free to do what we want …

7D.1

He doesn't work at night. He sleeps.
He doesn't work. At night, he sleeps.

7D.2

1 He wears a turban / because the desert sun's very hot.
2 They don't get many visitors / so they're excited.
3 Rajendra has to read it out / because she can't read.
4 The news is good / so she's happy.
5 Sometimes he has problems with his bike / so he has to push it.
6 I told him to come home / because I need some money.

7D.3

Well, um, I go to work six mornings a week. I'm a travel agent and I've got my own shop in São Paolo, and eh, when I arrive at work I, I switch on the computer, and um, because I get a lot of emails, so I check the emails. And then I make a cup of coffee and, I open the shop. I open the shop at nine. In the past, I had two people working with me in the shop. But now I work on my own, because there aren't so many customers now, um, because of the Internet. A lot of people buy their tickets on the Internet, and there are a lot of cheap airlines, so … But I sell a lot of holidays, you know, transport and hotels all together. Anyway, I close for an hour at lunchtime and then open again till five thirty. Um, at the end of the day, after the shop's closed, I do the paperwork. Ha ha, there's a lot of paperwork, and I hate it. But anyway, so I leave the shop at about 7 o'clock and go home.

7E.1

My last job was in an office and I hated it. I mean the boss, he was horrible, and you know, we weren't allowed to make personal phone calls or anything. And he read all our emails, and it was forbidden to drink coffee at your desk. Also I hated the long hours, starting at nine and finishing at seven in the evening. But it was nice to earn a salary every month, and of course, there were paid holidays. Um, yeah, and I enjoyed being with the others in the office, you know. We were good friends. Um, so yeah, but it's still better being self-employed.

8A.1

Tina Oh no!

Bill What's the matter?

T I'm so sorry, Bill, I've just deleted something by mistake.

B But why are you using mine?

T Well mine's broken, and I wanted to send a quick email, so …

B Uh huh … ?

T So I used yours, and um … oh, I'm really sorry!

B Well, what did you delete?

T I don't know – just a file that was open. I thought it was mine. Sorry, Bill!

B Oh, never mind. It wasn't important. Don't worry about it.

T Are you sure?

B Yeah, no problem.

T OK, thanks. I'm really sorry about that.

8A.2

A **Sorry!** I'm **sorry!** I'm **sorry** about **that!**

B No **problem. Don't worry.**

A **Sorry!** I'm **sorry!** I'm **really very sorry!**

B **That's** all **right. Never mind.**

8A.3

Zach What are you doing?

Jess I'm drying it. I'm sorry, Zach. It fell in the bath.

Z How did *that* happen?

J Well, I was having a bath and I dropped it. I'm really sorry …

Z Why are you sorry? It's not mine.

J Well, actually …

Z What?

J Yes, it *is* yours.

Z But why were you using *mine*?

J Well, I haven't got any credit on mine.

Z So you were using *mine* – in the *bath*!

J Yeah, I know, it was stupid. I'm sorry.

Z Oh well. Don't worry. I hope it still works!

8B.1

He's watched.. Passive
He watched … Active

They painted … Active
They're painted … Passive

They washed … Active
They're washed … Passive

It left … Active
It's left … Passive

They're moved … Passive
They moved … Active

8B.2

OK, well, first one. It's made of plastic and metal, and um, it works by electricity, it's … It's got a handle, and it's used for drying hair. It has two words, and the first word is *hair*, and the second word begins with the letter *d*.

And the answer is … It's a hairdryer!

8B.3

OK, number two, this is made of metal and plastic, it's big and it's square, and it's got a door on the front. It works by electricity and it's used for washing dishes, you know, plates, spoons, pans and whatever, so often it's put in the kitchen, anyway, the first part of the word is *dish*, D-I-S-H, and the second part of the word begins with *w*.

And the answer is … It's a dishwasher!

Right, next one. Number three. OK, this is made of wood and animal hair, um, it's got a handle, and the handle's made of wood. It's long and thin, and it's used for painting. Um, artists for example use these, and it has two words. The second word is *brush*, and the first word begins with *p*.
And the answer is … It's a paint brush!

OK, last one, number four. OK, these are made of glass and plastic, or glass and metal, and there are two pieces of dark glass, and they're round. Um, and these are worn in sunny weather, and you wear them over the eyes … There are two parts in the word and the first part is *sun*, and the second part begins with *g*.

And the answer is … They're sunglasses!

8C.1

I'll you'll he'll she'll it'll we'll they'll

8C.2

1 you'll
2 she'll
3 they'll
4 we'll
5 he'll
6 I'll
7 it'll

8C.3

We go to Spain.
We'll go to Spain.

They live in boxes.
They'll live in boxes.

I have lunch at two.
I'll have lunch at two.

They talk to us.
They'll talk to us.

8C.4

We'll go to Spain … future
We'll go to Spain … future
They'll live in caves … future
They live in caves … present
I'll have lunch at two … future
I have lunch at two … present
They talk to us … present
They'll talk to us … future

8C.5

We'll have very small ones in our ears. We won't have to dial numbers. We'll only have to think about our friends and

we'll be able to speak to them. We won't be allowed to talk about bad things. There will be telephone police and they'll listen to everything. They'll be able to make a horrible noise in your ear telephone.

8D.1

Receiving emails
If you double click on the *Email* icon, the email program will open. Now click on the *Send and Receive* button to download your messages. If it's junk mail, highlight it and click on the *Delete* button. Be careful – if the message has an attachment, don't open it. It could be a virus.

Sending emails
If you click on the *New Message* button, an email window will open. Write the email address and the subject at the top. Write your message and click on the *Send* button. The message will go the next time you're online.

8D.2

If you open the attachment, you'll get a virus.

If you click on this icon, a new window will open.

If you give them your address, you'll get lots of junk mail.

If we don't open the attachment, we won't get the virus.

If you don't watch your bag, somebody will steal it.

If Hugo gets your bank details, he'll steal your money.

If you don't want the money, I'll give it to someone else.

8E.1

Hi Jen, I'm sorry but I think I've sent you a virus by mistake, because I opened an email this morning, and I didn't know who sent it but the subject was just 'Good News!', and it had an attachment called 'Message from a Friend' and I opened it without thinking and it was a virus and I think it went into my address book and sent an email to all my contacts so if you got an email from me, DON'T open the attachment because if the virus gets into your computer, it will go to all the people in your address book and I'm really sorry about this, all the best, from Paul.

8E.2

Hi Jen
I'm sorry but I think I've sent you a virus by mistake. I opened an email this morning. I didn't know who sent it and the subject was just 'Good News!' It had an attachment called 'Message from a Friend'. I opened it without thinking and it was a virus. I think it went into my address book and sent an email to all my contacts.
If you got an email from me,

DON'T open the attachment! If the virus gets into your computer, it will go to all the people in your address book.
I'm really sorry about this!
All the best
Paul

9

9A.1

an orange
a sliced apple
a boiled egg
some grilled onion
some scrambled egg
an uncooked egg

9A.2

Kate What sort of food do you like?
Jon Um, I don't know … I like most things really … but I think one of my favourite dishes is fish pie.
K Fish pie?
J Yeah, it's fish in a pie with onion, um, potato, and grated cheese … Oh, and cream. And then you serve it with salad and lots of, um, lemon. Yeah, that's important, the lemon. What about you?
K Mmm, I really like Italian food, um you know, … spaghetti, and I really like a good pizza …
J Oh yeah? What's your favourite pizza then?
K Four cheeses, with lots of pepper and extra olives.
J I hate olives. Black or green, it just doesn't matter. I don't know how you can eat them.
K Oh, I love olives.
J So is there anything you really hate?
K Um … I don't like red meat, you know, like beef or um …
J What about fish? Do you like fish?
K Yeah, if it's cooked.
J Oh right. So you don't like Japanese sushi then?
K Ooh no! I mean, I've never tried it, and I don't want to!

9B.1

1 Frying a few fritters in Brazil.
2 Heating a little soup in the Himalayas.
3 Washing a lot of potatoes in a lake in Latvia.
4 Boiling some water in Wales.
5 Roasting a few chestnuts in China.
6 Barbecuing a few sausages on a roof in Seattle.
7 Grilling some corn in Croatia.
8 Peeling a few mangoes in the Middle East.
9 Chopping a lot of vegetables in Venezuela.
10 Pouring a little tea near Timbuktu.
11 Stirring some stew in South Africa.

9B.2

OK, well, first of all you have to boil some eggs. Then put them in some cold water, peel them, and cut them into pieces. Next, cut some lettuce and a few other salad leaves. Add some small tomatoes, a few pieces of tuna, and the boiled egg. Mix it all together and add a few black olives. Finally pour a little olive oil over the top.

9C.1

Presenter
So Dr Christie, tell us what the food pyramid means.

Dr Christie
Well, the food guide pyramid shows you how much of these different foods you should eat each day, and at the top of the pyramid, you see sweets, uh, you know, sugar, and that includes things like canned drinks and chocolate, or sugar in tea and coffee. You shouldn't eat a lot of sugar. Your body doesn't need much of these things. Also at the top you see butter and oil, things with a lot of fat. You shouldn't eat a lot of these things. OK, just below the top you see dairy products, you know, cheese and milk, and also fish, chicken, eggs and meat, dairy products. You should have two or three servings a day of these, and um, meat. Again, you should have two or three servings a day, and OK below that are vegetables and fruit, and vegetables, very important. You should eat a lot of vegetables, like three to five servings a day, and fruit's important too. You should have two to four servings a day. And finally, at the bottom you've got the carbohydrates, and these are the things you should eat most of, like bread and cereals, and um, rice and spaghetti, pasta generally. And these things, you should eat six to eleven servings a day of these things.

9C.2

You shouldn't eat a lot of white bread.
You should eat a lot of potatoes and pasta.
You should eat a lot of vegetable oils.
You should eat a lot of fruit and vegetables.
You should eat more chicken and fish than red meat.
You shouldn't put a lot of sugar in your drinks.

9D.1

In my country, you mustn't touch food with your left hand. It's OK to hold your glass or a bottle with your left hand, but you shouldn't pass things to people with your left hand. You must use your right hand to eat. You must wash it first. When you have started eating, you shouldn't offer your food, bread for example, to anyone else. It's fine to drink from a bottle, but your lips shouldn't touch the bottle.

9D.2

Q How should I set the table?
A OK, you put the knife on the right and the fork on the left, um, and the spoon or spoons, you put them at the top with the handle on the right.
Q How should I use my knife and fork?
A Well, in the European style, you should hold the knife in your right hand and cut with it, and hold your fork in your left hand.
Q Should I use my hands?
A Yes, it's OK to use your hands for some foods, like bread, fruit, olives, party snacks and so on. And er, barbecued meat.
Q When should I start eating?
A Start eating when everybody is ready, when everybody is served.
Q Is it all right to talk during the meal?
A Yes, of course. But don't talk with your mouth full of food.
Q Should I drink from the soup bowl?
A No, you mustn't do that. It looks very bad.
Q Is it ok to put my knife in my mouth?
A No, that looks very bad too. And you could cut your tongue.
Q Should I serve myself?
A Yes, but you should ask the host first, and offer some to other people. And don't reach in front of other people. Ask them to pass the bowl to you.
Q Which knife and fork should I use?
A Use the ones on the outside first and the ones on the inside after.
Q What should I do if I don't like the food?
A Best to keep quiet, and if your host asks, say you're not very hungry or something.
Q How should I leave my knife and fork at the end?
A Leave them lying next to each other across the middle of the plate.
Q If the host offers more, is it OK to refuse?
A Yes, sure. But it's best to give a reason. For example, say 'No thanks, I'm really full.'

10

10A.1

Nick Hi, I'm Nick.
Wendy Hi Nick. I'm Wendy.
N Where are you from, Wendy?
W Cornwall.
N Really? Whereabouts in Cornwall?
W Fowey.

10A.2

1
Nick Hi, I'm Nick.
Wendy Hi Nick. I'm Wendy.
N Where are you from, Wendy?
W Cornwall.
N Really? Whereabouts in Cornwall?
W Fowey. Have you been to Cornwall?
N Yeah, I've been to Newquay. Is it near there?
W Not far. It's about a thirty-minute drive. It's near St Austell.
N Oh, St Austell. I've been there.
W Yeah, it's just a short bus ride from St Austell.
N Oh, very nice. I love Cornwall. We used to go there on holiday when I was a child.
W Yeah, it's a good place to live.

2
L Where are you from?
W Fowey.
L Oh really? Whereabouts in Fowey?
W Do you know Fowey?
L I've been there a few times, yes.
W Do you know Place Road?
L Place Road? No.
W Oh. It's just up the hill behind the church.
L Oh right. So it's near the harbour, then?
W Yeah, it's a five minute walk from the harbour.
L I remember a pub near the harbour called *The King of* … um …
W The *King of Prussia*?
L Yeah, that's it – The *King of Prussia*. And I remember the castle.
W Castle?
L Yeah, behind the church, there's a castle.
W Oh I know what you mean. That's not really a castle. It's a house. It's called *Place House*.
L Oh, right.

3
E Where are you from?
W England.
E Oh yeah? Whereabouts in England?
W Have you been to England?
E Yes, a couple of times.
W Do you know Cornwall?
E I've never heard of it. Where is it?
W In the South-West.
E Is it near London?
W Not really. It's a four- or five-hour drive.
E Oh, quite a long way then. Is it a big city?
W It isn't a city. Cornwall's the name of the area. I live in a small town called Fowey.
E Oh, I see.

10B.1

I arrived at the airport.
I checked in my bags.
I went through security.
I went through passport control.
I went to the duty-free shop.
I went to the departure gate.
I boarded the plane.
We took off.
We landed.
I went through passport control again.
I collected my bags.
I went through customs.
I left the airport.

10B.2

Ben Hi Jess!
Jess Hi! Where are you?
B I'm at the airport.
J Have you checked in yet?
B Yes. I've just come through passport control. I'm in the departure lounge.
J Don't forget to buy me a present from the duty-free shop.
B I've already bought your present.
J Oh really? What is it?
B Aha! I'm not telling you!
J Ben! Where are you?
B We've just landed. The flight was delayed.
J Yeah, I know. Have you collected your bags yet?
B No. I haven't been through passport control yet. Have you been here long?
J Yeah, I arrived early. I've been here since three o'clock.
B Sorry about that. Read a newspaper!
J I've already read the newspaper!
B Crossword?
J Done.
B See you soon.

10B.3

Have you been on a Jumbo yet?
Have you been on a Jumbo jet?

'Yes', said Jess.
Jess said 'yes'.

This film's good, but yours is better.
This film's good, but '*Jaws*' is better.

10B.4

Have you been on a Jumbo jet?
'Yes', said Jess.
This film's good, but yours is better.

10C.1

Sandra Oh, you have to tell them about the seat-belt signs again.
Beth It's your turn. I did it last time. Oh, and don't forget to switch off the intercom when you finish.

S Ladies and Gentlemen, the captain has switched on the seat-belt signs. Please return to your seats and fasten your seat belts. Please take a moment to look again at the emergency instructions in the seat pocket in front of you.
B Very good. Very professional.
S Thank you.
B How long have you worked with this airline?
S For about a year. This is my first job. What about you?
B I've worked with them for three years, but I've been a flight attendant since 2003.
S Do you like it?
B Yes and no. I love travelling. I've loved flying since I was a teenager.
S So what's bad about it?
B The passengers. They're so stupid. The man in seat 3A for example. He's had that cup of coffee since lunchtime. And now he's complaining that it's cold.
S Ha ha, yes. And the woman in 10D. She's talking to her husband and he's been asleep since four o'clock!
B Ha ha. And that man in 8E. It's been dark for three hours and he's still wearing his sunglasses. He thinks he's so cool! Ha ha ha!
S Shh! Listen – why is everybody laughing?
B Oh no! You forgot to switch off the intercom!

10C.2

M How long have you lived there?
F For five years.
I've lived there for five years.
Since 2004.
I've lived there since 2004.

F How long have you been here?
M For four months.
I've been here for four months.
Since two o'clock.
I've been here since two o'clock.

M How long have you had this camera?
F For two weeks.
I've had this camera for two weeks.
Since last week.
I've had this camera since last week.

10C.3

Patrick Are you going to Athens on holiday?
Maria No, I'm going for work.
P Oh really? What do you do?
M I'm a tour guide.
P Oh yeah. What's the name of your company?
M *Golden Holidays*.
P Have you worked with them long?
M Since 2006. But I've been a tour guide since 2002. What about you? Are you on business or on holiday?

P Holiday. I'm with a tour company called *Sun Tours*.

M Oh really? I worked for them before I joined *Golden Holidays*! Are you enjoying it?

P Yeah. I've been in Europe for two weeks.

M Where have you been?

P So far I've visited France and Switzerland.

M Oh. I live in Switzerland.

P Really? Whereabouts?

M Geneva.

P Oh Geneva. I love Geneva! It was my favourite place! Have you lived there long?

M For about eight years.

P Wow.

M So where are you from?

10D.1

OK, you leave Geneva and you go along the north side of Lake Léman. It takes about an hour to reach Montreux at the other end of the lake. Then you follow the River Rhone. After that, you continue along the Rhone Valley for about 80 minutes until you reach Brig. Then you go through the Simplon Tunnel and cross the border into Italy. Finally you go down a valley and past Lake Maggiore until you reach Milan.

10D.2

used to
used to
use two
used to
use two
use two
used to

10D.3

They **used** to **use** francs in **France**
To **buy** their **milk** and **bread**
They **used** to **use** francs in **Belgium**
But **now** they **use** eur**o**s in**stead**

10D.4

My grandma was from Mallorca, so we used to go a lot, I mean every summer, and this was before cheap flights and everything, and the plane was really expensive, so we used to go by car, the four of us, my parents, me, and my little brother and, um, so we left London and we drove down to the coast to Portsmouth and took the ferry across to France, and then we went through Paris, and then we used to drive south and find a cheap place to stay in central France, then next day we used to get up and continue south until we reached the Pyrenees, and then we went across the border into Spain and down to Barcelona, and then finally we used to take the ferry across to Palma ... yeah and these days it's so easy, you just jump on a plane and you're there in two hours.

11

11A.1
1 I feel sick.
2 I've got a temperature.
3 I've got a cough.
4 I've got a sore throat.
5 I've got backache.
6 I'm aching all over.

11A.2

Dr Good morning, Mr Harker. You look well! Have you been out in the sun?

H No. I think I've got a temperature.

Dr Oh, very nice! So, how do you feel today?

H I don't feel very well. I've got a sore throat and a head ...

Dr Say 'Aaah!'

H Aaah!

Dr And are you still taking the pills?

H No, I stopped. They made me feel sick and ...

Dr Good, good. And how's your backache? Is it getting any better?

H It's worse. Now I'm aching all over and I've got a pain in the ...

Dr Can you put this in your mouth? Thanks. How's your mother?

H Mmm!

Dr Excellent!

H Doctor Stone ...

Dr Yes, Mr Harker? What's the matter?

H I don't think you're listening to me. You ask a question and then you don't ...

Dr Now, take these pills every four hours and come back and see me next week.

H But ...

Dr Next!

11A.3

Agnes Oooh, you look terrible! What's the matter?

Brad I don't feel very well. I think I've got flu.

A What are your symptoms?

B I've got a sore throat and I'm aching all over.

A Have you taken anything for it?

B No.

A Here, try these pills.

B *Flupast*?

A Yes, *Flupast*. Take two every four hours.

B OK, thanks!

A Get well soon!

(later)

A Wow, you look a lot better! How do you feel?

B I feel great! *Flupast* really works!

Presenter *Flupast* fights flu fast!

Read the instructions on the packet carefully. If your symptoms continue, get advice from your doctor.

11B.1

The artist's model in this painting is a young woman called Suzon. You are standing in front of her. She's looking straight at you, and she doesn't seem happy. She's working in a bar in Paris. There are lots of people in the bar – you can see them in the mirror. But she seems lonely. She doesn't really want to be there. Perhaps she hates the job. Perhaps she has problems in her life. We can see Suzon's back in the mirror, and the face of a man in front of her. The man doesn't seem friendly. You are standing in front of her, so of course, *you* are the man in the mirror.

11B.2

1 This girl's sitting for the artist. She isn't working or doing anything else, and you see her body from the side, but she's turning her head and, and she's looking straight at you, and it seems like she can really see you. She seems very calm and relaxed. Perhaps she's enjoying her job as an artist's model. Um ... It wasn't normal for women to wear head scarves in Holland at this time, so ... perhaps the girl is playing, or perhaps the artist wanted her to wear the head scarf or something.

2 OK, this is a girl working in a market in London. She seems happy, I think she's enjoying the moment. She's poor but, um, she isn't thinking about her problems. She's looking at something to the left. Perhaps she can see a child doing something funny. Perhaps somebody is calling to her. She seems to be moving quickly, she isn't standing still or sitting for the artist. Perhaps she is just a girl he saw for a moment and remembers.

11B.3

She's standing in front of you and she's looking straight at you. She isn't working or doing anything else. She's smiling. Behind her you can see countryside with a river. She seems very calm and relaxed. It seems like she knows your thoughts. I like this picture.

11C.1
agree
become
compare
decide
forget
prefer
pretend
promise
refuse
suggest

11C.2
exam
feelings
finger

lifestyle
problem
reason
singer
topic

11C.3

A Hmm, yeah, that's a difficult problem. Umm ... You could promise to think about it, you know. Why don't you ask him to give you more time ... ?

B Yeah, umm ...

C I think you should just refuse to do it. I mean you're too young, and what about your career and everything?

B No, but he's really nice, and I don't want to hurt his feelings.

C Yes, but he should try to understand *your* feelings too.

B Yeah, I know.

C And why does he *want* to get married, anyway?

B I don't know, maybe he thinks I want to get married.

A Anyway, you shouldn't agree to marry him if you don't want to, I mean, it's a very important step.

11D.1

Ben I was once an extra in a film, you know.

Kath Oh yeah? What film was it?

B It was *Emma*, with Gwyneth Paltrow.

K Did you meet her?

B No, I didn't even see her.

K What was it like?

B Well, I wouldn't do it again. We were taken to a place in the middle of nowhere and we had to stay there for three days.

K Wow! So you were given a place to sleep?

B Yeah, it was a hostel. And we were woken up at five every morning. I was given a really uncomfortable outfit and it was really hot.

K Oh no.

B And my face was covered in thick make-up, and I had to wear it for twelve hours.

K Were you given any time for meals?

B Yeah, we had an hour for lunch and we were given sandwiches in a big tent.

K Was it interesting?

B Not really. Mostly we just waited. We were only filmed for about half an hour a day.

K Were you given any lines to say?

B No, but we pretended to talk. It was a kind of party, and we were told to talk to each other, but just pretending, moving our mouths and saying nonsense.

K Oh. So are you shown in the film, then?

B Yeah, for about half a minute. I'll lend you the DVD and you can see.

K Yeah, I'd like to see it. Thanks.

12

12A.1

1 Would you mind giving me a hand with these boxes?
2 Excuse me. Could you tell me how to get to the station?
3 Excuse me. Could you show me how this works?
4 Sorry to keep you waiting. Would you like to come through now?
5 Excuse me. Would you mind giving me your autograph?
6 Sorry to trouble you. Would you mind answering a few questions?
7 Stop right there!
8 Would you mind stepping this way please?
9 In you go.
10 Stand up straight!

12A.2

Man Excuse me, would you mind moving your bag?
Woman Oh yes, of course. I'll just move it out of the way ...
M Thanks ... Um, sorry, would you mind changing seats? I like looking out of the window. If I don't, I feel sick.
W Well, um ... OK. I'm only reading, so ...
M Thanks. Sorry, would you mind letting me get past? I need to go to the toilet.
W What? Oh, um, OK, I'll let you out ...
M Thanks. Sorry about that. Is this your newspaper?
W Yes.
M Could I borrow it?
W Yes, go ahead. I've finished.
M It's a bit cold in here. Could you close the window?
W It's closed already.
M Oh. Would you mind lending me your coat?
W But I'm wearing it!
M That's OK. I don't mind. It'll be warm!

12B.1

station	information
action	competition
tradition	pronunciation
procession	congratulations

12B.2

1
A There's a spring festival in India called Holi, and it's really beautiful.
B Oh yeah? Why? What do they do?
A Well, there's a special day and everybody goes out into the streets, and they go crazy, throwing coloured stuff over everyone.
B What, like paint or something?
A Something like that, yeah, and coloured water, and they throw balloons full of water too.
B Sounds messy.
A Messy, but very colourful, you know, everything's covered in colour, and it's all over your face and in your hair and everything.
B Uh huh. What fun!

2
A Where's that picture taken?
B That's a place called Selçuk, in Turkey.
A Oh. But what's happening?
B It's a camel fight. They have a festival with camel fights ...
A Are they really fighting? I mean, do they get hurt?
B No, not really. And everybody watches and they try to guess which camel will win.
A How do you know which camel's won, though?
B Well, usually one camel runs away, and it runs into the crowd, and everybody has to escape fast, and that's the fun part!
A It's not my idea of fun, escaping from a camel!
B Yeah, but it's fun to watch!

3
A This is the *Festival of the Sun* in Cuzco, Peru.
B Wow, that looks amazing.
A Yeah, there's an enormous Inca ceremony with 500 actors, and one actor plays the Inca.
B Uh huh.
A And they carry the Inca up the hill on a chair and everybody walks behind, and there are flowers everywhere, on the streets and stuff.
B And what's this place?
A It's an enormous Inca castle on top of the hill, and everybody goes up there to watch the ceremony.
B What do they do?
A Well, the main thing is when the Inca kills an animal and takes out its heart, and this is to bring good luck for the next year.
B Yuck!
A They don't really kill an animal these days, it's just acting.

12C.1

A Date with Des
Des Are you doing anything tonight?
Lucy Oh, well I'm a bit busy actually ...
Oh no – I think he wants to ask me out!
D I'm going to see 'Bats' at the cinema. Would you like to come?
L I'd like to but I can't. I have to study for an exam.
I'd rather eat mud!
D Oh come on! You'll enjoy it, I promise! I'll collect you from your house at 7.30.
L That's very kind of you, but really ...
If you come near my house, I'll call the police!
D OK, I'll wait and we can go tomorrow.
L I'm sorry, but I'm meeting some friends tomorrow.
Thanks, but I'd prefer to sit in a box of fish!
D OK, will you go out with me next week?
L I'll think about it, OK? Can I help you?
D Are *you* doing anything tonight?
Cath Oh, nothing much. Why?
Oh great – he wants to ask me out!
D I'm going to see 'Bats' at the cinema. Would you like to come?
C Oh, I don't know ...
I'd love to!
D Oh, come on! It'll be fun!
C OK, I'll come!

12C.2

1
A Are you doing anything on Friday evening?
B Oh, nothing much. Why?
A I'm having a party. Do you want to come?
B I'd rather not. I have to get up early in the morning.
A OK then. Maybe some other time.

2
A What are you doing at the weekend?
B Oh nothing much. Why?
A How about going out for dinner?
B I'd love to. What time?
A Let's meet around 8 o'clock.

12C.3

I'd love to!   I'd like to ...
I'd like to ...   I'd love to!
I'd love to!   I'd like to ...

12C.4

1 I'd like to come ...
2 That's very kind of you ...
3 That would be lovely ...
4 Oh, I'd love to come ...

12C.5

1 I'd like to come, but I can't, I'm afraid.
2 That's very kind of you, thanks. I'll come.
3 That would be lovely. Where shall we meet?
4 Oh, I'd love to come, but I've arranged to go out with a friend.

12D.1

Ideal World
In an ideal world
People would be kind
You could just be yourself
And nobody would mind
We'd all make friends
We wouldn't fall out
We wouldn't have to cry
And we wouldn't have to shout

People in an ideal world
Living in an ideal world

In an ideal world
People wouldn't fight
In an ideal world
Snakes wouldn't bite
We'd all live together
We'd all live in peace
We wouldn't need lawyers
And we wouldn't need police

People in an ideal world
Living in an ideal world

In an ideal world
We'd live and let live
In an ideal world
We'd learn to forgive
And we'd all get along
With the neighbours next door
And people would be friends
With their mothers-in-law

People in an ideal world
Living in an ideal world

12D.2

If we lived in an ideal world, there would be peace in Africa. It's terrible there now, because there are so many wars there and the people haven't got enough to eat. I think those countries are poor because of wars. If there was peace, they would become richer.

If I could be a famous person for one day, I'd be someone like Shakira, the pop singer from Colombia, 'cause I'd really love to go on stage in front of thousands of people, you know. I think it would be really exciting, with everybody dancing and the lights and the music and everything.

12D.3

If I were an animal, I think I'd be a cat. I think cats are very independent, and I think they have a lot of fun, you know, they don't work too hard. They take it easy, and I think they're very intelligent. They're not stupid like dogs. Yeah, so I'd be a cat.

If I could live anywhere in the world, I'd live on a Caribbean island, 'cause the weather's great, and I think the people are friendly. I mean, I've never been there, but I've seen it on TV and it looks great. I'd live in a small town by the sea and eat lots of pineapples and mangoes and fish.

If I had a time machine, I'd visit Egypt at the time of Cleopatra. I think the Egyptian culture was very interesting and different, and there's a lot of mystery, there are a lot of things we don't know about Ancient Egypt, and if I went there I would discover things that nobody knows.

If I had a chance to meet a celebrity, I'd choose Brad Pitt. I think he'd be interesting to talk to. He does a lot of interesting things, charity work and everything. And of course, he's very attractive!

OXFORD
UNIVERSITY PRESS

Great Clarendon Street, Oxford OX2 6DP

Oxford University Press is a department of the University of Oxford. It furthers the University's objective of excellence in research, scholarship, and education by publishing worldwide in

Oxford New York

Auckland Cape Town Dar es Salaam
Hong Kong Karachi Kuala Lumpur Madrid
Melbourne Mexico-City Nairobi New Delhi
Shanghai Taipei Toronto

With offices in

Argentina Austria Brazil Chile Czech Republic
France Greece Guatemala Hungary Italy Japan
Poland Portugal Singapore South Korea
Switzerland Thailand Turkey Ukraine Vietnam

OXFORD and OXFORD ENGLISH are registered trade marks of Oxford University Press in the UK and in certain other countries

© Oxford University Press 2008
The moral rights of the author have been asserted
Database right Oxford University Press (maker)
First published 2008
2013 2012 2011
10 9 8 7 6

ISBN: 978 0 19 430479 5

Printed in China

This book is printed on paper from certified and well-managed sources.

ACKNOWLEDGEMENTS

Illustrations by: David Atkinson pp25; Cyrille Berger p18; Annie Boberg p48; Stuart Briers p110; Gary Bullock 126 (holiday picture), 132; Bob Dewar pp40, 127 (Lisa's house); Mark Duffin pp15, 53, 60 (bank & post office a/w), 75, 78 (making pencils & objects), 85, 90, 129 (drawing Lisa's house); Scott Garrett pp19, 29, 61; John Goodwin p56; Simon Gurr p62; Andy Hammond pp43, 59, 79; Peter Harper p102; Terry Kennett p36; Joanna Kerr pp13, 55, 129 (computer, holiday, journey etc); Ken Laidlaw p10; Gavin Reece pp46, 47, 100, 126 (film studio), 127 (the kitchen), 128 (what were they doing?), 133 (film studio & kitchen), 134 (what were they doing?); Mark Ruffle pp91, 107; Terry Wong p128 (robber), 129 (office), 134 (handbag thief & office).

Commissioned photography by: Gareth Boden pp38 (picture 'B'), 50 (Buying Jeans), 70, 106, 120; Mark Mason pp 8, 10

Thanks to the following for providing locations: Six TV, Oxford; Roberto Gerrards, Hertford.

The publishers would like to thank the following for permission to reproduce photographs: Alamy Images pp6 (Ericsson/vario images GmbH & Co.KG), 6 (McDonalds/Ferruccio), 6 (airplane/EuroStyle Graphics), 6 (Ford car/picturesbyrob), 6 (Schweppes advert/John Ferro Sims), 6 (Porsche/vario images GmbH & Co.KG), 6 (Dior shoes/PCL), 6 (Suzuki GSX750R/Motoring Picture Library), 6 (Fifth Avenue/Frances Roberts), 6 (Michelin logo/artpartner-images.com), 6 (Chanel/Andrew Holt), 6

(Honda logo/Gari Wyn Williams), 6 (Yamaha/Peter Coombs), 6 (Ferrari/Mick Broughton), 12 (watch/Synthetic Alan King), 12 (Allianz Arena/imagebroker), 12 (Cannon Hill Park/Images of Birmingham), 12 (match/Rob Walls), 12 (Maple leaf/imagebroker), 20 (Hyde Park/The Photolibrary Wales), 20 (winter/Robert Harding Picture Library), 20 (girls/Pegaz), 20 (Tower Bridge/SCPhotos), 20 (Siberia/Images&Stories), 22 (Cairo/Authors Image), 22 (Oriental knifes/FAN Travelstock), 22 (souvenirs/Jon Arnold Images Ltd), 22 (beerjugs/David Crossland), 22 (Soviet advertising posters/Iain Masterton), 22 (souvenir cups/Jack Sullivan), 22 (Egyptian souvenirs/Westend 61), 22 (Panama t-shirts/M.Timothy O'Keefe), 22 (fans/Robert Fried), 22 (baseball caps/Lightworks Media), 22 (postcards/Jeronimo Alba), 22 (keyrings/Stuart Crump), 22 (cairo/Authors Image), 26 (sky diving/StockShot), 30 ('Psycho'/Pictorial Press Ltd), 40 (spoon/Maximilian Weinzierl), 40 (sink/Patrick Eden), 40 (gas burners/Mark Sykes), 40 (cooker/Sam Morgan Moore), 40 (radiator/Leslie Garland Picture Library), 40 (tap/Stephen Cobb), 52 (keep off sign/Nick David), 52 (Prohibited sign/Kim Karpeles), 52 (admission sign/Paul Carstairs), 52 (sailing club sign/alam), 52 (St Elli shopping centre/Walespix), 52 (youth/Janine Wiedel Photolibrary), 58 (traffic lights/vario images GmbH & Co.KG), 58 (road sign/Chris Howarth), 58 (motorway/Tony Charnock), 58 (L Plate/Dominic Burke), 58 (dispatch rider/Ianni Dimitrov), 58 (zebra crossing/Paul Mayall), 58 (man on phone in car/Fredrik Skold), 58 (accident/Aspix), 58 (petrol station/Rob Walls), 68 (staffroom/Janine Wiedel Photolibrary), 76 (wireless symbol/Ewan Stevenson), 76 (Singapore/Eye Ubiquitous), 76 (frustration/David J. Green), 76 (drying mobile/Scott Hortop), 76 (mobile/Andrew Curran), 80 (schoolchildren/Sally and Richard Greenhill), 86 (fried egg/Jochen Tack), 86 (chicken/Michael Soo), 86 (scrambled eggs/foodfolio), 86 (egg/The Anthony Blake Photo Library), 86 (bread/D.Hurst), 88 (street vendor/David Leadbitter), 90 (food pyramid/D.Hurst), 92 (knife/Roger Eritja), 92 (India/Eye Ubiquitous), 92 (breaking bread/ArtMediaPix), 96 (England/David Gregs), 96 (Cornwall/Celia Mannings), 96 (public house/Graham Oliver), 98 (airport/joeysworld.com), 98 (check in sign/graficart.net), 98 (airport signs/Peter Horree), 98 (duty free/Helios), 98 (Airport gate sign/David R. Frazier Photolibrary.Inc), 98 (toilet sign/Wilmar Photography), 98, (Boeing 747/Gary Crabbe), 98 (airport sign/John Rensten), 98 (customs/geogphotos), 98 (exit sign/Oote Boe Photography), 102), (dragon on silk/Panorama Media (Beijing) Ltd, 102 (silk seller/Tamir Niv), 102 (Samarkand/Tibor Bognar), 108 (Girl with a Pearl Earring c1665/6 oil on canvas/Visual Arts Library London), 108 (Portrait of Lisa del Giocondo (Mona Lisa) 1503–1506 by Leonardo da Vinci/Dennis Hallinan), 108 (The Shrimp Girl c1745/Visual Arts Library London), 112 (Mar Adentro 2004 film poster/Photos 12), 112 (Jennifer Lopez/Photos 12), 113 (Emma 1996/Pictorial Press Ltd), 116 (clampers/Ruby), 116 (street canvasser/Gary Roebuck), 116 (police chase/Harry Sheridan), 118 (snow festival/Pacific Press Service), 118 (Moss Man Tribe/Doug Steley), 118 (rainbow/Keren Su/China Span), 118 (Berber men/Anders Ryman), 118 (carnival, Brazil/Sue Cunningham Photographic), 118 (Holi Festival/Keren Su/China Span), 118 (camel wrestling/Jeremy Nicholl), (Elephant football/Robert Harding Picture Library Ltd); Anthony Blake Photo Library pp40 (pint glass/ATW Photography), 86 (jacket potato/Norman Hollands), 86 (mashed potato/Scott Morrison), 86 (grated cheese/Tim Hill), 86 (frozen peas/Robert Lawson), 86 (grilled sardines/Martin Brigdale); Axiom Photographic Agency p94 (pumpkin seller/Sue Carpenter); Bridgeman Art Library Ltd pp60 (Drug Store, 1927 (oil on canvas), Hopper, Edward (1882–1967)/Museum of Fine Arts, Boston, Massachusetts, USA, Bequest of John T. Spaulding), 108 (A Bar at the Folies-Bergere, 1881–82 (oil on canvas), Manet, Edouard (1832–83)/©Samuel Courtauld Trust, Courtauld Institute of Art Gallery); Corbis pp6 (Maria Sharapova/Michael Cole), 6 (Bjork/Alessandra Benedetti), 12 (woman with dog/Tony West), 17 (Eiffel Tower/William Manning), 17 (London Eye/Skyscan), 20 (ice formation/Remi Benall), 24 (volcano & rapids/Hubert Stadler), 26 (ice climber/Beat Glanzmann), 26 (diver/Stuart Westmoreland), 26 (snowboarder/Mike Chew), 26 (waterskier/Rick Doyle), 30 (iceberg/Paul Souders), 42 (teens with pizza/C.Devan/zefa), 42 (mother & son/Freitag/zefa), 52 (rollerblader/Benelux/zefa), 67 (man serving/Patrik Giardino), 67 (tennis player/Joe McBride), 68 (cleaner/Shannon Fagan), 96 (Cornwall/Jason Hawkes), 98 (baggage/Patrik Giardino), 102 (desert/Keren Su), 118 (Tomatina/Reuters); DK Images p46 (swimming shorts/Dorling Kindersley); Getty Images (woman on mobile/Miguel Salmeron/Photographer's Choice), 6 (Gabriel Garcia Marquez/Piero Pomponi), 14 (female runner/Dirk Anschutz/Stone), 14 (smiling girl/Photographer's Choice RR), 19 (woman in glasses/David Young-Wolff/Photographer's Choice), 28 (Waikiki beach/Marc Schechter/Stone), 28 (Men surfing at Waikiki Club/Frank Scherschel//Time Life Pictures), 38 (broken egg/Harry Sheridan/Photonica), 38 (man in kitchen/Joos Mind/Taxi), 38 (woman clearing up/David C Ellis/Stone+), 38 (broken glasses/Dag Sundberg/The Image Bank), 38 (spilt

cereal/Philip J Brittan/Photonica), 38 (housework/Donna Day/Stone), 38 (spilt flour/Olaf Tiedje/Photonica), 38 (woman in kitchen/Trujillo-Paumier/Stone+), 38 (man with cleaning products/Didier Robcis/Stone), 46 (pants/Jacobs Stock Photography/Photographer's Choice), 46 (tights/Olle Lindstedt/Nordic Photos), 54 (Chinese New Year/Sylvain Grandadam/Stone), 68 (office/Gregory Kramer/The Image Bank), 68 (canteen/Yellow Dog Productions/The Image Bank), 68 (science class/Sean Justice/Photonica), 68 (computer class/Andy Sacks/Photographer's Choice), 84 (man with laptop/bilderlounge), 68 (woman cooking/Tai Power Seeff/The Image Bank), 88 (tent/Melissa McManus/Stone), 88 (potatoes/Petri Artturi Asikainen/Gorilla Creative Images), 88 (camping/Andrew Shennan/Taxi), 88 (barbecue/Riser), 88 (street vendor/Rich LaSalle/Photographer's Choice), 88 (preparing vegetables/Riser), 88 (tea ceremony/Bruno Morandi/Reportage), 88 (Ndebele woman/Martin Harvey/Gallo Images), 88 (mangoes/Livia Corona/Stone), 88 (kebab/Bill Arce/StockFood Creative), 89 (salad/David Loftus/StockFood Creative), 89 (egg salad/Chris Alack/StockFood Creative), 89 (pasta/Spencer Jones/StockFood Creative), 92 (eating/Todd Warnock/Stone), 98 (newspaper/amana images/Photonica), 102 (Jiayuguan Fortress/Keren Su/The Image Bank), 102 (Xi'an, China/Greg Elms/Lonely Planet Images), 102 (Pamir Mountains/David Sanger/The Image Bank), 109 (Detail from St. Augustine in his Study/Sandro Botticelli/The Bridgeman Art Library), 109 (Portrait of Paul Scarron (1610–60) (oil on canvas)/French School/The Bridgeman Art Library), 109 (Young Man with a Hat, 1888 (oil on canvas)/Vincent van Gogh/The Bridgeman Art Library), 112 (The Sea Inside 2004 film poster/Stephen Shugerrman), 116 (policeman/Peter Dazeley/Photographer's Choice), 116 (computer demonstration/Erik Dreyer/Stone), 116 (prison/Benelux Press/Taxi), 116 (waiting room/Silvia Otte/Photonica), 116 (army/Robert Daly/Stone), 116 (mature man/altrendo images), 118 (cheese rolling/Peter Macdiarmid), 122 (Les Saintes, Guadaloupe (oil on canvas), Claude Salez/The Bridgeman Art Library), 122 (Cleopatra (69–30 BC) on the Terraces of Philae, 1896 (oil on canvas), Frederick Arthur Bridgman/The Bridgeman Art Library), 122 (Be Free Three (oil & acrylic on canvas), Kaaria Mucherera/The Bridgeman Art Library), 122 (Shakira/Krafft Angerer/AFP), 122 (Brad Pitt/Piyal Hosain/Fotos International), 122 (First Carpet-Cat-Patch, 1992/The Bridgeman Art Library), 130 (family/Britt Erlanson/Stone), 133 (family/Britt Erlanson/Stone); KEO Films p20 (Dr Nick Middleton with an Afar cowboy en route to Dallol/KEO Films/Andrew Palmer); Kobal Collection pp32 (Laurel & Hardy/Hal Roach/MGM), 32 (Dracula 1931/Universal), 32 (Gone with the Wind/Selznick/MGM), 32 (Julius Caesar 1953/MGM), 32 (Psycho 1960/Paramount), 32 (Dr No/DANJAQ/EON/UA), 32 (Blade Runner/Ladd Company/Warner Bros), 32 (Titanic 1997/Twentieth Century Fox/Paramount), 33 (Laurel & Hardy/Hal Roach/MGM); OUP pp30 (tv/Chris King), 68 (school/Photodisc), 78 (wood/Photodisc), 78 (metal/Photodisc), 78 (material/Photodisc), 78 (colour hoops/Corel), 78 (glass/Photodisc), 78 (box/Ingram), 78 (clock/Stockbyte), 122 (young woman/Photodisc); PunchStock pp12 (trying on shoes/Corbis), 12 (coins/Brand X Pictures), 14 (woman/Stockbyte), 14 (woman/Valueline), 21 (smiling man/Photodisc), 22 (bags/Brand X Pictures), 26 (rollerblading/Digital Vision), 30 (illustration/Digital Vision), 36 (hotel receptionist/BananaStock), 36 (hotel room/BananaStock), 38 (rinsing finger/Image Source), 38 (cut finger/Image Source), 43 (young man/Digital Vision), 46 (socks/Photodisc), 46 (top/Photodisc), 48 (shopping/Corbis), 68 (youth/Brand X Pictures), 54 (Chinese boy/IZA Stock), 56 (mannequins/Digital Vision), 58 (car/Creatas), 58 (changing tyre/Stockbyte), 68 (teacher/Stockbyte), 68 (classroom/Stockbyte), 68 (class/Digital Vision), 74 (home office/BananaStock), 76 (spilt coffee/Digital Vision), 78 (ruler/Corbis), 92 (salami/Westend61), 98 (currency exchange/Creatas), 98 (departure board/Brand X Pictures), 98 (on time/Brand X Pictures), 98 (welcome home/Creatas), 102 (Mogao Caves/Digital Archive Japan), 104 (man/imageshop), 104 (man on dock/imageshop), 109 (Portrait of Giuliano dé Medici/Valueline), 115 (Federico II of Montefeltro/Photodisc), 116 (carrying parcels/Photodisc), 116 (autograph signing/image100); Rex Features pp6 (JK Rowling/Maggie Hardie), 6 (Jackie Chan/Maria Laura Antonelli), 6 (Wolfgang Peterson/Sipa Press), 30 (Anaconda/Columbia/Everett), 50 (Rebel Without a Cause filmstill/SNAP), 52 (heely shoes/SNAP); Science Photo Library p96 (Cornwall/M-Sat Ltd); Surfpix p28 (Rabbit Kekai surfing/Jim Russi).

The Publishers and Authors would particularly like to thank the following readers and teachers for their help with the initial research and piloting: Maggie Baigent, Jo Cooke, Ana Deptula, Jon Fitch, Anne Fowles, Rachel Godfrey, Amanda Jeffries, Colin Lockhart, Fiona McLelland, Marisa Perazzo, Graham Rumbelow, Enda Scott, Joanna Sosnowska, Meriel Steele, Carol Tabor, Michael Terry.

Recordings directed by: Leon Chambers
Words and music in songs by: Mark Hancock
Musical arrangements by: Phil Chambon
Vocals in songs by: Jo Servi and Jude Sim